Texts in Quantitative Political Analysis

This series covers the novel application of quantitative and mathematical methods to substantive problems in political science as well as the further extension, development, and adaptation of these methods to make them more useful for applied political science researchers. Books in this series make original contributions to political methodology and substantive political science, while serving as educational resources for independent practitioners and analysts working in the field.

This series fills the needs of faculty, students, and independent practitioners as they develop and apply new quantitative research techniques or teach them to others. Books in this series are designed to be practical and easy-to-follow. Ideally, an independent reader should be able to replicate the authors' analysis and follow any in-text examples without outside help. Some of the books will focus largely on instructing readers how to use software such as R or Stata. For textbooks, example data and (if appropriate) software code will be supplied by the authors for readers.

This series welcomes proposals for monographs, edited volumes, textbooks, and professional titles.

Natalie Jackson
Editor

Non-Academic Careers for Quantitative Social Scientists

A Practical Guide to Maximizing Your Skills
and Opportunities

 Springer

Editor
Natalie Jackson
Research Consultant
District of Columbia, DC, USA

ISSN 2730-9614   ISSN 2730-9622   (electronic)
Texts in Quantitative Political Analysis
ISBN 978-3-031-35035-1   ISBN 978-3-031-35036-8   (eBook)
https://doi.org/10.1007/978-3-031-35036-8

This Springer imprint is published by the registered company Springer Nature Switzerland AG
The registered company address is: Gewerbestrasse 11, 6330 Cham, Switzerland

Contents

Introduction: Surveying the Landscape of Industry Jobs

Natalie Jackson

Earning a PhD is a massive undertaking, and anyone who completes one should be proud of their accomplishment. That does not change, no matter where you work after completing the degree. The fact that you are reading this sentence shows that you have accepted that social science PhDs do not necessarily *have* to go into academia. Maybe you realize that some do not even *want* to. Maybe you are that person with a social science PhD, or a current graduate student, nervous about the state of academia or simply not enjoying it, wanting to know your options. Maybe you are in academia advising those students. You are in the right place. This book is for you.

Sometimes graduate students and academics struggle to see how their studies and skill sets could possibly be applicable outside of academia, but there are a lot of satisfying career alternatives outside of academia that utilize and place high value on the skills you learned in the process of getting your PhD. Several chapters of this volume serve as introductions to some of those alternatives.

Other chapters focus on simply speaking the language of nonacademic jobs. In countless conversations over the decade-plus that I have been in various nonacademic positions, the overarching theme that has emerged is understanding differences in language between academic and nonacademic positions. Academia has its own language for research, conferences, presentations, publications, teaching, service, and how it all comes together to form a career. So does every field. Many of the skills are the same, however, if you know what jargon to use to talk about them. One example: Have you written a dissertation? Guess what – that means you are an expert at managing large projects. In fact, every research project you have is an exercise in project management. Another: Every class you teach is an exercise in supervising, mentoring, guiding, and holding people accountable – not unlike managing a team of people in a nonacademic job.

N. Jackson (✉)
Research Consultant/National Journal, Washington, DC, USA

© The Author(s), under exclusive license to Springer Nature
Switzerland AG 2023
N. Jackson (ed.), *Non-Academic Careers for Quantitative Social Scientists*,
Texts in Quantitative Political Analysis,
https://doi.org/10.1007/978-3-031-35036-8_1

These are simplifications, and there are key differences beyond the language, of course, which the authors in this book discuss in detail. But you are much more qualified for many positions than you might think.

The decision to go into academia vs. looking for nonacademic jobs has a lot of factors – some of which are completely out of your control (notably, all job markets, whether academic or not, can be fickle and extremely frustrating). This book is about introducing some of the types of jobs out there beyond academia and explaining what you need to know about nonacademic jobs that you might not learn in graduate school. You will still have plenty of questions after you finish reading it, but hopefully you will have a better understanding of the types of opportunities and how to prepare for a nonacademic career.

The book proceeds in two sections. The first section focuses on types of nonacademic jobs that are available to social science PhDs, particularly (but not exclusively) to those with quantitative research training. These examples intentionally focus both on job opportunities and the authors' individual journeys into those spaces and, in some cases, into other job opportunities later. No individual career pathway is replicable or necessarily desirable for any other person, but the point in sharing the stories from a personal angle is to illustrate how everyone's path looks a little different. Each person has different things they want out of life and a career. These stories are some of the ways in which these authors have accomplished their goals – whether it was the goal they set out to accomplish or a goal they discovered along the way.

Career Paths

The first section offers a wide swath of career paths and descriptions of how the authors got where they are and how their PhD skills were useful in pursuing that path. Substantively, the career options discussed in the first section are not comprehensive. No single volume could contain the full breadth of career options outside academia available to social scientists. Also, in putting this book together, I relied upon the authors' desire to contribute to knowledge on the topic of their career. It should be noted that most of these contributors had nothing to gain career-wise by writing a chapter for this volume. That is a key difference between academia and nonacademic jobs: in the latter, there is often little incentive to publish or write book chapters. Additionally, some employers (generally larger companies) considerably restrict what their employees publish or have substantial permissions processes, making contributing to a volume like this onerous, if not impossible.

Those considerations shape the types of jobs represented in the chapters, and I am extremely grateful to all of the contributors. Many of the major types of jobs and sectors in which a social science PhD might find opportunities are represented, including alt-academic jobs (at a college or university but not in academia), data science, working for government, start-up life, survey research, and market research.

Chapter 2, from Dr. Juan Manuel Contreras, describes how to think about and prepare for a career in data science. He argues that data science needs social scientists in the field and provides examples of the skills that make social scientists particularly valuable on data science teams. Contreras then walks through how to prepare for a career in data science – a field that includes a huge variety of opportunities with many types of employers – and how to set yourself up to be a good candidate for those jobs.

Dr. Schaun Wheeler highlights how his training in cultural anthropology set him up well for his 15 years of experience as a self-taught data practitioner in Chap. 3. He hacked himself into a builder and leader of data science teams across the defense and intelligence, travel, investment, education, and advertising industries, eventually culminating in his founding a mobile engagement start-up as a technical co-founder. He addresses the inherent industry biases against researchers with "soft" science backgrounds, offers up ways to circumvent these biases, and argues that, in fact, his "nontraditional" background is exactly what allowed him to thrive in industry.

In Chap. 4, Dr. Bethany Morrison describes her pathway from PhD to an alt-academic career in educational development. "Alt-academic" refers to full-time jobs at colleges and universities that are not the typical tenure track or teaching academic jobs. The alt-academic sector is a frequently overlooked source of jobs for PhDs who do not necessarily want to be an academic but enjoy the academic atmosphere. In Morrison's case, a love of teaching led to a postdoctoral career that focuses on teaching by helping academics be the best teachers they can be.

In Chap. 5, Dr. Susana Supalla offers a look into working for tech start-ups. The start-up life can be quite appealing due to its fast-moving and exciting atmosphere and the opportunities to be creative and entrepreneurial. At the same time, it can be an unstable career, as many start-ups have high turnover, although Supalla points out that the experience is still extremely valuable. She outlines her own transition from academia to start-ups and then helpfully lays out five dimensions on which one can evaluate potential start-up opportunities.

Chapter 6 is my own story of going into survey research as a career, along with the myriad opportunities that practical survey skills open up for PhDs. I discuss some of the various types of employment for survey researchers – government and government contractors, nonprofits, private companies, politics and elections, media, and alt-academic positions. Then I suggest a few ways to develop skills in survey research, whether you are in graduate school or in an academic position.

Dr. Michael Gibbons writes about his transition from academia to market research – and back to academia – in Chap. 7. In addition to a description of what is different between the sectors, this chapter will be of particular interest for anyone with the question of "can you go back into academia once you leave?" For Gibbons, the answer was "yes," but it was not necessarily easy. Along the way, he also discusses his experience working in market research with clear eyes, including the perks and the downsides.

In Chap. 8, Dr. Annie Pettit discusses her journey of overlooking the traditional academic and clinical psychologist routes and instead working in government, small and multinational companies, foreign companies, start-ups, and private consulting. From an insider's perspective, she outlines the relative advantages and disadvantages of each and how to get what you want once you're there. She shares the ideas of rejecting "the grass is greener on the other side" syndrome and saying yes to potential opportunities even when your current situation is bright.

Dr. Thiago Marzagão discusses working as a data scientist in government in Chap. 9. Government employment comes with unique limitations and circumstances, and Marzagão explains how the job might be more varied and challenging than working at larger companies, as well as the various entry points for working for and with governments as a data scientist. Importantly, he also describes how career development and moving into management work in this sector.

Dr. John Bordeaux explores the world of quasi-government research at Federally Funded Research and Development Centers (FFRDCs) in Chap. 10. These are contracts held by nonprofits or universities (typically) doing research to help the government understand the emerging challenges and opportunities affecting many aspects of life in the United States: education, technology, national defense, government reform, environmental science, hydrology, and more. The quantitative social scientist is a vital contributor to this work, and while the day-to-day work can resemble an academic environment, the researcher is challenged to help advance the public interest.

In Chap. 11, PhD candidates Daniel Casey and Mark Fletcher write about their decision to go back to academia to work on doctoral degrees after several years working in the Australian Public Service. They discuss why they did not immediately pursue the doctoral degree but decided to after some time, as well as how their experience in the APS has shaped their research. They argue that the reverse pathway – from industry to academia – offers as many advantages for academia as academia has to offer industry. Casey and Fletcher also discuss what their options might be after completing their degrees and what factors will affect their decision to go back to the public sector, stay in academia, or take a different pathway altogether.

In Chap. 12, Dr. Sarina Rhinehart discusses her experience working in state government and shares tips for understanding how the skills learned during a PhD can be applied in state government work, especially in emerging fields where the adaptability of a social science PhD serves as an advantage in new positions where few have the degree or specific experience to fit the needs in an emerging data field. She has found tremendous growth areas in new and upcoming data fields including data governance, data quality, data literacy, data privacy, and data analytics – fields not always or often found as majors in universities' academic catalogs but areas where state agencies across the country are investing their money and staff.

Advice for Nonacademic Job Success

The second section of the book is about how to position yourself as a candidate for nonacademic jobs, an employee, and resources for learning more.

In Chap. 13, Dr. Laura Schram lays out some excellent general advice on how to market yourself for a nonacademic career. Importantly, the first step is to understand your own goals, strengths, and desires before setting out on a job search so that you end up in a career you are likely to be happy and successful in. Equally important, she explains how to tailor your materials to the jobs you are applying for and how to talk about your skills in ways that are relevant to nonacademic hiring managers.

In Chap. 14, Dr. Analia Gomez Vidal shares her experience navigating the academic and nonacademic job markets and reflects on how being an international student and worker in the United States has shaped and informed this process. From thinking ahead about visa requirements to identifying her true interests and skills in the midst of countless rejections, she breaks down the steps she took and the mindset that helped her (or not) navigate the job market. She also shares more about resources, including career coaching, which has empowered her to advocate for herself and pursue her own vision. The chapter is geared toward the specific challenges international students face, but it has good information for everyone.

In Chap. 15, Dr. Matthew Barnes shares practical tips for making the leap from academia to a career in the technology sector. He describes two primary shifts in mindset required to make the leap and be successful: a shift from ideation to execution and creating value and understanding the core function of your new job is engineering. He also discusses how to develop skills and tools, crafting a résumé, and preparing for interviews for tech jobs.

Chapter 16 offers a different pathway out of academia. In it, Elisa Rapadas describes the circumstances and thought processes that led her to leave academia before completing a PhD. She discusses how and why this was the right decision for her and provides tips for leveraging university and free resources while working on an exit strategy. She offers valuable tips on converting a C.V. to a resume and emphasizes how internships can help.

In Chap. 17, Dr. Robert Oprisko discusses what happens when academia did not work out as a career path despite all his best efforts. He ultimately transitioned from political theorist to agile product management strategist, and he describes the ways in which he set himself up for that transition while he was still in academia. This chapter does not shy away from hard truths about pursuing careers in academia and the private sector and provides plenty of tips and tricks for how to find a pathway forward when the one you wanted does not work out.

Chapter 18 is a conversation among four colleagues about their transitions from academia into data science jobs. Matt Bernius and Drs. Laurel Eckhouse, Amelia Hoover Green, and Kerry Rodden discuss their pathways, including why Eckhouse and Green left tenure-track jobs to go into the private sector. They discuss approaches to translating academic research into case studies and portfolio pieces that you can use in interviews as well as their experiences in getting hired and doing the hiring. They share ideas for navigating interviews and communicating your skills and approach to planning, conducting, and presenting research to both data scientists and the people you will be interacting with from other disciplines.

Chapter 19 moves on to what happens once you have a nonacademic job, with Drs. Susan Navarro Smelcer and Meredith Whiteman Ross writing about how to thrive in a nonacademic environment as a trained academic. They point out that you will have knowledge gaps and how to navigate them, discuss how to think about the various audiences you are communicating with in a nonacademic job, and address ethical issues that could arise in data use and analysis, noting that the nonacademic environment often uses data for quite different purposes than academia.

Drs. Catasha Davis and Mackenzie Price used their research skills to conduct interviews with women about getting their *second* nonacademic jobs, and they summarize those findings in Chap. 20. The reality is that most people will not keep the same job for their entire career for a wide variety of reasons. This chapter covers the reasons for making a change, how job search strategies change with your level of experience, and how to make transitions between jobs.

Finally, in Chap. 21, Dr. Angela Fontes talks about how to remain "relevant" in academia while in a nonacademic job for those who want to remain engaged and connected to the academic conversation in their field. She provides tips based on her experiences with balancing a "day job" and academic publishing, including seeking out academic coauthors and the unique perspective nonacademics can add to the academic research process.

You may find all, some, or none of the advice in this book useful and relevant to your journey. That's okay; take what is useful and leave the rest. No one says this is an easy path; authors do not shy away from sharing the difficult parts of their journey. But the diverse perspectives will offer a variety of starting points and hopefully leave you more informed about what is out there, how to prepare for it, and how you might find career satisfaction over time.

Part I
Career Paths

Data Science Needs You, Social Scientist

Juan Manuel Contreras

Technology continues to advance into more and more areas of our lives. And it expands and deepens its influence, if not outright control, in many of these areas. From what news we consume to who we date, modern life depends on technology and, in turn, on the algorithms that personalize it for us.

But convenience has a cost. Over the past few years, we have become increasingly aware of the unintended harms that algorithmic influence and control of our lives has brought and will continue to bring if unexamined and unchecked. The solution to this problem will be multifaceted. But it will surely benefit from having more social scientists in the profession that designs, deploys, and can govern these algorithms: data science.

Data science needs you, social scientist. The complex challenges at the intersection of algorithms and social policy are tackled best by a data science profession filled with practitioners who hail from intellectual traditions that understand human behavior and know how to study it rigorously but ethically.

I urge you to consider becoming a data scientist if this profession has what it takes to satisfy the curiosity that brought you to academia. To this end, I share my advice for transitioning from academia to data science. This profession is not easy, but it will play a critical role in defining how well we will meet the challenges of integrating algorithms into our lives.

J. M. Contreras (✉)
Uber, Washington, DC, USA

© The Author(s), under exclusive license to Springer Nature
Switzerland AG 2023
N. Jackson (ed.), *Non-Academic Careers for Quantitative Social Scientists*,
Texts in Quantitative Political Analysis,
https://doi.org/10.1007/978-3-031-35036-8_2

Research Data Science as a Profession

Your doctoral advisor and fellow graduate students have probably been academics all their lives. But they may know data scientists, including alumni of your department and university. Ask for introductions to these people.

But don't be afraid to cold message data scientists. You can find them in your alumni directory and on social media. Most of us were helped in our transition from academia and will gladly pay it forward to someone like you.

When you talk to data scientists in your network, ask them about their experience as data scientists. What is most fulfilling and rewarding about their work? What is least enjoyable and stimulating about their work?

I most enjoy the tricky interface between the technical work of data science and the policy applications of its use. This interface is large and continues to evolve as algorithms grow and expand their role in society. Doing this well requires using nearly all of my skills. It also challenges me to learn new skills, especially the interpersonal ones needed to bring about change in organizations, and the managerial ones to lead well.

It's hard to express in words the lived experience of a job. But the better you understand it, the more confident you'll be that you'll be happy with the job once you get it.

Understand the Subdisciplines of Data Science and Find Your Best Fit

As the technology industry has evolved, so has data science as a discipline. *Data scientist* was once one job but now has specialized in different subdisciplines that vary in what work they perform and what background they require.

Data scientist increasingly refers to people who perform large-scale descriptive analysis. *Applied scientists* are the people who use machine learning in production. *Research scientists* perform more exploratory work to create new data science methods. And data science tasks that interface and overlap with engineering have given rise to *machine learning engineers*.

This typology is imperfect as these terms are used differently between and within companies. And they change over time, slowly but surely, potentially making the descriptions above outdated by the time you're reading this. (*Prompt engineer*, anyone?) For example, the increasing understanding of how algorithms create unintended harms will likely give rise to new titles for the people whose work will detect and mitigate these harms.

I'll stick with the term *data science*, but job descriptions are often more helpful than job titles to make sense of a given job. Most data science job descriptions suffer from too many technical terms, but don't let this discourage you.

Good data science managers write straightforward job descriptions that clarify the competencies they need. They don't vomit specific technical jargon that's de rigueur today passe tomorrow.

You don't meet every requirement of the job description. That's fine; most applicants won't. You only have to fit enough of them to pique the recruiter or hiring manager's interest. You want them to know you can overdeliver in enough requirements to compensate for those you don't.

And don't worry about wanting to change subdisciplines later. It's possible to transition between them, and these transitions will contribute to the breadth of your experience as a data scientist.

Tell Your Story Clearly and as Often as You Can

Resumes are stories. Recruiters and hiring managers will spend no more than half a minute on your resume on a first pass so write a story that piques their interest enough to want to hear more of it in an interview.

Many hiring managers don't fully know who makes for a good data scientist and shudder at hiring someone they won't be able to help to perform well. They will favor an application from a data scientist over one from a newly minted Ph.D. like you. Overcome this bias by writing your resume with the language you read in job descriptions, including the specific competencies you could already bring to the job.

But don't just tell your story clearly; tell it often. Hiring markets – including in data science – are broken in many ways, including in the incentive structures of job applications.

A job application costs nothing more than the time it takes to submit it. This cost is trivial compared to the benefits of a potentially curious recruiter pulling out your application from the black void to which most job applications go to die.

Although this makes the population of data science job applicants worse off, it benefits you to apply broadly.

Finally, if you know someone at an organization to which you're applying, ask them to refer you internally. A referral moves your application to the top of the black void. You're still not guaranteed an interview, but your application is likely to be considered.

Show Them Who You Are as a Technician and as Their Potential Teammate

Forget MATLAB, Stata, SPSS, and other proprietary statistical software you used in graduate school. Learn an open-source alternative like Python (to make it easier to venture into the no-man's-land between data science and engineering). Also, learn

SQL, the dopey pseudo-language that looks easier and less important than it will be to you as a full-fledged data scientist.

Learn these concurrently with job applications because it's not clear when you've learned enough of them and going through technical interviews in Python and SQL will hone your sense of what matters learning and how.

Technical interviews will consist of take-home assignments, live-coding exercises, and conversational interviews that involve thinking through technical problems. They are relatively random samples from a virtually infinite population of possible tests of your ability to demonstrate technical skill within interview parameters. They're not ideal, but they're the means interviewers use to evaluate your skill as a technician.

However, you're not getting hired to work from a locked room, being fed contextless data science problems, and passing your technical solutions for faceless others to implement.

You're interviewing to be a teammate to peers across functions, from data science to design. So you'll have to demonstrate the nontechnical skills that make data scientists successful at their job. Specifically, you can work with people (interpersonal), get stuff done (project management), and tackle new situations (problem-solving).

You've likely had to develop and refine these skills to get through your Ph.D. unscathed, particularly in delivering your dissertation. You only need to describe specific examples that clearly and effectively show this to your interviewers.

Understand Who Is Hiring and Why

Learn as much as you can about the hiring manager and your immediate coworkers during the interview process. It's not easy being a first-time data scientist. A more senior and experienced manager – ideally a former practicing data scientist – can make a big difference in setting your career on the right path.

The same thing is true of your more senior colleagues, especially if the manager has fostered a collaborative culture in their team, and you'll end up learning much and often from these colleagues.

Finally, figure out the hiring manager's location in an organizational chart and how their team's priorities get set. This information gives you a better sense of what you will work on and why. It will also help you compare different job offers when you have them.

Conclusion

Data science needs you, social scientist. Our profession needs your deep understanding of research on human behavior and expertise in the quantitative, rigorous, and ethical study of human behavior.

Your background as a social scientist will not only serve you well as a data scientist. It will also benefit the profession in navigating societal questions about the role and governance of algorithms in our daily lives.

If you choose to join us, I hope this advice helps you transition as effectively as possible.

Juan Manuel Contreras, Ph.D. is an applied science manager at Uber leading a team at the intersection of technology, policy, and law. He was trained as a social psychologist and cognitive neuroscientist at Harvard University and Princeton University. The opinions in this essay are personal and do not necessarily represent or reflect the views, opinions, or policies of Uber.

How to Thrive in the Data Industry Without a Traditional STEM Background

Schaun Wheeler

I had worked 3 years as a data scientist when the term "data scientist" entered popular usage. People started sending me Thomas Davenport and DJ Patil's "Data Scientist: the Sexiest Job of the 21st Century" in the *Harvard Business Review*, with notes that said, "this is what we've been doing!"[1]

When I started to call myself a *data scientist,* my younger coworkers looked confused, and my older coworkers rolled their eyes. My trendiness didn't impress them. "A data scientist is just another name for a quant," dryly remarked the new VP of Marketing when at promotion time I asked for the title of *Director of Research and Data Science*. While they might have expressed skepticism about the label, no one doubted the value of my skills. I could pull insights out of the production database without needing an engineer to build me a report. I could predict churn or define customer segments without the company needing to hire a consultant. Colleagues brought me their boring, repetitive tasks, hoping I'd automate them away.

I did something most of my coworkers hadn't previously realized was possible, so they rarely asked about credentials. Sometimes, in casual conversation, it would come up that I had a Ph.D. in cultural anthropology, that I'd conducted ethnographic fieldwork in a former Soviet republic in Central Asia, and that I'd written an absurdly long dissertation on identity formation in populist social movements and its implications for the concept of culture as a theoretical construct. They'd look at me sideways and ask, "how did you go from *that* to doing…data stuff?" I had a hard time explaining that it took every ethnographic skill in my toolkit to cobble together a

---

[1] Davenport, Thomas H. and Patil, DJ. "Data Scientist: The Sexiest Job of the 21st Century." Harvard Business Review. October 2012. Accessed 23 November 2022 at https://hbr.org/2012/10/data-scientist-the-sexiest-job-of-the-21st-century

---

S. Wheeler (✉)
Aampe, Inc. Raleigh, NC, USA

© The Author(s), under exclusive license to Springer Nature Switzerland AG 2023
N. Jackson (ed.), *Non-Academic Careers for Quantitative Social Scientists*,
Texts in Quantitative Political Analysis,
https://doi.org/10.1007/978-3-031-35036-8_3

customer segmentation that our marketers supported and our salespeople accepted that wouldn't tank our 20-year-old customer relationship management system.

Over time, the questions shifted from "how did you come to do data science?" to "how come you think you can do data science?" Universities and bootcamps discovered a whole lot of tuition money in offering data science credentials. I'd become a data scientist in an environment where the most important question was "what can you do for the business?" Increasingly, however, data scientists defined themselves in terms of what tools they could use instead of how they tackled business problems.

For a short time, the rise of credentialism in data science felt threatening. The early data science programs were often appendages to math or statistics departments, so new data scientists came into the market with a much heavier background in matrix algebra, probability theory, and other domains in which I was entirely self-taught. On several occasions, potential employers rejected my job application because I didn't have a STEM-heavy academic pedigree.

I've competed with, worked with, hired, managed, and sometimes fired many STEM-heavy data scientists. Over and over again, I've seen my "nontraditional" background from the social sciences do more than allow me to just keep up with my more math-y counterparts. It's allowed me to demonstrate value in ways others can't and in ways that, so far, have proven much less automate-able than other parts of the job.

I've built data science teams in a wide array of industries: defense and intelligence, travel, investment, education, and advertising. I've been a technical co-founder in a mobile engagement startup. Every last one of my skills in statistical analysis, machine learning, data visualization, data cleaning and wrangling, and programming is something I taught myself from blog posts, books, docs pages, and tinkering, always because I needed the skill to tackle a pressing business problem. Those skills were necessary but not sufficient for me to find success in my career. I'm a data scientist, but I'm still, first and foremost, an anthropologist. Ethnographic skills have been and continue to be the main thing that makes my technical skills useful.

What Is Ethnography?

I define ethnography as iterated, negotiated storytelling. When I have a research question, I find someone willing to talk. They tell me how the world works according to them. I take notes, and eventually I craft a story that explains the assumptions and contexts that make their story reasonable and logical to me. I share that story with the person who helped me develop it. They tell me all the ways my story is wrong. I recraft the story based on their criticism, and after a few iterations, I usually end up with something that my partner can accept. Then I find a new storytelling partner and, starting with the story I've already crafted, resume the cycle.

Moving through additional iterations, with additional storytelling partners, I craft a story (or stories) that most contributors recognize as reasonable.

Ethnography is more than just the straightforward compilation of information, and it's more than the methods employed to collect information. I base my stories on interviews, observation, participant observation, surveys, and any other methods that come in handy, but no single one of those methods is strictly required to produce an ethnography. I often fill in the gaps between individual contributors' stories with my own subjective understanding. I defend my contributions to the story as much as my other contributors defend theirs. Together, we negotiate a story that blends my views and their views, my priorities and their priorities, until we can all accept the whole even if each of us doubts parts.

Ethnography is my job – I don't know how to do data science without it. Every business problem is people looking for a story they can all agree to. Crafting that story – solving the problem – involves multiple rounds of back-and-forth and give-and-take.

Shipping Value

Data science has a dirty little secret. Eighty-seven percent of data science projects never make it into production.[2] Seventy-seven percent of businesses don't achieve "business adoption" of their ML initiatives.[3] Eighty percent of analytics insights don't deliver business outcomes, and 80% of ML projects "remain alchemy, run by wizards."[4] Plainly put, most data science never sees the light of day, and most of it that does doesn't make a difference.

There are a lot of reasons for this. Sometimes, the algorithm you need doesn't exist. Sometimes, you don't have the skills to use an existing implementation, or you don't know if your usage of the existing implementation is any good. Many algorithms require that data be "labeled," or categorized, and lack of trustworthy labels (or lack of any labels at all) is a constant problem. Most often, however, data science work is abandoned for the simple reason that the people who are paying for the work decide it's no longer worth the investment.

This failure carries costs. Dropped data science work often results in increased but unproductive investment – for example, stakeholders aren't willing to change business processes to accommodate a new ML-augmented workflow, so they end up investing time and money in messy workarounds and half-fixes. They didn't find enough value to justify making the changes – often, legitimately hard changes – that

---

[2] https://venturebeat.com/ai/why-do-87-of-data-science-projects-never-make-it-into-production/

[3] https://designingforanalytics.com/resources/failure-rates-for-analytics-bi-iot-and-big-data-projects-85-yikes/

[4] https://blogs.gartner.com/andrew_white/2019/01/03/our-top-data-and-analytics-predicts-for-2019/

would have allowed data science to deliver on its promises. The data science work already completed is added to a garbage heap, where it stands as a constant reminder of wasted time and money. This creates the vicious cycle of lack of stakeholder support: if you don't get the buy-in needed to put the system into production, the system gets put on the garbage heap. As the garbage heap grows, it becomes harder and harder to get the buy-in needed to put new systems into production.

Moving data science projects from development to production is a trust issue. Failure to "ship" our work – moving it from design and implementation to a stage where it actually impacts the business on a regular basis – creates a trust gap, and a trust gap creates future failures to ship.

For data scientists, "trust" can mean several different things:

1. We can trust the model – in other words, that our model produces reliable results.
2. We can trust the data – in other words, that our data doesn't reflect a systematically biased data-generation process that might carry adverse side effects for the business.
3. We can trust the problem – in other words, that our work reflects the priorities of the people who paid to have the work done.

Throughout my career, I've seen data scientists from traditional, STEM-heavy backgrounds fixate myopically on the first issue, only touch on the second issue when something goes wrong, and seem largely unaware of or uninterested in the third issue. I've built my career by thriving in their blind spots.

Trust in the Model

The first challenge is to become confident that the model produces reliable results. This is largely a solved problem – so much so, that big companies like Google Cloud and Microsoft Azure as well as relatively small companies like DataRobot have largely automated it away. This can be an immediate impediment and an eventual career threat for a data scientist straight out of a master's program or bootcamp, because model evaluation might be the only one of the three trust issues they ever learned to solve.

The metrics module of the scikit-learn Python library contains dozens of ways to evaluate the performance of a model.[5] None of these metrics are truth-tellers, of course. They're storytellers. Metrics give us information from which we construct a story about how good our model is.

For example, when I founded a data science team for a network of charter schools in New York City, one of our tasks was to classify students by their intervention needs. Some students struggled with the subject matter to the point that they would benefit from extra help and attention and perhaps a more formal kind of help such

---

[5] https://scikit-learn.org/stable/modules/classes.html#module-sklearn.metrics

as an individualized education program. Other students easily surpassed the material presented in class, to the point that they benefit from interventions to keep them engaged and challenged. Other students needed no intervention at all.

We had plenty of data from student assessments, and it's not hard to find an implementation of any number of good classification algorithms – I believe we used a random forest. Assessing the performance of a classifier is straightforward: we choose a standard approach, calculating precision and recall and then using a harmonic mean to combine those metrics into an F1 score.[6]

None of this helped our school administrators make decisions about which students needed more resources, because a model can make different kinds of mistakes, and, when it comes to getting kids an education, not all mistakes are created equal. One kind of mistake is a false positive: you decide a student needs extra help and give it to them, but they actually would have been fine without it. Another kind of mistake is a false negative: you decide a student doesn't need extra help and so don't give it to them, and then they fail where they otherwise might have succeeded.

We needed to work with our school administrators to negotiate the story we wanted the model to tell. Some quick back-and-forth on hypothetical scenarios involving false positives and false negatives revealed that our administrators were willing to accept around ten false positives (giving help where it wasn't really needed) in order to avoid just one false negative (withholding help where it wasn't needed). Our model performed very differently within that story than it did within the simple, unnegotiated story where we ran the metrics calculations and took the results at face value.

The metrics didn't tell us our model was good. We *said* our model was good, and we used the metrics to give the model a voice to contradict us. In this case, the model *didn't* contradict us, so we could keep telling the story that our model was good. We don't often think of model evaluation metrics as storytellers, but they are what allow the model to speak up and tell us something we might not want to hear.

This example may seem trivial, but it tells a core truth about the difficulty of doing data science in a business context: we build the best models when we can be contradicted. If we build, say, a house, the contractor or the owner can look at what we were doing and tell us when we've built something they don't want or can't use. When we build a machine learning model, however, the people we're building for don't have the background or intuition to contradict the story we tell. Model evaluation metrics give the model a voice to contradict us, but it's the data scientist that has to tell the metric what kind of opinion it's being asked for.

In my experience, STEM-trained data scientists are much more inclined to take model metrics on trust – the metrics are a set of tests, and of course you need to run tests before you ship. Tests, in this view, are *requirements*, not stories. I've built trust among nontechnical stakeholders by recognizing that even an F1-score calculation can and should be negotiated.

---

[6] If you're unfamiliar with the concepts of precision and recall, it's worth at least a cursory read of the Wikipedia article on the subject: https://en.wikipedia.org/wiki/Precision_and_recall

Trust in the Data

Several years ago, Bloomberg did an investigation of Amazon's rollout of same-day delivery to various parts of the United States.[7] The decision on where to provide same-day delivery had apparently been made algorithmically, and the algorithm was apparently racist: poorer, high-minority neighborhoods were consistently excluded from same-day postal shipping across many US cities.

Obviously, Amazon's engineers and data scientists didn't set out to exclude minority communities from same-day shipping. I'm sure the model produced reasonable evaluation metrics, indicating that Amazon (and, by extension, all of us who rely on Amazon) could trust that the model captured actual signal from the data and wasn't simply over-fitting to noise.

It seems that the training data, however, was generated from past customer activity. Customer activity depends, at least partially, on household finances, which in turn depends on the economics of those households' surrounding communities. The data-generating process itself had a systemic bias, and Amazon didn't catch it before putting their model into production.

This is a perennial problem across the industry. Wired showed how child-abuse protection algorithms tended to target poor families – the abuse indicators the algorithm tried to take into account (not having enough food, having inadequate or unsafe housing, lacking medical care, leaving a child alone while you work, etc.) blurred the lines between neglect and poverty.[8] In another example, researchers from Carnegie Mellon created fake users that behaved in the same way and whose profiles only differed in their gender. Google's ad display system tended to show ads for highly paid jobs much less often to the users whose profiles indicated that they were women.[9]

In general, the toolset for negotiating a story about data trust just isn't nearly as robust as the toolset for telling stories about model trust. Some tools do exist. Researchers at the University of Chicago developed a tool that looks at the representation of different classes in both the training and test datasets and the training and test prediction outcomes.[10] If a class makes up 2% of your data but 30% of your positive predictions and the predictions determine who gets flagged as a threat (as is the case in models that predict criminal recidivism), then you have a problem. And there are other tools that come at this problem more obliquely, such as methods to identify Simpson's paradox, where a relationship between variables systematically reverses direction among certain subsets of the data.[11]

---

[7] https://www.bloomberg.com/graphics/2016-amazon-same-day/

[8] https://www.wired.com/story/excerpt-from-automating-inequality/

[9] https://www.theguardian.com/technology/2015/jul/08/women-less-likely-ads-high-paid-jobs-google-study

[10] http://www.datasciencepublicpolicy.org/our-work/tools-guides/aequitas/

[11] https://github.com/ninoch/Trend-Simpsons-Paradox/

In most cases, however, trust in the data-generating process depends entirely on what we tend to call "exploratory data analysis," which in daily practice is mostly just another term for "I'll poke around and see if I notice anything weird." Cases like Amazon show that if we build trust in our data based only on histograms, heatmaps, and measures of central tendency, we're going to build models that are consistent, but which consistently distort the way our systems deliver results.

For example, I worked for an ad-tech company where I designed systems to use geolocated records from mobile usage data to understand users' behavior patterns in the physical world (such as where they like to shop for groceries). We got hundreds of millions of new records a day, but not all of that data was usable. Specific Internet service providers, apps, devices, or device configurations would report pinpoint geo-coordinates that were actually the location of a data center, or the centroid of a geographic administrative area, such as a postal code, rather than the actual location where they were shopping. Taking that bad coordinate at face value could lead to drastically wrong conclusions about user behavior.

At the start, the problem seemed pretty straightforward: flag coordinates attached to an unusually high number of unique devices. For example, if most of the coordinates in an area see between one and ten unique devices a day, but one coordinate pair has 1527 unique devices, then that one coordinate pair is probably spurious. The company had used that kind of simple outlier identification for several years by the time I was asked to take a look at the issue and see if I couldn't improve it. There was little to be gained from stakeholder conversations in this case – no one knew any more about the data than I did. But there's no rule that says ethnographic story-telling partners need to be human. Our data was the result of one or more underlying data-generating processes, and those processes needed a voice.

I matched up shapefiles of US administrative divisions (states, counties, cities, and zip codes) with the device coordinates data to identify geolocations that were outliers given the distribution of device location visitation within each geography. I didn't know what the data had to say about what outlier behavior looked like, so I had to do a lot of listening – or, rather, watching, since data doesn't have its own voice. I designed a visualization workflow and then spent a couple weeks paging through maps with dots on them.[12]

I remember seeing the outlier data from Fort Worth, Texas. It was a grid. There were a couple points that didn't fit the grid, and other parts of the grid were missing, but I could easily see a definite pattern. I kept paging and soon had similar examples from Boise, San Antonio, and Colorado Springs. I stopped recording the locations after I'd found a couple dozen. The visualization from Manhattan was particularly striking – a full grid of around 20 dots covering the entire island, all evenly spaced, and no dots missing.

This took me in a whole new direction. I worked up an algorithm to identify the grids – to approximate what I was doing with my eyeballs. I found grids all over the United States and Canada. In most places, the grid was made up of roughly

---

[12] https://github.com/vericast/theto

meter-wide patches separated from other nodes by at least 1 kilometer. The distances and angles differed in different places – it was hundreds of very-similar-but-not-exactly-alike grids, all made up of coordinates that saw unusually high mobile-device visitation.

I looked for attributes to differentiate these coordinates from other coordinates. I discovered that grid coordinates were much more likely to come from weather apps – in particular, apps operated by the Weather Company. Those apps, however, created far more coordinates that *didn't* fall within a grid than coordinates that did, and many of the apps involved in the coordinates weren't obviously weather-related. Still, the most plausible story I could negotiate with my data was this was a weather grid. I spent the better part of a week researching and downloading projections from the US National Weather Service. None of them matched up, but the exercise made me realize that my grid data wasn't actually a grid – any three adjacent points in *my* "grids" formed more than just 90-degree angles and straight lines.

I'd tried to negotiate a story with my data. My data told me I might be looking at a weather grid. I took that story from the National Weather Service data. The NWS data told me my story was garbage. It happens. But neither my company's proprietary data nor the NWS data could have told me anything if I had not built a visualization workflow to give that data a voice. None of the patterns I discovered were evident from simply frequency statistics or histograms.

My data and I did finally negotiate a story we could all live with: it took me another week to finally realize that a grid is not the only way to systematically place coordinates. Instead of Googling "weather grid," I Googled "weather mesh." Apparently, the Weather Company (owned by IBM and owner of both the Weather Channel and Weather Underground) collaborated with the climate group at Los Alamos to develop a mesh that could be stretched to have higher resolution at some places in the world and shrunk to have lower resolution at others.[13] Their implementation of that mesh is proprietary and possibly subject to change over time as their forecasting needs change. And the Weather Channel hosts an API that allows other apps to serve weather, which explains why so many other apps end up falling into the hexagon centroids as well. However, weather apps have tons of hits outside of these centroids, which suggests they only provide centroid data sometimes, perhaps only when location services are disabled on a device.

Painstakingly negotiating a story about the data-generation process allowed me to design algorithms that substantially increased the validity and precision of our geolocation data. The process I went through to get that understanding went far beyond "debugging," and my breakthrough ultimately rested on a set of tools that literally put dots on maps so I could stare at them. This wasn't a technical breakthrough. By building tools to give data a voice – to show me in rough but intuitive terms what the coordinates looked like under different assumptions of how many devices were considered "outliers" – the problem changed from an analytic problem

---

[13] https://mpas-dev.github.io/atmosphere/atmosphere.html

to a design problem. Once I solved the design problem, the analytic solution practically suggested itself.

I solved a problem none of my colleagues had been able to solve, not because I knew math that others didn't, or used a model others couldn't, or wrote code better than anyone else. I solved the problem because I used simple tools to give my data a voice and then kept negotiating until I could make sense of the story it was trying to tell and could reconcile that with the story I needed to tell.

Trust in the Problem

Geoffrey Hinton (who, along with Yann LeCun and Yoshua Bengio, won the 2018 Turing Award) said in 2016, "We should stop training radiologists now, it's just completely obvious within five years deep learning is going to do better than radiologists."[14] The US Food and Drug Administration approved the first AI algorithm for medical imaging that same year, and there are now more than 80 approved algorithms in the United States and a similar number in Europe.

The number of radiologists working in the United States, however, *increased* by about 7% between 2015 and 2019.[15,16] Only a third of radiologists get help from any type of machine learning, and those who do tend to use it for work-list management, image enhancement, operations, and measurements. Only about 11% of radiologists use it for image interpretation in a clinical practice, and 72% of those who do not use it have no plans to change. Of those who do use it, 94% say its performance is inconsistent.[17] All of this even though analyzing images for signs of disease seems like something machine learning should be good at.

Andrew Ng recently summed up the situation:

> When we collect data from Stanford Hospital, then we train and test on data from the same hospital... [the algorithms] are comparable to human radiologists in spotting certain conditions... Take that same model... to an older hospital down the street, with an older machine, and the technician uses a slightly different imaging protocol, that data drifts to cause the performance... to degrade significantly. In contrast, any human radiologist can walk down the street to the older hospital and do just fine. So even though at a moment in time, on a specific data set, we can show this works, the clinical reality is that these models still need a lot of work to reach production. ... All of AI, not just healthcare, has a proof-of-concept-to- production gap.[18]

The problem here isn't a poorly fit model, and it's not systematically biased data. It's a bad problem. The task isn't to simply classify images. The task was to classify

[14] https://www.youtube.com/watch?v=2HMPRXstSvQ&t=29s

[15] https://www.aamc.org/data-reports/workforce/interactive-data/number-people-active-physician-specialty-2015

[16] https://www.statista.com/statistics/209424/us-number-of-active-physicians-by-specialty-area/

[17] https://qz.com/2016153/ai-promised-to-revolutionize-radiology-but-so-far-its-failing

[18] https://spectrum.ieee.org/andrew-ng-xrays-the-ai-hype

images that (1) show a wide range in quality, stemming from the age and quality of the machinery as well as the nature of the medical problem, and (2) will be acted upon by people who vary widely in the attention and skill with which they interpret information. Researchers told a simplistic story about the problem, which caused them to collect insufficiently varied data and also caused them to build tools with insufficient appreciation for how the models based on that data would get used.

Before we ask if we trust our data, and certainly before even thinking about asking if we trust our model, we need to ask if we trust our understanding of the business problem we're trying to solve. No data is big enough, and no model advanced enough, to solve a problem that no one wants solved.

I co-founded Aampe, a company that uses messages like push notifications as an experimentation engineer to learn user communication preferences.[19] From the time we founded the company, I validated a lot of models and explored a lot of data, but the grand majority of my work building Aampe's machine learning systems focused, ultimately, on problem definition.

Channels like push notifications are of high value for companies: they land directly on the customer's phone, and no customer ever looks at a push notification and asks "how did they get my contact information?" When a person downloads an app, they expect to get push notifications, and if they don't want them, then they can turn them off in their phone settings.

We started out thinking we were solving a problem of competency. Companies had this channel to send messages directly to their customers, but what do you send? A typical clothing retailer has a dozen or so major product categories containing tens of thousands of different products. And once you decide what to send, how do you word it? You could just offer a discount with every message, but one study showed that as many as 49% of discounted grocery sales would have occurred even if the customer hadn't been offered a promotion.[20] Let's even say you've decided on your topic and your text – What about the timing? When do you send the message? Different people do their shopping on different days at different times and under different circumstances. Figuring out how to inform and encourage without pestering is a legitimately hard problem.

We built a tool where users could write a message and then tag parts of each message to add meaningful variation. So if you're selling shoes, you might write a message for high-tops, and then tag "high-tops," and add alternates for "low-top," "sandals," "slippers," and so on. You might write a sentence that says "Check out our great deals!" for someone who cares about cost, but then tag the sentence and replace it with "Put together a style that's all your own." for someone who cares more about expressing themselves or "Find fashions from top designers." for someone who cares about prestige. And then we took all these tagged variations and ran massive continuous experiments, trying out a variation with a customer, seeing how

---

[19] https://www.aampe.com/

[20] https://www.marketing-interactive.com/49-of-discounted-groceries-would-have-occurred-without-promo

they responded, using machine learning to generalize those results to the whole customer base, and then use those predictions to decide what to send each individual person next. The whole thing was elegant and sophisticated and beautiful.

No one wanted it. No, that's not true. Not *enough* people wanted it *enough* to pay us *enough* money that we could meet *enough* our payroll and expenses. Startups never face problems of yes or no. Startups always face problems of *enough*.

We invested more in our sales efforts, tried to come up with more convincing pitches, and played with our pricing – none of it was enough. We were starting to run low on funding from our investors. That caused some soul searching. What if, we wondered, this isn't a problem of competence? What if our potential customers don't care that they can't make good decisions about what and how and when to send messages to their customers? What if the problem is simpler than that?

What if they're just drowning under constant requests for more messaging from all the stakeholders in their company and simply can't keep up? We stumbled on this possibility talking to one of our customers. He'd devoted two employees to writing enough messaging to feed our experiment system. They'd only written messages for their beauty line. It had taken them 2.5 months. He loved the product and wanted to expand it to luxury and sportswear lines, but he was assuming each of those would also take 2.5 months. He didn't have that time. *We* didn't have that time.

So we did something we'd been reluctant to do up to that point. We started looking at GPT-3, a text-generation model offered by OpenAI. Generative models are problematic. Asking a generative model to write your messaging is kind of like asking Twitter to write your messaging – things can go bad real quick, before you even notice it's happening. Also, those models tend to suffer from "drift" – if you ask it to write five sentences, you very often encounter at least one sentence that pairs fine with the sentence immediately prior, but makes no sense combined with the sentences before that one. Also, generating the number of unique messages we would need to feed our system would cost thousands of dollars a month in API fees.

We'd already solved a lot of those problems, however, without realizing that's what we were doing. We didn't work with whole messages – we worked with discrete parts. We could generate a bunch of offerings, a bunch of value propositions, a bunch of calls to action, a bunch of fun facts, and a bunch of emoji and then mix and match them to get the scale we needed. The AI could do the work of putting together single, coherent sentences, and our algorithms could do the work of figuring out which pieces appealed to which customers and combine those appealing pieces into a sentence.

Using our system to do that recombination brought our API fees down to around 31 cents per month per customer, and suddenly customers could write millions of messages in minutes. In fact, we started coming to sales demos with hundreds of thousands of messages already written for a customer. We didn't have to tell them that it was easy to message with us – we could show it.

All of our experimentation pipelines and learning algorithms are wonderful – they represent some of the best data science work I've ever done. But by themselves, they solved the wrong problem. Once we figured out the right problem, we could combine what we had built with additional tools, and that's when we were able to make a difference.

Play to Your Strengths

I was trained as an anthropologist, but my job title has never been "anthropologist." I bill myself as a data scientist because, to the people who work with and employ me, that label embodies desirable skills and experience, while the label of anthropologist simply does not. The companies that have hired me have never recognized "anthropologist" as something that would be of value to them. I don't blame them for that. If anything, I'm inclined to blame anthropology (the profession, not the body of knowledge). At any rate, I have interesting work and a good job, so I'm not going to quibble over a title.

That being said, I think a lot of the value I've been able to add as a data scientist is directly the result of my being an anthropologist. I approach problems differently than most other data scientists I've met, and I can see how many of those differences stem from the skills and perspectives I developed before I ever learned how to code.

I think data science needs anthropology. I don't mean that people whose job titles are "data scientist" need to join forces with people whose job titles are "anthropologist."[21] There are certain ways of trying to understand the world–ways I discovered when I was learning to be an anthropologist and developed further over the course of my career – that don't seem to be learned by most people who call themselves data scientists, and I believe the profession of data science is unnecessarily fragile because of that.

There's an ethical component to this as well. Historically, anthropologists benefited professionally from information given by people–for a long time actually referred to as "informants" –who were never given a say in how that information would be used. Informants were described in and on the anthropologist's terms, not their own. That should sound familiar: the automated compilation of personal data that characterizes data science does what anthropology did, except at scale. The people whom the data represents rarely have a say in how it is used and are often unaware that it was collected in the first place, and too often they receive only marginal benefit. It's hard to imagine two professions less similar on the surface, but in this particular aspect, they have a lot in common.

There was no clear watershed moment when anthropology started to try to move away from the practice of benefiting from others' voicelessness – and, of course, no one can claim that that movement is an accomplished fact today.[22] Data science, however, hasn't really done much of that sort of moving at all. A few in the profession briefly talked about maybe writing up a professional code of ethics, but those efforts fizzled after no one was willing to demand anything more than a promise to watch out and not do bad stuff.[23,24]

---

[21] I appreciate the motivation behind such initiatives (e.g., https://www.epicpeople.org/data-science-and-ethnography/), but I think on the whole they tend to be pretty barren.

[22] Bennet, John W. 1998. "Classic Anthropology," American Anthropologist, Vol. 100, No. 4 (Dec., 1998), pp. 951–956. Last accessed on 28 November 2022 at https://www.jstor.org/stable/681819

[23] https://towardsdatascience.com/ethical-codes-vs-ethical-code-fea118987a5

[24] https://towardsdatascience.com/an-ethical-code-cant-be-about-ethics-66acaea6f16f

The data scientist in me recognizes the clear benefit of data science products – the personalized experiences, the convenient inferences about my preferences, and the time savings – but research generates information, and information facilitates action, and the anthropologist in me holds an entrenched conviction that any such action should be made to benefit,or at the very least in no way withhold benefit from,those who ultimately made that action possible. This is especially true when that information was gathered from people without their full knowledge, under-standing, and consent. It's not enough to try to get more opinions on an approach or product, though naturally we should do that. Data science operates at scale, which means we need a way of revoicing people *at scale*.

Treating our data science work as ethnographic work first and engineering work second doesn't fix all those problems, but it's a start – a step in the right direction. I've benefited immensely from being a data scientist who came from the social sciences. For me, however, this is more than just a matter of career progression. Data science has and will continue to change the world we live in. If we're going to create that change, the least the world can demand in return is that we be responsible stewards.

Alt-Academic Career Paths

Bethany Morrison

You can be a professor, or you can be a data scientist. That's it. Those are the options. I don't know if my graduate program *really* intended to communicate this message to me, but it was the message I received. As a first-generation college student, I learned it from the experiences of the students ahead of me in my graduate program, and I learned it from the faculty who advised and mentored me. The message I received was that my PhD in political science prepared me for a career on the tenure track. If I **had** to do something other than the tenure track, then I could use my quantitative methods training in government or the private sector.

Here's the problem with that alternative to the tenure track: I was in it for the teaching. Teaching was my passion. Good teachers changed the course of my intellectual and professional life and I wanted to do the same. I experienced that elusive feeling of "flow"—of being fully immersed and deeply energized—when I was teaching. When I thought about the alternatives to the tenure track, such as working in government or the private sector, I felt discouraged. Why did I even go to graduate school—why did I run this gauntlet—if teaching wasn't at the finish line?

The summer before my last year in graduate school, my dissertation adviser suggested alternatives to the professoriate within the academy. This path has been colloquialized as "Alt-Ac" or #altac, short for alternative academic. It characterizes the career path of PhDs working in nonfaculty professional positions within academia, often in fields outside their dissertation field. Initially I dismissed him out-of-hand. I wanted to teach, and teaching meant being in front of a classroom of undergraduates. Lucky for me, the conversation sparked another conversation, which led to a set of experiences, which led to my current career as an educational developer—a great fit for me.

B. Morrison (✉)
University of Michigan, Ann Arbor, MI, USA
e-mail: morrisbe@umich.edu

© The Author(s), under exclusive license to Springer Nature
Switzerland AG 2023
N. Jackson (ed.), *Non-Academic Careers for Quantitative Social Scientists*,
Texts in Quantitative Political Analysis,
https://doi.org/10.1007/978-3-031-35036-8_4

What My Career Looks Like Now

Educational developers, also known as faculty developers, are usually housed in a university's teaching and learning center. Alternatively, they may be found in the institution's faculty development center or employed directly by schools, including public policy schools, or university programs. My day-to-day work involves consulting with faculty as they work to improve their teaching practices. Sometimes this work takes place one-on-one, in conversations or classroom observations. Other days I lead more formal programs, such as a one-time 75-min workshop or a semester-long faculty learning community.

An example: A faculty member approached my center with a teaching concern. She was a petite young woman teaching graduate students. Some of her students were older than her. Some had careers prior to returning to graduate school. Her principal concern was that she was not projecting confidence and authority in the classroom. I suggested a classroom observation.

The classroom observation is one of my favorite parts of my job. I love critically reflecting on what's working in the classroom, what isn't working, and why. In fact, when I was still a student, I often found myself reflecting on those questions in class sessions. *She is such a soft-spoken professor in a male-dominated field. Why is it that we all are so rapt?* And *it's interesting that my classmates come to this class so prepared, but don't do the same in our other class together. What is it about the instruction that encourages this behavior?* I like to think it was an early sign that this career path was a good fit for me.

During a classroom observation, I observe with a few areas in mind, such as organization, interactivity, instructor delivery, and inclusive teaching practices. One example of a skill that falls under organization is whether the instructor shares her objectives for the class and whether she returns to them at the end of the period. This practice helps students parse out what information is important and the hierarchy of information. Interactivity refers to interactions between students and the instructor and among students. For example, how did the instructor respond to questions? Did she incorporate activities that allowed the students to learn from each other? This practice builds classroom community, along with giving students the opportunity to practice with concepts and material they are learning. Delivery characterizes her presentation skills. Could she be heard? Were her slides easy to read? Lastly, inclusive teaching practices describe building an environment where all students feel like they belong. For example, does the instructor use all the students' names and pronounce them correctly?

Let's return to the instructor with concerns about her authority. In my observation with her, I noticed a lot of strengths, particularly when it came to her organization and clarity. I wanted to be sure to highlight those strengths—not only because it feels good and builds goodwill to highlight strengths. I want her to recognize it as a strength and reinforce it. I thought she encouraged a lot of interaction between herself and the students but could use more opportunities for student-to-student interaction. Because I sat in on the class, I was able to brainstorm particular moments during the class that were opportunities for more interaction. And her concerns about projecting authority? She was soft-spoken, but her students seemed respectful. The graduate program was a professional one, and she had valuable work experiences in the profession before teaching. I noticed how rapt the students were when she related the skills they were practicing back to her own experiences in the profession. While I didn't see evidence of a lack of authority, I encouraged her to provide more connections to her experience in the field to address her concerns.

What about the other part of my day-to-day—leading more formal programs for instructors? One example is that in my center, we run a faculty learning community for new faculty members. It is a voluntary experience and usually around 15 faculty members sign up. We met four times over the course of the first semester. There was a common reading assignment from the excellent *How Learning Works* (Ambrose et al. 2010). The chapters reviewed the science of how learning works with regard to a particular area—for example, how prior knowledge affects learning or how course climate affects learning. Then it suggested concrete teaching strategies aligned with the science. In our meetings, we'd discuss what we read, debrief on their first semester of teaching, and try to draw connections between the two. New faculty build relationships on campus and learn about best practices for teaching. With each program, we build a university climate that values teaching.

One-on-one consultations and formal teaching programming are the core of a position in faculty development. I do, however, have other responsibilities. For example, I'm responsible for keeping up-to-date with the existing literature on evidence-based practices in teaching and learning. I may be asked to write or develop resources for faculty on teaching and learning for our website or published materials. Faculty developers may serve in an advisory capacity as department leaders and institutional leaders make decisions that impact teaching and learning on campus. For example, if a department is reconceptualizing its introductory-level courses to encourage more majors, the department might ask a faculty developer to weigh in.

Within these additional roles, I have opportunities to utilize some of the research design and methodological skills I developed in political science. I have designed, fielded, and interpreted the results of university-wide surveys of faculty and students. I've helped faculty with research design when they wanted to investigate the impact of a teaching intervention on student learning. I have built a relational database and developed a data collection protocol, so we could track the work of our teaching and learning center and make data-informed decisions about our programming.

While I work as a generalist, some educational developers are more specialized. For example, some educational developers work primarily with graduate students and postdocs, preparing them to teach and for future careers as faculty. Some educational developers are dedicated to particular segments of the faculty, working primarily, for instance, with STEM faculty or business school faculty. Some positions work on particular subject areas within teaching and learning. For example, our center has positions dedicated to diversity, inclusion, and equity in classroom contexts and other positions dedicated to research and assessment.

How to Become a Faculty Developer

There isn't one path into a career in educational development. It is common for folks in faculty positions (on the tenure track or not) to transition into a role at teaching and learning centers. Think of this as the mid-career path into faculty development. I took the early-career path. Both paths are well-trod.

When my dissertation advisor suggested that I look at alt-ac positions after graduation, I **nearly** dismissed him out of hand. As I mentioned earlier, I wanted to teach, and I thought alt-ac meant being an *administrator* (you'll have to imagine my judgmental nose wrinkle at the term). An opportunity emerged for an "informational interview," i.e., an informal conversation over coffee, with someone who had moved from a tenure-track position into educational development. That seemed low-stakes enough, so I pursued it. That's my first suggestion: ask folks in the field to chat over coffee. Your university likely has a teaching and learning center, so that's a natural place to start.

My PhD institution's faculty development center had a few positions for graduate students, one fulltime fellowship and a handful of 10-h-a-week assistantships. My next tentative, low-stakes step into the field of educational development was to apply for one of these assistantships. It was an opportunity to learn about the profession without closing any doors to traditional academic positions. That's my next suggestion: look for these opportunities.

I loved the work environment at that faculty development center. I was learning lots about the field of educational development. I decided to take another step down the path. I applied for postdoctoral positions at centers for teaching and learning. A couple of things to keep in mind as you consider this suggestion: There are not tons of postdocs at teaching and learning centers. It is a relatively new idea, and most centers are not large enough to support one, so postdoc experience is not a deal breaker on the job market. Where do you learn about these positions? Well, at the time I am writing this, the profession's main way of communicating with each other is a Google group called the POD Network Open Discussion Group. The POD (Professional and Organizational Developers) Network is the professional organization to which educational developers belong. Yes, it is lo-fi, but every position in the field will be mentioned there.

Both my graduate assistantship and my postdoc were opportunities for me to learn about the profession, while keeping the door open to academic jobs. That was the main reason I pursued this path, but there was another benefit. As you already know, there are too many PhDs and not enough faculty positions. My experiences in faculty development gave me an edge in the application process—I knew more about the profession relative to the other PhDs fresh out of graduate school in the application pool. In addition, I was able to communicate a story other than "I'm applying for everything because the tenure track market didn't pan out." I had an established interest in the career path.

That said, you can apply for entry-level positions in educational development out of graduate school without these experiences and be successful, particularly if you have experience teaching and can demonstrate that you are reflective about teaching. These entry-level positions go by different names, depending on the institution. These include, but are not limited to, "educational developer," faculty developer," "instructional consultant," and "teaching support specialist." In many small centers across the country, the entry-level position has the title of assistant director.

There are a few very good reasons to pursue a career in educational development. Being on a team of smart folks from a wide range of disciplines is intellectually stimulating. The work environment is warm, equity-focused, and family-friendly. Working one-on-one and in close communities of faculty as they develop as instructors is immensely rewarding. It's a place where your passion for teaching can be shouted from the mountain tops, rather than held as a closely guarded secret. If you want to promote evidence-informed teaching practices in higher education, explore a career in educational development.

From the Academy to Tech Startups: Considerations and Opportunities

Susanna Supalla

As a graduate student coming out of 5 plus years of an academic program, considering a job at a startup may feel akin to planning a trip to Mars. Yet a PhD program and the startup environment have many similarities, and the ways in which startups differ from academia may feel refreshing.

Graduate programs and startups are both hubs of innovation, where creativity and drive are rewarded. Startups often require collaboration and teamwork and a commitment to a common goal – a notion that may be absent in graduate school, where a lot of work occurs in isolation and PhD students must often compete for funding and research opportunities.

Startups are hardly a monolithic type of entity, though, and differ along a number of dimensions, notably including the extent to which they value academic experience. In this chapter I discuss some of the biggest similarities and differences between startup and academic life and then delve into five dimensions along which startups vary. I hope this chapter will enable readers to better determine whether startup life would be a good fit for them and, if so, will spark valuable questions for readers to ask potential employers in the application and interviewing process.

Choosing your post-academic work environment can be daunting, but keep in mind that if you choose tech startup life, you are likely not choosing a permanent position. LinkedIn reports that the technology sector has the highest turnover rate of any sector.[1] Attrition is higher in high-growth startups than in the tech industry

---

[1] Booz, Michael. (2018, March 15). These 3 Industries Have the Highest Talent Turnover Rates. Retrieved from https://www.linkedin.com/business/talent/blog/talent-strategy/industries-with-the-highest-turnover-rates

---

S. Supalla (✉)
Staff Data Scientist, Hinge Health, Washington, DC, USA

© The Author(s), under exclusive license to Springer Nature
Switzerland AG 2023
N. Jackson (ed.), *Non-Academic Careers for Quantitative Social Scientists*,
Texts in Quantitative Political Analysis,
https://doi.org/10.1007/978-3-031-35036-8_5

overall, according to Founders Circle surveys of its members.[2] One positive aspect of that is that there is no such thing as choosing wrong, as a startup job that is a poor fit can still offer valuable lessons, and a short tenure at a single startup will hardly destroy your future potential. So should you choose startup life, realize that it does not need to be your whole life and, like academia, can remain simply a part of the whole.

In addition, if you have caught the entrepreneurial bug, and you yourself want to start a business down the road, serving in the leadership of a small company will offer experiences you will never have in academia or big tech. Consider it your further training in entrepreneurship, enabling you to act on your dreams.

My Own Academic-to-Startup Transition

I started graduate school in political science like many, with a goal of joining the professoriate and spending the rest of my life in academia. I had already developed some research questions and was looking forward to crafting a research agenda, as well as learning to pursue answers with rigor. As a former undergraduate computer science minor, I was eager to further develop my technical skills in statistics and formal modeling and apply my programming skills to answering important social questions. I dreamed of writing books challenging the status quo, testifying before Congress in my areas of expertise, and delivering powerful lectures to mold young minds.

The realities of graduate education soon set in, as I toiled away doing research and writing papers largely alone, with a small audience of fellow graduate students and professors. Once I started assistant teaching, I had a few star pupils and many other students who behaved like homework was imposing on them when they had better things to do. I watched the more senior graduate students and newer professors in my department battle for publication after publication, never sure what would be enough to get that dream job, much less keep it. I calculated the number of years I would need to endure before I would maybe, just maybe, reach that dream where I could challenge the status quo. The number was high.

As I worked on my PhD, I thought back to those years before graduate school, when I had worked on political campaigns, every day making a difference. I realized I didn't need a PhD to challenge the status quo. Yet now I almost had a PhD. I knew I could go back to what I was doing before – fundraising and managing political campaigns – but I had so many new skills that I wanted to contribute. And then a job description came into my email from the Political Methodology listserv. It was for a "Senior Modeling Analyst" position at a new data analytics and technology company formed by Obama for America alumni, including two political science PhDs who were building predictive models and conducting field experiments to improve outreach for progressive causes and candidates. It brought my entire set of skills and experiences to bear in one position. I applied, tested, interviewed, interviewed again, and ultimately got the job.

Since then, I have worked as a data scientist at four startups in politics and in healthcare, working alongside other PhDs, as well as brilliant technologists in software engineering, data science, product management, user research, and UX design. I have conducted national surveys, built machine learning models to predict voter turnout and candidate support, and designed field experiments to measure outreach program effects. In healthcare, I have predicted who would be eligible for subsidies for Obamacare so they could be encouraged to apply for healthcare, worked alongside oncologists to design interventions to improve patient care at a lower cost, published articles calling for methodology changes in Medicare value-based care payment programs, and collaborated on cross-functional teams to build software platforms enabling healthcare practitioners to explore their patients' Medicare claims. My work is challenging the status quo now, and I still have the opportunity to persuade key stakeholders and mentor colleagues – they're just often doctors instead of members of Congress and other data scientists rather than undergraduates. If anything, I'm closer to the action I had dreamed of than I would be in academia.

Not everything has been smooth sailing. I've been laid off twice. On one of those occasions, the company dissolved entirely. I've faced workplace injustices, big and small, and tried to stand up for myself or my colleagues and lost. I've earned less money than my big tech counterparts. I've overworked myself and been overworked by others.

I've also been a part of fantastic teams with wonderful, talented colleagues. I've had the opportunity to build and belong to such tight-knit groups that accomplished feats together. This is the experience I have realized was what I most desired and did not find fulfilling in academia.

I didn't set out on my career path seeking to join a startup. I wasn't looking for a way to make a lot of money. But I found a set of small companies that shared a commitment to innovation and creativity. The fact that they all needed to battle for funding made them scrappy and that they were small gave me the opportunity to quickly serve in leadership roles and deliver feedback directly to the CEO. When there are few staff members to accomplish big dreams, after all, everyone quickly gains the experience to meaningfully and transparently contribute to those dreams.

Ultimately, working for others for several years also reminded me that I still had my own questions and wanted to craft my own agenda. So I started my own data science and analytics consulting company. I now choose which projects to take on and have the opportunity to seek out the kind of work that challenges the status quo in the way that I want to challenge it. If it doesn't work out, I know there will be other startups seeking data scientists for years to come, and I've built a solid network of former colleagues to help me find my place.

Dimensions of Startup Jobs to Pay Attention to When Applying

It is unusual to see a single job description for a single company, find it to be the perfect fit, and then get the job. Ultimately, you will most likely read many job descriptions, apply to many jobs, interview for several, and, if you apply for long enough, consider multiple offers. How should you go about filtering through all the startup jobs out there? Here I outline some dimensions of those jobs, based on my own experience of tradeoffs across companies, to consider when choosing where to apply and where to accept a position.

Expert Versus Beginner

Founders of a new company may come to their chosen industry as either a knowledgeable insider with an innovation derived from expertise or as an outsider who gleans ideas from other industries or trades. Similarly, startups may look to you, a potential hire, as bringing expertise in the field or as bringing a beginner's mindset. A startup working to categorize legislative bills using machine learning may highly value your dissertation research on the same topic. Or, you may bring your machine learning knowledge to the insurance industry with little knowledge of how claims are adjudicated, but also no limiting assumptions. In any job, you will likely find aspects in which you are knowledgeable and others in which you are not.

As a PhD, the expertise you will bring to any job is the experience of having amassed knowledge on other subjects before. You spent 5 years (or more) developing your research on a specific area, and now that you have done that once, you can do it again. The degree to which you will enter as an already-accomplished expert or a naive beginner will vary from job to job, just as startups as a whole vary in their placement on this dimension.

When considering different jobs, weighing the kinds of expertise you bring to each, as well as the types of things you would have to learn, may differentiate them and allow you to better consider alignment with your preferences.

Short Term Versus Long Term

The time horizon on which a startup operates could be critical to your happiness in a role. Does the company have many small projects on which it delivers services or technology products on a short timeline? Or does the company have a single large product that will take multiple years before it reaches the market? Considering such questions and your own preferences for working on short-term versus long-term projects may inform the kinds of jobs you find fulfilling.

In academic work, the dissertation is for many a long-term project. Did you enjoy spending multiple years on a single goal? Or did you prefer to think of your work as smaller deliverables and celebrate milestones along the way? Do you prefer to work on big research questions or to research small issues at a time, maybe on many different subjects? Answers to these questions may inform the types of jobs in which you would be happy.

Implementation Versus Development

Another version of the short-term versus long-term dimension is whether the startup or role focuses on executing existing analyses or products or researching new methods. A company or job may involve new applications of existing technology, or the production of new technology, or some balance of the two. Implementation-focused positions tend to align with short-term deliverables, while research and development positions often build more long-term solutions, though this is not a hard-and-fast rule.

Your preference for concrete versus abstract thinking, and the kinds of work you preferred doing in graduate school, may inform where on this dimension your preferred role would lie.

Services Versus Products

Startups may focus on services or technology products or both. Services tend to be solutions customized for each client, while product technology is often generalized to meet multiple users' needs.

As an example, a client who is implementing a program and wants to measure its treatment effects can be served with either a custom analytics solution – where the company acts as a consultant for the client, learns about the particular program, and measures the treatment effect – or a software product where the client can enter sizes of control and treatment groups and the outcomes for each. If you work at a company that produces the first type of solution, you will likely be implementing short-term projects and working more with customers. If you produce the second type of solution, you may work more with software engineers and other technical team members on the backend of the software product that the customer never sees, and you may produce and fine-tune your product over a longer time horizon to meet the needs of more users.

The kind of work the company does has implications for what your work life will be like – who you will work with most often, on what time horizon you will be expected to complete projects, and the types of skills you will be expected to know and learn. The intersection of these dimensions may also provide some insight into the pace of the startup. If they are working on multiple products, customizing each product for a different set of customers, and delivering each product on a short time-line, that may lead to a more chaotic (or exciting!) atmosphere.

Hierarchical Versus Holacratic

Finally, the structure of the company itself, and how its employees interact, is a criti-cal ingredient in a startup's culture. Because so many startups are founded by lead-ers chosen because of their great ideas (and not necessarily their management potential), the organizational structure of a startup may have come about intention-ally or more organically. In either case, a company's structure and associated pro-cesses can reveal a lot about what it will be like to work there.

Some companies form as more collaborative groups of equals, while others highly value chain of command. Many levels of hierarchy can make communication routes and authority and delegation clear, as well as create clear paths for career advancement, but they can also impede the flow of information and individual employees' feelings of ownership over their work. Meanwhile, holacracy can empower employees, offering them more claim over the company's future and more information on its direction, but it can also lead to chaos with unclear roles and responsibilities.

While companies can belong somewhere in the middle between hierarchy and holacracy, they may also seesaw between the two, with crises of confidence leading to frequent reorganizations and leadership changes. While neither structure is per-fect, a startup will be in better shape if it is aware of its own structure, as well as the associated benefits and limitations. Even better yet, if the company has introduced processes to counteract the downsides of its chosen structure, you may find it to have a great culture no matter your own organizational preference.

Practical Questions

Now I turn to some of the elephants in the room surrounding startups, namely, com-pensation and career trajectory. It's common when discussing startups to hear the term "unicorn" – that rare software startup that is expected to be bought for a zillion dollars, making all of its employees and equity holders millionaires and hot com-modities as potential future founders. Aileen Lee, the founder of Cowboy Ventures, coined the term in 2013, and over the next 5 years, the number of unicorns in the USA grew to 145.[3] The vast majority of startups are not unicorns, just like most academics will not win the Nobel Prize in their field.

---

[3] Clark, Kate. (2018, November 16). Unicorns aren't special anymore. Retrieved from https://tech-crunch.com/2018/11/16/unicorns-arent-special-anymore/

Startups involve a degree of risk that is not present in taking a position at a larger company. The company has not existed long enough to have a proven track record, and if the company has sought investors, the investors will expect the company to exit and return that investment – either by selling to another company or going public.

That can be good and bad – more career transitions are common for people in startup life, either adapting to new roles in the same company or changing companies entirely. You may also be unemployed after funding runs out or a role doesn't work out. That risk may also provide more opportunity – for trying new things, and different kinds of work, for different companies, in different fields.

Startup life requires flexibility, creativity, commitment, and a sense of adventure. If you keep up your technical skills in your startup roles, it's often easy to transition into big tech for more stability if your life circumstances or outlook changes.

Often the tiny potential for a huge payoff is reflected in salaries: startups commonly have compensation packages that are part salary and part equity. For some companies that will never realistically have a successful exit, company valuations and equity are meaningless. But startup salaries in general, even if you ignore the equity portion, can be better than an academic salary.

I think we all hear of those startups where the founders ask you to work for stock options only and no salary whatsoever. That certainly presents a red flag, but for a company that has real potential, that may be what they need to do to get it off the ground. That doesn't mean that you should ever count on a payoff from those stock options. A great way to value your compensation package is to use those quantitative social science skills to calculate your salary expectation, given the probability of a successful exit. But, also remember to take into account the time horizon of those payoffs and the practicalities of paying rent and other bills in the short term.

Ultimately, as a PhD, you have put extensive time into training that gives you a long list of transferable skills, as other chapters in this book discuss. Your base salary will likely be less in a startup than in a big tech position, but as a PhD, you are far from entry level, and your compensation and position should reflect your experience. However, startup salaries are far from standardized, and they will look different from industry to industry, city to city, company to company, and even from first employee hired to fifth employee hired at the same company. Negotiating for a startup position is a little bit like planning that trip to Mars, whether you're coming from academia or a tech incubator program. Rather than seek out certainty, seek out solidarity with people who have been through the experience before.

Lastly, What About Starting Your Own Company?

Working in a small startup is excellent preparation for starting your own company. As a PhD graduate, you already know how to develop an idea and market it to a small group of stakeholders – your dissertation – from proposal through execution. That may not have gone perfectly, but you have experience in the kind of long-term planning and production that others outside the academy may never get to do.

But now, instead of distributing your idea freely to the world as an academic, you need to generate money from it. You also may need to build a whole team to execute the idea, rather than doing so yourself. In many startups, regardless of your position, you will feel the stresses of needing profitability. You may be asked to repeatedly iterate on work or pivot completely to satisfy a paying customer or prospect. You may need to explain your work to nontechnical audiences who are holding the pocket strings. I'm not talking about getting rich. But I am talking about building a product or selling services that are good enough that someone will pay money for them. That's a hurdle you don't ever need to jump as an academic.

There is no better preparation for trying to sell your idea than trying to sell someone else's. And if you're that person in graduate school who was like me – busting at the seams to *do* something and change the world, rather than write about it – you might be an entrepreneur yourself. PhD programs in the social sciences are poor preparation for the mechanics of starting your own business. And those are also things you will not learn in big tech roles. But those are things you can learn while being an excellent addition to someone else's small business or startup.

Ultimately, as a social science PhD, you are well positioned to be a top-notch contributor in any startup you choose. And ultimately, when you are applying for jobs at a startup, you are choosing the company as much as the company is choosing you. Joining a startup carries risk, and it is up to you to assess and weigh that risk against other options. It might be the right adventure for you, and if not, this volume has many other avenues for you to explore. Enjoy the ride, no matter which planet is your destination.

Opportunities and Pathways in Survey Research

Natalie Jackson

The study of social science is essentially the study of human behavior. One of the best ways to get information about human behavior when it cannot be directly observed is to ask humans questions and get their answers. Survey research is the study of just that – how to ask questions and get answers in ways that inform research questions on an infinite range of topics to achieve an equally infinite variety of goals.

Survey research is not only used in social sciences, however. It is utilized in any field in which human input is necessary. The range of uses for survey research skills makes it worth investing in when opportunities arise in graduate school. The range of jobs in which the skills can be used can make for a flexible and satisfying nonacademic career. This chapter will explore the various uses of survey research skills, the types of places that hire survey researchers, and how to learn practical survey research while in graduate school and beyond. But first, a little about how this author got into a long and happy career in survey research.

My Pathway

I had applied to PhD programs in political science with a goal of going into academia with a teaching focus – I wanted to get into a program with funding and a teaching assistantship. When that did *not* happen, it turned out to be the best thing that ever happened to me. The University of Oklahoma was the first program to make an offer to me – but it did not come with a teaching assistantship. It came with a research assistantship at the OU POLL (Public Opinion Learning Laboratory). I

N. Jackson (✉)
Research Consultant, District of Columbia, DC, USA

N. Jackson (ed.), *Non-Academic Careers for Quantitative Social Scientists*,
Texts in Quantitative Political Analysis,
https://doi.org/10.1007/978-3-031-35036-8_6

43

was crushed that I wouldn't be teaching right away, but I took the position with the idea that I would try to switch to teaching as soon as I could.

When I got to OU POLL, I barely knew what survey research was, but I very quickly learned. OU POLL in 2006 was a full-service telephone survey field house staffed by students and led by two graduate assistants and a director. I got a crash course in how to conduct research interviews, how to train and supervise staff, and how to analyze survey data. I spent time on the phones making the calls for a few shifts and then many hours monitoring and supervising as students collected data on all sorts of topics – economic studies of regions in Oklahoma, follow-up calls for the 1–800-QUIT-NOW tobacco cessation programs, surveys for potential jury pools and litigation, and public policy issues. The assistantship was set up to be a 2-year rotation, but I stayed on a third year to help ensure continuity during a director change. By my fourth year in graduate school, I had stopped trying to leave – I had gotten opportunities to be a teaching assistant in addition to the survey work, and I was hooked on doing survey research.

My intent was still to go into academia, though, until I was at a postdoc at Duke University and, for the first time in 5 years, not conducting surveys. I was *consulting* on surveys campus-wide, but not doing the data collection or following through on the projects myself. I missed doing data collection terribly. That realization shifted my focus to working outside of academia in survey research, rather than going on the academic job market. I had been aware of my options in this regard for a few years. I was very fortunate to have been connected with the American Association for Public Opinion Research (AAPOR) early in my graduate studies. That network, and attending the conference each year, showed me the wide variety of jobs out there for PhDs who love to find out what people think and do not necessarily want to do that from an academic vantage point. I had seen that it was normal to have a PhD and work outside of a university.

As my career has progressed, I have shifted focus within the broad survey research umbrella a couple of times, going from political polling at a liberal arts college to elections and forecasting at a major media organization, to business-oriented research at a nonprofit, and back to public policy polling in a different nonprofit. There are countless other roads I have not taken, but could, with this skill set.

What Does Survey Research Consist of?

As previously mentioned, survey research is quite literally asking people questions and getting their answers. That can take place in a variety of contexts and can be both quantitative and qualitative in its nature. Qualitative survey research consists of – but is not limited to – focus groups, in-depth interviewing, cognitive interviewing, and the like, anything where responses are free-form and *not* designed to be coded into data (although that can be, and often is, done later). A particularly salient example of qualitative research is user experience research. "UX" is a quickly growing sector of qualitative survey research that any company making a product for mass consumption can benefit from and involves systematically interviewing people about products and services.

Quantitative surveys are likely what most often comes to mind when the topic of survey research comes up. These are large-scale question-and-answer designs that immediately transform answers to questions into data that can be analyzed using statistical analysis. It can be easy to think that anyone can do survey research without specialized training (or on-the-job training, as I had), but there is an art and a science to asking people questions that begins with the very concept of who you want to talk to and how to reach them. Most quantitative surveys are designed with a goal of generalizability to the population concerned, but rarely can that entire population be surveyed.

As a complicated communication strategy, one that needs to be carefully designed in order to get reliable, valid, generalizable results, there are quite a few opportunities for specialization within survey research. The best way to think of this is the total survey error paradigm (Weisberg 2005) – basically, any one source of survey error can be a specialization. Coverage refers to how comprehensively (or not) you are able to cover your population in your potential sampling methods, sampling refers to how the sample is drawn, measurement is how questions are asked and answered, nonresponse refers to both sampled units declining to respond at all and refusing to answer individual questions, and post-survey refers to weighting and analysis. Errors at any of these stages – known and unknown – could render your survey result farther from the true population value. As such, each one can give survey researchers a career full of research – and heartburn.

Any one of those categories can become a survey researcher's specialty, or they can focus on substantive questions and explaining certain beliefs or phenomena (although the latter still requires thorough knowledge of the former). The directions within survey research are myriad, and perhaps the best part is that you need not choose a single one and stick with it for the rest of your career. There is ample opportunity to move and grow in different directions.

What Are the Opportunities for Survey Researchers, and Who Hires Them?

While asking people questions and analyzing their answers for meaning is a practice that dates back to ancient philosophy, survey research as a formal field has mostly developed in the last 80–90 years. In that relatively short amount of time, though, it has become common practice in a huge variety of industries – including academia, government, private, and nonprofit sectors. Any business or enterprise that has deals with people – serves people, wants people to buy something, wants people to vote for them, or needs to know things about people to allocate services – has a need for professionals who know how to gather opinion data and analyze it.

This means there are lucrative nonacademic careers available to survey researchers in fields as disparate as medicine (surveying patients about their health, symptoms, or experiences with a clinic or doctor) and political campaigns (surveying constituents about what makes them support a candidate).

Government and Contractors

The governments of many countries have large agencies to collect data on the people in their borders – and sometimes outside their borders – in order to allocate services to people and know about living conditions in the country. The US federal government, for example, has more than a dozen separate statistics agencies – basically all of which require collecting data from US residents to carry out their missions.[1] This does not count agencies that exist at the state or municipal level, many of which require their own data collection processes – and, therefore, hire survey researchers.

The vast quantities of work that government agencies need done give rise to a network of contracting companies – private companies that largely function to conduct government research that the agencies themselves do not have the capacity to support. These contractors might work with other nongovernment clients, but frequently the largest projects are done on behalf of federal agencies.

Private Sector

As the tech sector has grown over the last three decades, social scientists of all stripes have seen demand for their knowledge increase in private companies. Survey research is no different. Companies that sell things need to know what people are looking for in those sales, they need to know if products are working well for customers, and they need to keep tabs on their brand's reputation, among many other possible needs. They also might employ survey researchers to work internally – to survey company employees about satisfaction and job performance or to find out what the company should do to enhance the culture or improve employee retention.

Another part of the private sector is market research, usually conducted by market research firms that specialize in talking to consumers and helping companies understand what will resonate with their desired customers. Sometimes a company will have these analysts in-house, but separate market research firms can provide external assessments of how to connect with customers. The following chapter will look more closely at market research work and opportunities.

---

[1] https://www.ncbi.nlm.nih.gov/books/NBK447392/

Nonprofit Sector: Including Policy and Advocacy

The nonprofit sector is also a key employment area for survey researchers, as many "think tanks," policy institutes, and advocacy organizations need to understand both how people think about the issues they are interested in and, in the case of advocacy organizations, how they might use messaging to change minds and get people on board with their causes.

These jobs can be more substantive than statistical, since the organizations are often attached to specific issue areas. Or, the organization covers many areas, but researchers generally work on specific topics. These positions can be as much about assessing research others have done and determining good research from bad to make recommendations as about conducting original survey research – although often both are involved. While typically paying less than private sector positions, these jobs can be particularly rewarding for those who want to pursue survey research on a specific issue and those who want to leverage that research into advocacy efforts.

Politics and Elections

For the true political junkies of the world, political polling offers many career opportunities for survey researchers. One area of this, campaign work, is partisan – meaning, in the USA, Republican or Democrat – and sometimes attached to specific politicians. A position attached to a specific politician's campaign is unstable by nature, of course, subject to the candidate's successful election, but there are also independent (meaning, not attached to a candidate) partisan data firms, polling groups, and research organizations that work for many candidates or the party itself.

Outside of campaigns and elections, there are some independent political polling organizations that work specifically on political topics, but are not attached to campaigns, candidates, or parties. These organizations vary widely in their size and scope, and some nonprofits fit into this category.

Miscellaneous Other Possibilities

There are quite a few other types of opportunities in survey research, as the study of asking questions and analyzing answers is a useful skill in any forum where humans are involved. To mention just a couple of additional ones not covered above, jobs can sometimes be found in media, as well as alt-academic setups in colleges and universities.

Large media outlets sometimes hire survey researchers – often in the political realm – to conduct their own research on what the public thinks and inform their coverage. These positions are distinct from the behind-the-scenes product development and customer management positions that large media companies also have, in that these roles are public-facing and generating data and research for editorial purposes rather than business purposes. Particularly around elections, media will use survey research data to assess which candidate is winning (the horserace) and explain other political trends. They need experts to make sense of that data and its quality.

Alt-academic positions are those at colleges or universities as staff roles, rather than academic faculty. Some colleges and universities have survey research centers that do public-facing research on the state or nation. These roles resemble running a survey research shop, but with the critical distinction that part of the mission is to support student education. Often, even without such centers, colleges and universities will hire people with survey research expertise to work internally with alumni associations, students, staff and faculty, and other stakeholders to do survey research on matters related to the institution itself.

What It Looks Like to Work in Survey Research

The day-to-day work of conducting survey research varies considerably by sector and job function, but there are a few overarching themes. Your days are likely to be consumed by questions about how to contact people, including people who are difficult to contact. You will likely become at least somewhat obsessed with how questions are worded and how even the most minor wording changes could affect responses. I have literally argued – vigorously – over where to place a "the" in question wording. Above all, you likely want to know what makes people tick and how they think about certain topics. As a survey researcher working outside of academia, you will often have to work on the topics others assign you, rather than choosing what to work on. Hopefully you will be able to find a position that is in a general field you find interesting and that aligns with your goals, but as with all nonacademic positions, you are likely to be working on someone else's agenda.

In general, survey researchers will work with other teams to create products – whether in the form of knowledge, such as reports and press releases, or in the form of developing actual consumer products. Survey project development is, and should always be, collaborative. No one person will ever be able to guess all the possible ways the population might think about an issue or product, necessitating working with others to design the project. This is not solitary work.

Survey research is a very complex field in the twenty-first century, as contacting people has become more varied and people have become more resistant to unknown contact attempts. If you are designing survey projects with the general public as your target, some portion of your work life will likely be consumed by considering the tradeoffs in various methods of conducting surveys. These are not simple questions. The most thorough methods generally require lots of money, but there are also plenty of cheaper options that could be fit for your particular research purpose.

How to Learn Survey Research?

I never took a single class in survey research, and that background is more common in the industry than you might think. A strong quantitative methods background – such as most social science PhD programs have – is enough to get started post-degree. Many of the particulars of survey research can be learned on the job, as I did, plus a genuine curiosity about how people think and how to communicate with them. Every survey is a social interaction. That said, if you know that survey research is a skill set you want to build, either for the job opportunities or because you are really interested in how to ask questions and get answers, there are good ways to develop those skills while you are still in graduate school or while you are applying for jobs if you are already out.

Obviously while you are in graduate school, courses on survey research are the best way to explore the field. Look in social science departments throughout your institution to see if they are available, and look at the work professors in those fields do to see if anyone is a survey researcher. Even if a course is not available, independent study might be possible. If you cannot identify a pathway at your university, look outside. Programs such as the Joint Program on Survey Methodology, at the University of Maryland and operated as a consortium with the University of Michigan and some corporate and government survey research firms, often have courses that are open to those outside of their programs.[2] Separately, the University of Michigan offers a summer program in survey research.[3] In some cases, you might be able to get credit at your program for taking these external courses.

Additional options for learning survey research include non-course opportunities at your university, including in-house survey research centers like my experience working at the OU POLL. Internships with survey research firms can also be an excellent way to make connections, learn about the field, and possibly get a job later on. And finally, simply being exposed to the wealth of opportunities in the field is invaluable. For that, I strongly recommend getting involved with AAPOR or a regional chapter and attending a conference or event. You will be introduced to a community of researchers, many of whom have PhDs, who work in a wide variety of contexts – from academia to government, to private sector tech firms, to small think tanks, and beyond. In my experience, people in the survey field have been kind and willing to share their thoughts on the profession.

In sum, if measuring how people think about the world around them – any aspect of it! – appeals to you, survey research might be a good career path for you, with plenty of different options for employment.

---

[2] https://jpsm.umd.edu/

[3] https://si.isr.umich.edu/

Marketing Research with a PhD in Sociology

Michael Gibbons

I earned my PhD in Sociology from the University of Notre Dame in 2002 and taught at the University of Evansville until 2006. I left academia for a job in a marketing research and strategy consultancy serving the pharmaceutical and healthcare industries. At the time I had a spouse and two daughters, was 35 years old, and had lived in Midwestern cities for the entirety of my life. I worked at the consultancy for 3 years, until the 2008 recession hit the industry and led to my eventual layoff. I looked for work in both industry and academics and was fortunate to find a Visiting Assistant Professorship that eventually renewed for 3 years. This was good because it took the whole 3 years to find a tenure-track job as an Assistant Professor in Macon Georgia. I've been at Middle Georgia State University for 10 years now, more than half of them in administration.

This chapter details that experience in hopes it will help other academics realize their industry potential. I focus on the structure of the industry and the things I needed to unlearn and relearn differently.

Let me caveat this entire chapter by saying this is really a story of my own growth over these fairly different work experiences. You may not have had the same assumptions and ignorance coming out of graduate school as I did. After my PhD this was the most important experience I had for career development. It was far outside of my comfort zone, but it also showed me how much room I had to grow in both knowledge and professionalism.

M. Gibbons (✉)
Business Value Services, Higher Ed, Oracle Software, Macon, GA, USA
e-mail: michael.gibbons@mga.edu

N. Jackson (ed.), *Non-Academic Careers for Quantitative Social Scientists*,
Texts in Quantitative Political Analysis,
https://doi.org/10.1007/978-3-031-35036-8_7

Academic Frustrations

While I loved universities, my discipline, and the life of the mind, I found academics as a career limiting in a few ways. The first was relevance. As a grad student, the highest aspiration was to publish research in the best journals. By the time I was an Assistant Professor, I was already off of that track. I could still do research and publish in lower-tiered journals of course, but who reads those? Truthfully my research was likely to be limited to conference presentations. But here in the corporate world, there was the possibility that the work I did could inform brand strategy and guide multimillion-dollar decisions.

The second was location. I am from the Midwest and have a certain appreciation for small cities on the plains. Going into a PhD, I didn't think I would mind not getting a posting at Berkeley or Madison or Cambridge. However, I failed to recognize that the small rural colleges I would get offers in were not MY small rural colleges. My extended family was in Nebraska and Minnesota. But the jobs I was getting were in Indiana, Pennsylvania, and Georgia. I even interviewed in Alaska. Those are all fine places, but they were far from family, far from where things were going on. All of the downsides of small rural places, but none of my personal upsides.

The third was financial. For context, I was a professor 3 years into my current job and 6 years into teaching. I spent a lot of mental energy wondering about the mortgage payment on my small affordable home in a neighborhood with a less-than-awesome public school for my kids. We had a used Toyota Corolla for me and my wife, I was bicycling to campus to avoid buying another car, and I was worried about that payment on the Corolla. Even though we had tried to be frugal, having children in grad school meant that there was student debt. Frankly, as a professor I didn't see a way to increase my income to the point I would be able to meet those obligations.

Industry Hopes

I first learned about the position in an ad in the American Sociological Association listings, which is itself a little unusual, as there are very few industry jobs in their job bank.

This job was in Philadelphia, which is big enough for national concerts, museums, professional sports, and headquarters of lots of big companies. With a hub airport, I could likely afford to fly home to see my family.

The interview was straightforward, but surprising in its brevity. As an academic I was used to marathon interviews where I had an hour with one group of faculty, another hour with another faculty, an hour with a dean, an hour with the provost, an hour presentation, and so on. With this firm, I only needed to meet the two managers of the small business unit (SBU) that I was interviewing with. That took 45 minutes.

I met a few other people as they walked me around the office, but that was about it. They flew me halfway across the country and put me in a nicer hotel than any academic all for an interview that was essentially a couple hours.

The second thing that stood out was the lunch that concluded the interview, where a manager of another SBU met us.

Recalling my financial concerns, it's worth pointing out that we rode to lunch in my future boss's Maserati. The person joining us showed up in his brand-new Cadillac. The three of them wore two Rolexes and a Breitling. Suddenly I was a little self-conscious of my Timex. I would like to think I'm not a materialistic person, but given my concerns at that point in life, I paid special attention when one of them talked about the first time his bonus check was larger than his year's salary as a professor.

Interestingly, this firm was a collecting place for ex-professors and was full of PhDs. Among them were institutional/organizational psychology, which was the most common, but also neuropsychology, political science, and sociology. Many had taught for a little while before deciding they needed to make a better living. One important difference was that many of them had some exposure to this kind of firm or industry while they were in school. I however had not. I knew such researchers existed, but other than an old PBS Frontline on Ethnography and kids' "coolness," I didn't actually know anything about this industry.[1]

As an aside, this always bothered me. I knew that there were these kinds of research and firms where sociology students would fit well, but my path through the discipline had been so traditional that I had no exposure to them. Even though my undergrad was 90 minutes from Minneapolis/St. Paul, which has a strong consumer-packaged goods industry, when I asked my favorite professors where to work, none of them had any idea. I ended up in the boneless skinless breast room at a poultry factory as my first postcollege job.

For all these reasons, I was excited to be exploring this industry and this side of research.

Starting

At 7:45 am I sat in the parking lot of a small office complex with my stomach in my throat. I went in, and the administrative assistant told me I was an hour early.

Starting the job was like visiting a foreign country. First it was in a suburb of a big East Coast city, and I was a Midwesterner through and through. I drove into a small plaza of small offices hidden in trees – quite different than the manicured campuses and large buildings of my years in academia. They handed me a Blackberry, a nice new laptop, and docking station – I didn't have to buy my own. I

[1] PBS *Frontline*. "Merchants of Cool". 2001

sat at a fresh desk and chair from IKEA and had no idea how in over my head I actually was.

One hurdle I had to overcome was a basic shared knowledge gap. I had read lots of social theory, had taken and taught methods and stats classes, but never looked into business literature at all. I didn't really take business literature seriously.

But now I was finding that I did not have the background knowledge and shared language my colleagues did. I started by looking at the company president's bookshelf. He was a well-read PhD and maintained a library we were free to take from. Since the company was a marketing research and strategy company, the first titles included Ries and Trout *Positioning: The Battle for Your Mind* (2001) and *Differentiate or Die* by Trout and Rivkin (2000). These were good starts, and shared some conceptual overlap with my sociological background, specifically with culture and social psychology.

Next were Seth Godin's books. These are small and focused on a single idea. They do tend to be somewhat commonsensical and, from an academic background, extremely underdeveloped. But that makes them easy to digest, with the benefit of being fairly trendy. Reading these helped me sound more up-to-date immediately. Classics include *Purple Cow* and *Permission Marketing*.

Then there were consumer behavior books, such as *How Customers Think* (Zaltman 2003) and *How Doctors Think* (Groopman 2008). While Kahnemnn had not yet published *Thinking Fast and Slow*, some of his earlier work with Tversky (see *Heuristics and Biases,* 2002) was percolating around. Both clients and our consultants were discussing the emotional drivers of decision-making on a regular basis.

Some of the popular business books were useful here too. Malcolm Gladwell's *Blink,* for instance, was popular because of the focus on nonrational decision-making. While I hadn't found it yet, *The Lords of Strategy* (Kiechel 2010) would have been wonderfully helpful for laying the groundwork for my new industry and its shared ideas. Finally, since I didn't have all that much time for reading books, I followed the blogs and writings available from Wharton and Harvard Business Schools and their faculties, as well as white papers from notable consulting firms such as PWC and Deloitte.

Relevant Skills and Things I Needed to Relearn

Presentation Matters

There were a host of things I had internalized from academia that were not only unhelpful in this new job, but that I actually had to relearn. The first perhaps was attitude and professionalism. As a sociologist, there aren't a whole lot of reasons to wear a suit. There really is no reason to own three or five of them. Now, I may have been exceptionally naïve, but I have to admit I went to my first year of graduate studies wearing cutoff jean shorts and handwriting title pages to my papers because

I thought it was creative. I believed the work would stand on its own, but truthfully, my work was entirely adequate. The aforementioned lunch with the marketing company boss cemented that in this new world I had to dress my best, iron my shirts, and wear ties, and that was that. Looking like a full professor squeezed into a 10-year-old suit for a donor dinner was not going to cut it.

Writing and Communicating

That goes beyond dressing too. Much of our writing was on PowerPoint, which to that point I had only used sparingly in teaching. None of it could be sloppy. Details mattered. Typos were not acceptable. Outlines and bullet points need to be consistent throughout. Tables had to be formatted a certain way. Text boxes needed to be in the same place on every slide. Branding needed to be correct. Plain Excel and PowerPoint graphs weren't good enough. The colors had to be consistent throughout. Best if they complemented the client's branding. If you wanted something specific, you had to be creative about how the data was arrayed in your data field to get your charts to look that certain way. The same went for documents prepared in Word.

One of my most important learnings on professionalism was "closing the loop." As a graduate student, I did my projects alone. I talked to my faculty and did what they said. As an instructor, I tried to respond to my students in a timely fashion. I tried to communicate effectively with my Chair. But in business, I was not prepared for how much checking back in was really required. More than once I ran into trouble because I didn't touch base when I thought things were settled (a painful lesson – doublecheck with an email) or didn't call quick enough when running into trouble on a project. But also, I had to recognize that working in teams and groups is fundamentally very different than working as a solo graduate student finishing a dissertation or a solo professor plowing through grading. Now I try to close the loop – send lots of follow-up emails, and call the person.

Writing for clients turned out to be very different from writing as an academic. As different as it was though, it still consisted of all the same pieces – but in a different order. Where a conference paper might go:

1. Introduction to the Problem
2. Literature Review
3. Methodology
4. Results
5. Discussion and Conclusion

The reports we delivered proceeded:

1. Executive Summary
2. Research Question
3. Methods
4. Results
5. Conclusion and Recommendations

Mostly the same pieces, but in different order and with a different style.

The executive summary says in just a few PowerPoint slides what the main findings were and what their implications were. The research questions were just a couple pages to restate what was being investigated and with enough background for the client to have faith you understand the business problem. Importantly, research objectives are laid out with a laser focus. Methods again are just a page or two. The results can be as long as necessary, and the conclusions and recommendations are kind of a formality – since you have likely summarized them into the executive summary at the front.

An academic paper is linear – here is the problem, how other people have addressed it, how I tried to address it, what I found, and what that means. A client-based paper is action-focused – the most important findings come first.

This points to a key difference in writing style – incidentally one that has helped me in administration. Be brief and actionable. It may at first seem that if a client is paying you for a bespoke product, they are going to want as much information as possible. But in fact, the client is paying you to distill all that information into actionable points. It's the exact opposite of telling a student to fill up 20 pages of text. It's telling the student to get all the pertinent information into three pages.

As it turns out, this style of writing is tremendously difficult. It is a challenge to distill the important information, including action points and challenges, into as few words as possible. Don't overcomplicate it!

This also applies to methodology. For all of my time troubleshooting SPSS code, trying to get LISREL to work, trying to remember why heteroscedasticity matters in linear regression, what our clients generally need can be answered with compared averages. It's not sexy, but the point isn't to do sexy methodology – it's to provide actionable intelligence to the clients. The compared means, crosstabs, and linear regression any undergraduate sociology degree plan should have are plenty.

There also has to be a recognition of meaningful compromises. You may not have a perfectly representative sample – in fact you won't. You and the client don't have the resources to do that. You may find that your p-value is greater than 0.05. It might not be enough information for journal publication, but do you have enough information for your client to act on? How much more money do you have to spend to move from a stratified sample to something more appropriately random? How much more do you have to spend to move beyond the research facility's call list and broaden the research pool? How much larger does your sample have to be to move your p-value to be small enough?

This can get philosophical fairly quickly. Even $p < 0.05$ is really only saying "we're pretty certain this isn't made up." It's still not known (T)ruth. So, if your science isn't good enough for journal publication, does it mean you're peddling falsehoods? I find that upon deeper reflection, most of life can boil down to making decisions and acting with imperfect information. Finally, while more complicated methods are cool and make us look smart, are we getting closer to (T)ruth with them? And can we explain that (T)ruth to a reasonably intelligent nonscientist? Because as a consultant, your job is to help clients decide and act with the best information they can afford.

My communication with clients also had to change. As a professor, how many times did I say "It's in the syllabus!" to students who wouldn't read the syllabus? What I have since learned as a consultant and as an administrator is that students aren't the only ones who don't want to read lengthy documents. And while I can get frustrated with students and send them back to the syllabus, I cannot do that with clients, my faculty, or my current college's vice presidents.

Our clients were extremely intelligent people, but they all thought a little differently and communicated a little differently. I had to adjust my communications to match. Some I had to call on the phone and answer fairly straightforward questions. Some would want bullet point emails. Quite often what they were asking they might have answered by rereading the contract, prior emails, or the report we had sent them. But my job was to make sure it was clear to them, which included delivering reports, presenting at their office, summarizing in bullet-pointed emails, and answering questions over the phone. Sometimes the questions they were asking seemed basic, but it had been a while since they had taken statistics. Or they wanted to walk through from the bottom up. By the time I left, I had gotten to think that simply stating "it's in the syllabus" is a pretty entitled response from a faculty person.

Roles

There are many different kinds of research firms out there, and my experiences were a representation of the firm that I worked for. The firm was small, high energy, did bespoke research, and charged boutique prices. When I joined the company, it was being acquired by one of the big three global research firms. That gave me the opportunity to see how the two different kinds and scales of firms worked. The company I started with was small, flexible, and entrepreneurial. The company I finished with 3 years later was large, bureaucratic, with clearly defined roles within the business. I had to learn the different roles of this world, both within the company and the company in its own larger context.

External

The roles of the different companies were highlighted when we were behind the glass in a research facility. In an in-person interview or focus group setting, the moderator and the respondents would sit in the interview room, and all the rest of us would be behind the glass observing. For hours. In the dark. If the client had a question, someone on the research team would write it on a slip of paper and unobtrusively walk it in to the moderator. Behind the glass there would be at least one representative from the research company, supporting the moderator and managing the client. There would be a few representatives of the brand team – three or four in the early stages of the project, maybe just one in the later stages. If we were doing advertising research, there would be representatives from the advertising company. All these relationships needed to be managed.

As the research team, we were by default critiquing the advertising company's projects. It was useful to keep an ear on how the advertising team was communicating about the research with the client. If a concept was not standing up in research, but the advertising team liked it, they may try and reinterpret the results for the client right there in the backroom.

At the same time, the research team had to host the client and make sure the client was getting what they needed out of the field experience. Sometimes this meant you were managing the client's expectations. Sometimes it meant you were ensuring the client's preconceptions didn't drive the research off-track. Sometimes it meant you were helping the client digest hard-to-hear responses. It also meant really straightforward stuff like ensuring the facility prepared the right lunches and ordered out Starbucks for the client.

We also had to be sensitive to the internal politics of the client company. While we were technically working for a large brand, we were contracted by that particular brand manager. We needed to guide that brand manager to making good decisions with the research. That brand manager would be working with people on her own team who had different opinions about which direction the advertising or the product could go. That manager also usually worked in a larger corporation with other brands and herself had a boss she reported to.

We needed repeat business with brands over time. There are a lot of ways to politically screw that relationship up. If we managed to make that brand manager look stupid to the rest of her company, to make bad decisions, or didn't help her pushback gently on superior's poor decisions, that could be the end of that relationship – and income stream – so we gave them the tools to do all those things deftly.

Internal

There were also a variety of internal roles, which, as a college professor or PhD student, I previously filled on my own. The company was organized into small business units, and each unit had a vice president as its head. Within each unit were senior consultants, consultants, and analysts.

Analysts were the youngest, newest hires. They did a lot of the basic work including writing PowerPoints, running stats, and making graphics. Consultants would be writing the research documents, surveys, discussion guides, and screeners. They would also do a lot of moderating. At first that would be telephone interviews, growing into in-person interviews. A moderator had to be pretty refined by the time you would put them in an interview room in front of clients.

Senior consultants would often do the interviews early in a project, in front of the client, and then pass the later in-person and all the telephone interviews off to a consultant to finish. Senior consultants would also start managing clients and beginning selling some projects. After selling beyond a certain threshold, they could transition to a VP and run their own small business unit.

Aside from the people inside your small business unit, we also had access to a field department. These folks managed the relationship between field vendors and our researchers. Having done my own fieldwork for my academic projects, I found this to be a wonderful service. They would contract with the research facility who would provide the research suite and recruit a sample of respondents to meet our specifications. If qualitative, they would schedule all the interviews, record them, and host both us researchers and our clients. If quantitative, they would handle the survey hosting, recruiting the sample, and the data collection and provide some basic statistics as well as the raw data.

A large difference from the projects I had worked on as an academic was the amount of teamwork that was involved. As mentioned, a senior consultant would often start a project, ensure the client was happy, and then pass it off to another consultant. Depending on budget, you could pull other consultants and analysts into your project, and they would bill you for the work they did. This meant that on any given project, you could have a senior consultant, a consultant, a couple analysts, and field. On any given day, you would be contacting any of these people on from three to five projects. This was far more interactive than sitting in my library carrel writing my dissertation for a year. And because you're working on three to five different projects at a time and sharing the work with a half dozen other people, I accumulated experience much more quickly, working on 20 or more projects per year.

One of the more important things I learned at this job is the value in being able to bridge different groups. Being able to understand the research process and findings and then being able to clearly communicate that to clients is a very valuable skill. Similarly, being able to read a client and know from what they are saying what they *actually* need and convey that to researchers is the same skill. It's been my experience that being able to take information effectively across groups is *more important* than being an expert in either of those groups. This is also just a different version of being a teacher.

Lifestyle

This was a job that is easy to glorify, and I still reference it if I need bragging rights. But truthfully it had its ups and downs, and it is important to be honest.

First the good: We traveled a lot. Research facilities are in large cities across the USA and the world. During those few years, I went to New York, Philadelphia, Washington DC, San Francisco, Chicago, Atlanta, Boston, and even New Jersey many times. I got to know all these cities – at least around the research facilities. We stayed in very nice hotels – nothing I ever could have afforded on my own. When flying internationally we flew first class. We took car services (limousines) and taxis everywhere when we traveled.

As a college student, I wanted to study abroad for a semester, but financial aid wouldn't cover it. While at the firm, I oversaw the fieldwork on three projects in Europe. For 6 weeks I visited Hamburg, London, Pairs, Rome, and Madrid while staying in unbelievable hotels and eating and drinking on an expense account. They told me to try and keep it under $40 k. That was more than my first teaching contract.

I enjoyed that we had multiple clients. It was like we zoomed in, helped them answer their questions, and took off again. We were like the fixers. It also wasn't like our bosses were watching us punch the clock. As long as we're billing a minimum of hours to cover our salary, they were happy. Which I did by working on lots of projects with other consultants in the firm. I did have a few of my own projects, and I just needed to ensure they stayed profitable.

My favorite story: I was taking a break from research in Manhattan and going outside to call my wife. I grabbed the Starbucks the facility had provided and headed out. The facility was right next to the New York Public Library and it was a beautiful spring day. As I was talking to my wife on my Blackberry, holding the Starbucks, standing on the corner of the NY Public Library, a group of tourists asked me where the Starbucks was. I indicated that I didn't know, and they walked away annoyed, muttering something about New Yorkers under their breath. I was a Midwestern kid in an off the rack suit from Kohl's and they thought I was a New Yorker blowing them off!

The bad was the same as the good. We traveled a lot. Some of my strongest memories from the period are feeling deeply lonely, sitting in an airport at 6:00 am with only a couple other travelers in business suits. That trip to Europe was something I would have never gotten to do, but my wife and young kids were at home, with enough of a time offset that even talking on the phone was difficult. To this day I hope to go back to some of the same places with my wife, so I can properly enjoy them.

It was also hard to maintain some level of health. When traveling it was very challenging to work out. And while you can get whatever you want from restaurants, I found maintaining my weight on restaurant food all but impossible. That's all aside from the stress.

There was a fair amount of stress. Some was contextual, but some was a legitimate part of the job. Contextually I had managed to get in over my head and had to get up to speed. The company was in the process of being bought and assimilated, and so our high earning VPs left to start their own thing. This left everyone scrambling to hire new VPs and bring in more business. Finally, 2008 was just stressful for everybody.

Pertaining to the job though, dealing with clients is stressful. Managing clients' feelings and expectations is your first priority since you need to build relationships and bring in repeat business. We would have several projects at once, and you wanted each client to feel like they were your only priority.

Managing projects is stressful on its own, and then more so with simultaneous multiple projects. Your boss wants you to keep costs down, the client wants more than they paid for, and field wants to keep good relationships with their vendors. And as the research consultant, you are balancing all these competing interests.

Additionally, something always goes wrong so you have to be nimble enough to solve problems on the fly. That might be prodding the research vendor to find more recruit at the last minute; it might be picking up a project in the middle after someone leaves. It might be hours of fixing SPSS code because the survey variables were laid out poorly by a junior researcher.

One thing I missed about academics was its cyclical nature. School started in the fall, and it was exciting. You worked hard and got a break for winter. Then spin work back up again for spring, and everybody gets a breather come June. This was not like that. There were no week-long fall and spring breaks. As faculty, of course you do work in those times, but you don't have to go to campus unless you elect too. Over winter break you are prepping spring semester, but fall semester is done and in the books and spring hasn't yet started. With summer you have the choice to teach extra and make some money or spend time research and writing.

As a consultant, my projects were always at different stages. There was never a point when they were all done and I got to breathe. One wrapped, and that was nice, but I was on three others. If I was on too few, then I worried about billing and not making bonus. If I was on too many, then I was just hamster-wheeling like a madman to get through it all. If there is no clear pipeline of work, that's not a sign of a rest period coming; that's a sign of not having work in a few weeks.

The Road Back to Academia

Getting back into academics was difficult and uncertain, and I have been extremely fortunate. However, the experiences from marketing research made me a much better professional and laid the foundation for the skills that got me into administration and helped me succeed here.

My time at the firm ended with the financial crash of 2008. I made it through a couple rounds of layoffs, but on the third, they laid off our whole business unit. This was not entirely a surprise. We had watched the financial crisis unfold. Our client companies pushed back and cancelled work while they laid off tens of thousands of employees. Because of this, I already had applications out, both at other firms and colleges.

At this point I had very conflicting feelings about what to do next or even how much choice I might have in what to do next. When I left academia, I thought to myself "If I'm going to be a cog in a machine, I might as well make some money doing it." While I had started in a firm with tremendous potential, after the buyout, I was looking at lots of career researchers, who were cranking out brand concept testing, message testing, and ad testing. If I was only looking at a middle-class income to do this journeyman's work, it didn't carry as much appeal. Again, I didn't know which way my career was going to go at this point, but I did recognize that at a college, "if I'm a cog in a machine, I might as well open a couple minds while doing it." I also recognized that the stress of consulting was taking a toll on me.

At colleges, I had applied for tenure-track jobs, and several weeks later, one of them called me back. They had already started the hiring process for the tenure-track job but were calling because they had a visiting assistant professor as a sabbatical replacement, and it was in medical sociology. Since the firm I was laid off from was in pharmaceuticals and healthcare, they thought I would be an interesting fit. I took the job, and we relocated to the small town that college was in. I didn't feel like I had much choice at that point.

In many ways, the following years were some of the best of our lives. We lived in a ratty house near the college, our income went down, but after the stress of the consulting job, which was compounded by the acquisition and the ongoing financial crash, the professor's life was deeply enjoyable. As a VAP there was no publication or committee expectations. I did fun projects with my students, got a little writing done, wasn't on the road so I saw my kids every day, and even worked out and got in better shape.

While a wonderful reprieve, it wasn't sustainable. The college liked me enough to extend my time through 3 years of sabbaticals, but after everyone had taken their leave, my time was up. Perhaps naively, I had thought I would be extra competitive on the job market at that time. I had more than 6 years of teaching under my belt, I had a couple publications, but I also had the critical answer to "What are you going to do with a sociology degree?"

But of course, that meant also there were 4–6 years of new PhDs, all of whom had potential. I may be mistaken but it felt like there was a bias toward the new graduates. I came in second at a lot of job interviews. I could almost feel that I was becoming "cold product."

While I applied all over the country, the one area I had left out was the South. I just didn't know anything about it and hadn't given much thought to living there. But with a countdown timer on my contract, southern schools went on the list too. With two on-campus interviews, I was second (again) at one, and I finally got a tenure-track assistant professorship at the other. In essence, almost starting back at the beginning.

Teaching and Administration

Moving my family to the South was as big a culture shock as moving my family to the East Coast 6 years earlier. But thankfully, things have worked out, and we've prospered. As it turned out, the adjustments, growing, and learning I had to do to pass as a marketing research consultant gave me the skills to be working in administration within 5 years of hiring at the new school. I fully understand that my success as an administrator comes from the experience I gained in those years as a consultant.

The most apparent learning from consulting that helped in teaching was in running research methods classes as if they were consulting projects. Typically I would find a local nonprofit who might have a consulting need to partner with. I broke the classes into smaller research teams and sent them out to do the fieldwork.

I had them write up their results in mini-reports and then aggregated them into a full report that could then be shared back with the local partner. I eventually formalized this into MGA's Center for Applied Research and Education in the School of Education and Behavioral Sciences.

This research capability is what drew me into administration. I applied for the position of Director of Institutional Research and was granted an interim role, which after a year converted to the official role. In this position we both report out all the relevant information needed by the National Center for Educational Statistics and all the other surveys (Peterson's, USNews, etc.) and provide decision support to the executive leadership of the university. This is a good fit for sociology grads, and I am aware of several who are in these roles. Beyond that however, learning to communicate research results to clients as actionable information has made me more effective at presenting university information to our stakeholders and decision-makers.

As mentioned elsewhere, better presentation has been an important step forward for me.

Coming back to the classroom, even though I took the liberty of wearing jeans sometimes, I was always far better dressed than when I taught before. My presentations and documents that get shared around are also far more polished. I pay extra attention to consistent tables. I try hard to declutter graphs, charts, and documents. In many ways communicating with executive leadership inside the university is no different than communicating with an industry client. The provost and president are my clients now, and I want to have what they need, in intuitive formats, so they can make the best decisions possible.

I try to keep communications brief. I try to include clear action items if necessary, with links or whatever makes those items easier to do for the recipient. I consistently try to close the loop. When someone asks for information, I will usually send them that info and doublecheck that it meets their needs. When a project is stalling, I'll circle back every week with a nudge asking about progress.

Another element that was a bit of a surprising crossover was the familiarity with business language and thinking. At the executive level, there aren't as many academics in university administration as one might think. There are HR people, finance people, and marketing people, along with the academics. These representatives are far more likely to be familiar with business literature and ideas than I would have been in the past. Being able to not just reference the literature and language but truly understand their perspective has been one of the more important communication tools I developed.

In Closing

I don't want to mislead with a "happily ever after" ending. In those 3 years on the market as a VAP after reentering academia, I put in nearly 300 applications all over the USA and Canada and at least 1 European country. I got dozens of nibbles and many on-campus interviews and, as stated above, kept coming in second. I'd like to think that what got me my job finally was my essential awesomeness, but in truth the applicant pool was likely small. There is something to be said for persistence, but I had started to make backup plans in case academics didn't work out.

There are good sellable skills a social science PhD brings to the table. Qualitative and quantitative analyses are needed in every organization. Marketing research is a large and global industry. There isn't a notable product that gets released that isn't researched as scientifically and thoroughly as possible. From inception, when opportunity exploration helps drive acquisition of a new product, through a wide variety of user research to tweak the product to meet the needs of the intended audience, to the development and tailoring of the marketing to communicate the product to the customer, scientific social research happens at every step through the life cycle of a product.

As a consultant, I learned higher professionalism, to include closing the loop, distilling information, and making things actionable. I also understand that the ability to translate between different kinds of roles and users is one of the most important skills out there. Taking those research and analysis skills and combining them with the knowledge and professionalism of a business can make you a strong candidate for a rewarding career.

Say Yes to Cultivating Your Future

Annie Pettit

I pondered becoming an academic for about 10 minutes.

Instead, I said "yes" to the first grown-up job offer that came my way. As the years progressed, I continued to say yes as other opportunities arose, and I haven't regretted any of those decisions for a moment. To get things started, I'll share a quick timeline of my journey:

1. While still in graduate school, I said yes to a provincial government position where I developed and validated police employment tests for a couple years.
2. To broaden my experience, I took a position at a marketing company that had a small research department to support and validate its own products.
3. After seeing the potential of market research, I leapt at the opportunity to join a global consumer research company where I handled access panel analytics and survey data quality for a few years.
4. I then said yes to an unexpected opportunity to join a technology start-up building a social media listening market research tool from scratch.
5. Our start-up was acquired by a global market research company where I stayed for a few years supporting the social media listening tool as well as social media sample.
6. After being laid off from the global company, I became a private consultant for several years supporting research companies with their communication efforts and writing research reports.
7. As of this writing, I am now the sole Canadian researcher at a quickly growing, foreign-run market research company.

A. Pettit (✉)
Annie Pettit Consulting, Toronto, Canada
e-mail: AnniePettit@gmail.com

© The Author(s), under exclusive license to Springer Nature
Switzerland AG 2023
N. Jackson (ed.), *Non-Academic Careers for Quantitative Social Scientists*,
Texts in Quantitative Political Analysis,
https://doi.org/10.1007/978-3-031-35036-8_8

All Skills Are Transferable

Throughout undergraduate and graduate school, I never took a single business, economics, or politics class, and it never occurred to me to do so. Rather, I actively trained to become an experimental psychologist and eagerly signed up for every psychometrics, computer programming, statistics, and research design class in the psychology department. I had created a very precise and logical path to become a psychometrist.

Even though my first job was exactly what I had planned for, the rest of the positions I took were not. Looking back, though, I can see that my university training was directly relevant to every position I've held:

- A degree in psychology helped me understand the complexity of human behavior and perception. Market research is simply the application of psychology to the perception of products, brands, and companies.
- My psychometrics classes taught me to design valid, reliable, and unbiased scales and items. In the marketing research industry, we call those same things questionnaires and questions.
- Even though my dissertation is now hilariously outdated, understanding the validity of online questionnaires is directly relevant to creating data quality metrics for marketing research questionnaires.
- In graduate school, I learned the syntax versions of Turbo-Pascal and SAS, not the menu-driven versions. When I eventually needed to learn SQL to manipulate huge access panel datasets at a research company, I already had the foundational programming knowledge that made learning a new software language much easier.
- Writing a dissertation honed my written communication skills, an essential skill for writing blog posts, conference papers, white papers, marketing materials, website content, book chapters, and much more. Never undervalue how important your writing skills are.

No matter how niche or out-of-date your academic career is, it has prepared you for a nonacademic position. Take the time to identify your unique skillset. And if you can't, find a mentor who will help you do that. There are thousands of potential mentors on LinkedIn.

Doing Good for Others

When I said yes to my first real job in the government, I recognized it as a great way to contribute to my community in a positive way. My training in psychometrics, statistics, and research design was a perfect match with building psychometric tests to ensure that police officer candidates were well equipped to take on a dangerous and mentally challenging role. As one person among many others in the system, I helped people find rewarding careers, and I helped make my community safer for everyone.

This government position even came with unexpected enrichment. I went on field trips to the city morgue (no, we didn't see any bodies) and the jail (I felt like I was invading people's privacy), and I was invited to stay at the police training academy for a few days while running workshops.

I worried that leaving a government role for private business meant I was also leaving behind doing good but that wasn't the case. I soon discovered I could volunteer for the national and international ethics and standards bodies in my industry. Now, I am part of global teams of experts helping to make sure my colleagues around the world understand the high standards of practice they need to commit to in order to ensure the public is treated fairly and respectfully.

I also found ways to do good for my community on my own schedule. To counter the dearth of diversity at conferences, I actively recruit and mentor people who belong to marginalized communities to speak at marketing research conferences. As someone who's taken the stage more often than most people, I'm in a unique position to mentor brand-new speakers and help build a more diverse pipeline. And I've supported my academic colleagues by giving talks at local colleges and universities.

No matter what company you work for, private or public, large or small, you can always find or create opportunities to do good for others.

Pivot to Market Research

When I was in graduate school, I didn't realize that marketing research was a career. I certainly didn't realize it was a perfect match with my interests in psychometrics and human behavior. I don't remember how, but early in my first job, I became aware that marketing research could be an interesting career. I saw the wide variety of research methods and statistics it incorporated. I saw it included research about consumer products, business services, social services, government, healthcare, and much more. The opportunity to practice a far broader range of research methods and research topics piqued my interest, and I decided to pivot away from my formal career choice. Good-bye psychometrics! Or so I thought.

I moved to a global marketing and social research company where I found and cultivated a niche for myself just as I had within the government. Rather than using SPSS to build and validate tests to select police officers, I used SQL to manipulate massive databases to understand the human behaviors that led to good and bad response behaviors on questionnaires. I leveraged the SPSS, SAS, and Turbo Pascal skills I had gained in university as a foundation for learning SQL. Same skills, different application. I loved it all.

But after a few years of that fun, I was invited to join a start-up. It was a big decision. Should I leave a comfortable position at a company I admired for a job at a nonexistent company that might go bankrupt in 6 months? Should I keep playing with data quality metrics that directly related to my dissertation research or jump into social media data, a new data source that no one understood?

As I pondered the pros and cons, I realized I would probably never be presented with an opportunity like that again. I didn't want to look back and regret saying no to something that could have been. The decision was difficult but, at the same time, also very easy. I said yes to the unknown.

Being part of a start-up was exciting but not easy. Rather than helping someone else build products and services to their specifications, our little team made all the decisions ourselves. We designed and built a social media market research tool to our specifications as there was no similar product on the market to compare ourselves to. There were no guidelines to stay within and no metrics to replicate. As the lead researcher on the team, it was a wonderful feeling to know I was being trusted to create a valid and reliable research methodology.

Despite all that fun, it was stressful to have no paying clients during the development phase. We had to support ourselves financially long enough to finish the product and market our services. I prepared myself for possible failure and built a more robust personal emergency fund. Just in case. Fortunately, we found clients and ended up getting acquired.

Despite the financial uncertainties, saying yes to joining a start-up was a great decision. I'd never spoken at a conference before, but this intriguing work meant that I was being invited to share our learnings on the global stage. I'd never been part of a global committee before, but this work led me to be invited to become a member of the ISO (International Standards Organization) market research committee as an expert on social media listening tools. It was strange to go from being completely unknown to having people seek me out at conferences and meetings. Ok, it wasn't Beyoncé recognition but it was an interesting experience!

Being Your Own Boss

As an employee, you should expect to be laid off or fired at least once. When I was made redundant and laid off, it was an unwelcome surprise, but I packed up my box of knickknacks, my small (forbidden!) area heater, and headed home without a plan.

Instead of jumping straight into job hunting, I decided to take 6 months off. Why? Two reasons. First, I realized there would be few times in my life when I would have the opportunity to slow down and observe the world. If your finances permit it, I highly recommend taking a longer break if the opportunity arises. Second, I wanted to broaden my expertise. Having been a part of the research industry for a number of years, I saw how broad the field was and how little I knew about much of it. I decided to attend as many free online webinars and conferences as I could in those 6 months. I got out a crisp new notebook and became a full-time student of the Internet.

Those 6 months, however, were shortened to 3 months. I took on a few consulting projects to help some friends which turned into 5 years of being a busy private consultant. It turned out that working at a couple global research companies, giving lots of conferences presentations, and being active on social media had created a fantastic network of friends, colleagues, and connections. I was in a fortunate position where I didn't have to source paying projects or prove myself to unknown prospects. It wasn't because I was lucky. It was because I had unknowingly played the long game.

Even though I didn't have to worry about finding clients, I still had to struggle with other aspects of the freelancing life. It's no fun to track minutes per project per client, prepare invoices, go to the bank during business hours, save receipts, and assign them to the right categories. Even without an administrative assistant, paperwork must be done and it's never fun.

Another huge challenge of freelance roles is determining your rate. While it's tempting to accept any paying project that comes your way, you must know your worth and use the word "no." Just because competitors accept minimum wage jobs doesn't mean you have to. Figure out the annual salary you intend to earn and create a payment structure that will match (or exceed) that. If you need any inspiration in this regard, do a quick Internet search for Cindy Gallop (https://cindygallop.com/). She'll advise you to ask for the highest number you can say out loud without bursting out laughing. Make that your goal.

Freelancers also need a lot of mental strength when it comes to the wise use of time. This was definitely not my strength. I would view every minute as a billable minute. If I was taking time for lunch, going for a walk, or grabbing something from the kitchen, I would fret over that lost billable minute. Ten minutes every day over 50 weeks is 40 hours. Forty billable hours that generate zero income. Sure, as a freelancer, you can take whatever breaks and holidays you wish but is it really a break or holiday if you're fretting about nonbillable hours? After 5 successful years as a consultant, this was one aspect of the arrangement I was happy to say good riddance to.

Embrace an Unfamiliar Culture

In the marketing research world, working for a company based in a developing nation can come with stigma despite the fact that most global research companies have, at a minimum, an operations team there. In fact, both of the global companies I had already worked for had large teams in various developing nations.

When the opportunity arose for me to join a company based in India, I did my homework before saying yes. I soon became the sole Canadian among more than 200 Indian colleagues. Despite living in Canada's largest city where non-white ethnicities are actually the majority, I quickly learned how limited my worldview had been.

When dealing with clients, you may have to counter erroneous stereotypes about the ethics and work quality of your company. Of course, like any unknown business anywhere else, it's hard for people to know whether they're dealing with an ethical business that values its team members and pays its suppliers promptly or an unethi-cal business that never pays its people or suppliers. And some people are uncomfort-able supporting companies that "steal" jobs from people in their own country. As if people in other countries don't also deserve jobs that pay a living wage. Be prepared to address stereotypes and call out racism.

When your personal culture is the minority at your company, you'll no longer know the meeting routines, the text messaging protocols, the daily pleasantries, and the holiday traditions. You'll have to actively correct your ignorance with plenty of Internet searches and respectful conversations with a few trusted colleagues. Don't be shy about asking for help. Your new colleagues will be eager to teach you their culture and some of their language, and you'll definitely need to learn the phrase for thank you – Dhanyawad!

Most importantly, rarely seeing your colleagues face-to-face means you'll have to take special care to be kind. Humor doesn't translate well over email and texting, and silly jokes can be overlooked or interpreted literally. Even worse, when things go wrong, not having a lot of face-time makes it much easier to assume negative inten-tions. If you've never used smiley emojis before, now is the time to overuse them.

An Introvert in an Extravert's World

I'm an introvert. Very much an introvert. But people who've only met me on Twitter, Facebook, and LinkedIn rarely believe it. It can be hard to accept that people who are talkative in the online world aren't also talkative in the offline world.

As a freelance consultant or the sole employee in another country, you can glee-fully escape many of the office extravert moments. You don't need to make small talk in the kitchen with anyone besides your dog and your partner. You don't need to feel bad about eating lunch by yourself at your desk or on the porch. If you prefer to have music on while you work, you can easily do so. However, you'll never be able to escape phone calls and video chats with clients and colleagues who can't proceed with their work unless they're talking at someone's face. Them's the breaks.

Conferences can also be tough on introverts. But that's where putting years into building a broad network really helps. When people know you from the online world, you never have to worry about where to sit or who to sit with. Someone will always recognize you and invite you to join them. You'll still have to make small talk but you'll have a common point of interest to chat about!

Own Your Career

Historically, people would join a company and stay there until they retired. Today, it's perfectly acceptable to change companies every few years. I've changed compa-nies every 4–5 years and it's not been a deterrent for any hiring companies. I'm not saying you should change jobs every 5 years, but you do need to actively curate your career.

While creating my future, I learned a few important things:

- Don't settle for the bare minimum. Whether it's a government job, a start-up job, a freelance job, or a job with a massive global company, you have the right to review your contract, scratch out the noncompete clause (now finally starting to disappear from all contracts!), start the health plan immediately, increase the number of paid holidays, and request a higher salary. In general, your biggest raises will come when you switch companies so don't let 20% raises (every 5 years plus compound interest) pass you by just because you want to be loyal to a legal entity. Be loyal to yourself and your family first.
- Don't wait to be asked. If you want a raise or a promotion, it's your responsibility to document the specific things you've done to warrant them. With that in hand, set up a meeting with your boss and initiate the discussion. If that discussion doesn't land where you'd like it to land, get your resume in order and start working your connections.
- If you want to attend and speak at a wide range of conferences, create that path. There are plenty of opportunities for thought leaders in private business and there's room for you too. Volunteer to run team meetings and webinars. Write blog posts and papers for your national associations. When speaker calls are made, volunteer yourself as a speaker. Again, don't wait to be asked.
- Be present in social media. Personally, I owe my career to the 3-hour daily commute I had early-on. I didn't care to sit on the bus doing nothing so I started writing short blog posts about questionnaires, surveys, and research design. My little blog became popular and my network of friends and colleagues around the world grew.
- There is no perfect job. Every single job, no matter how amazing it looks from the outside, has a downside. You will have to work with colleagues and clients who make you cringe. You will have to fill out paperwork and complete projects you hate. The perfect job does not exist. However, you can find or create a job that balances the good with the bad and makes you happy much more often than not.

The PhD Stigma

Let's be honest. Earning a PhD comes with privilege. If you've got those letters after your name, somehow you managed to collect the time, money, and support to complete high school, undergrad, and graduate school. It may have been excruciatingly difficult, but now you're in a position to benefit from a future of higher pay grades and more flexible opportunities. Take the PhD stigma with a huge grain of salt.

After more than a decade of attending university, it feels amazing to have that piece of paper in hand and to be able to call yourself Doctor. You worked hard for it and you earned it. Congratulations!

Unfortunately, calling yourself Doctor has a downside. At my very first job in the government, I witnessed the repercussions of that. A colleague, rightfully proud of their newly gained accomplishment, would remind colleagues to address them as "Doctor." Even though everyone else went by their first names. That reminder wasn't appreciated by colleagues who were 20 or more years their senior and who had far more relevant knowledge than the new graduate. It created an uncomfortable and unhappy atmosphere for them.

The quiet path I took was much smoother. Where specialized expertise was essential, someone would inevitably ask me about my qualifications. Hearing that I had a PhD would reassure them that, yes, I was qualified to be developing psychometric tests for the selection of government employees. I never asked anyone to call me Doctor and no one did so except during formal introductions with senior leaders. Taking a modest path created a much smoother and kinder experience for me.

In private business, however, having a PhD might be seen quite differently. I still never overtly mention my PhD but sales people love to trot out a colleague who has an advanced degree. Since clients don't always trust sales people to know the intricacies of research, I'm occasionally brought in to share an unbiased opinion. Of course, the sales person never knows if I will corroborate their claims about appropriate sample sizes or product capabilities, but clients always appreciate getting an honest, educated opinion.

In recent years, I've become more open about letting people know I have a PhD. Despite all the hard work our society has done to promote equality, there remains a segment of people who need an in-your-face reality check that women are smart. And it's important for girls to see successful women who are valued for their intellect and contributions to the business world. On top of that, it's important to show people that there are unlimited career opportunities for PhD researchers outside of academia. The corporate world is not a disappointing back-up plan. It is an exciting world to look forward to.

I'm still not comfortable brandishing the PhD in every situation where I could legitimately do so, but, for those reasons, I've decided to do so in certain circumstances. Today, all of my social media channels clearly say PhD or Dr.

While you contemplate whether to use your title in interpersonal interactions, remember this. Whether someone has completed a PhD or an apprenticeship or has labored their entire career in a service position, every hard worker has a unique set of skills and expertise that is worthy of praise and admiration. Your PhD does not make you a better person nor more valuable than them.

Though my early plan to become a psychometrist actually came true, my career pivoted as unexpected opportunities arose. I found joy working for both large and small private companies, as well as with the government and start-ups. I said yes to unknown companies, to joining committees, to speaking at conferences, and to giving guest lectures at universities, and all of it was exciting, entertaining, and educational.

Do I wish I'd said yes to academia? Well, my career isn't over yet!

Working in Government

Thiago Marzagão

So You Want to Make a Difference

Data scientists who choose to work in government often do so out of a desire to be relevant. They want to use their quantitative skills to improve millions of lives, and they see in government work a chance to do just that. What better use of your deep learning knowledge than reducing poverty or fighting climate change? To socially minded data folks, that kind of work sounds more rewarding than, say, refining recommendation algorithms to make people click on ads.

High expectations come at a price though. Most quantitative work in government is not about reducing poverty or fighting climate change. The reality of government-flavored data science is quite mundane. Every government generates tons of paperwork – food stamp applications, court rulings, and diplomatic communications. A lot of the work – perhaps most of the work – involves training classifiers that help organize that paperwork, so that documents can be queried and retrieved and so that aggregate statistics can be compiled.

You may also be required to do a fair bit of software development. That is particularly common in small teams, where the lines between data science and software development are often blurry and one is expected to be versatile. On top of training document classifiers, you may also be required to "appify" them – i.e., to turn them into apps. Appifying your models often takes much longer than training them, so you may find yourself becoming much more proficient in JavaScript than you ever wanted to. You may spend many hours trying to center HTML tables. That may trigger some soul searching if you joined the government to help reduce poverty.

T. Marzagão (✉)
Fitbod, São Paulo, Brazil

N. Jackson (ed.), *Non-Academic Careers for Quantitative Social Scientists*,
Texts in Quantitative Political Analysis,
https://doi.org/10.1007/978-3-031-35036-8_9

Naturally, classifying documents – and performing the myriad of other mundane tasks data scientists perform in the government – can be immensely valuable. To give just one example, that is the only way to know what products and services the Brazilian government buys. Public procurement data is a mess in Brazil (though it has been improving lately); without a properly trained text classifier, it would be impossible to know how much is spent on office paper or defense contracts or university libraries. Training a classifier to handle government paperwork may not feel world-changing but without it the government is largely blind.

The point here is: yes, you can make a difference when you work in government, but you cannot expect to run a regression 1 day and see fewer poor people in the streets the next day. You need to care about the intermediate steps of policy making: helping organize information, making your models usable by nontechnical government employees, and automating manual processes.

Here and there you get to do work that directly impacts people's lives. Depending on where you end up, you may get to train a model that detects corruption in public procurement, or that helps prioritize who gets food stamps, or that uses satellite images to find deforestation. This is the sort of quantitative government work that sometimes makes the news and that the head of your agency may hear about. These high-profile projects help you become known beyond the small circle of data folks you normally interact with, and that can be rewarding to prestige-oriented people – and can help you advance your career, if you want to climb up the bureaucracy ladder. But they are not representative of what data folks do in the government most of the time.

Getting In

There are different ways to do quantitative work in government. Some agencies hire project-specific contractors and consultants. That is a good way to familiarize yourself with the work and environment and assess whether government work is for you. In developing countries that type of hiring often happens through the United Nations Development Programme – check the UNDP website for open positions.

Full-time work positions with benefits (such as vacation and sick days) are a different matter. You often need resident status to apply, which may severely limit your choices. And sometimes resident status is not enough – the latest data science positions announced by the US Office of Personnel Management all required US citizenship. Hopefully residency/citizenship requirements will become a thing of the past as remote work gets normalized, but for now they are still in place.

The way to get a full-time position doing data science work varies widely from government to government. The latest data-related positions announced by the US Office of Personnel Management all involved a multiple question exam, resume review, and work sample assessment. In Brazil, on the other hand, the government does not normally recruit data scientists; it recruits auditors, managers, or other types of positions, and by sheer chance some of the recruited people happen to have an interest in data science. To get one of these positions, you have to memorize dozens of arcane pieces of legislation that have nothing to do with data science and then take an exam.

In short, there is no single formula for getting a quantitative job in government. You have to research how it works in each country you are interested in.

Your Model's Worth

Machine learning models are usually evaluated based on metrics like accuracy or recall. Those metrics are well understood by data scientists, but nontechnical people often struggle to understand them.

In practice, a good project can get a bad reputation because of a single false positive or false negative. If your model says that internal affairs should investigate Jane but the investigation does not find anything on her, investigators may question the usefulness of your model – even if its overall performance is fine.

You may be asked to explain specific false positives; why did Jane get flagged in the first place? This can be challenging in many ways. Depending on the algorithm you are using and on the number of features you have, knowing why Jane got flagged may be outright impossible. That can further reduce confidence in your model, as people are often wary of using tools they do not fully understand. That can also fuel preexisting anti-AI (artificial intelligence) sentiments; it might give the "old guard" just what they want – "See? We told you this AI idea would not work."

That's why it is important to collect data on your model's real-world performance. The answer to "why was Jane flagged?" question is that investigations started because of your model find x% more fraud than investigations started because of other reasons – assuming, of course, that that is indeed the case. You have to shift the conversation toward the big picture.

To do that you need to know how your model is performing – not in your validation or test set, but out there in the wild. Hence it is vital that you do not forget about your model after you release it. You need to find out who exactly is using (or supposed to use) your model, reach out to those people, and arrange for them to periodically send you data updates. That can require you to cross bureaucratic borders, as your users may be in another department or even in another government agency altogether. That can also require you to implement anonymization strategies – this is often the case when personally sensitive data is involved, as you may not have clearance to fully access it.

One difficulty that often arises is that you have no control over whether your model is used at all. You have trained your model and now it is out there, generating predictions and whatnot – but the putative users are not bound by those predictions and can do whatever they want. How can you know your model's real-world performance when your model is not being used in the real world?

One way to go about it is to sit down with the users and try to understand why they are not using the model. Maybe they do not trust it? If so, why? Or maybe using the model would require taking extra steps – filling out a form or something? Maybe it is just the model tries to solve a problem that they do not have? Whatever it is, understanding it is the first step.

Sometimes a model just cannot be saved. You trained it, performance on the validation and test sets was good, but bureaucratic inertia prevailed and no one is using it. Time to pull the plug and move on. Pulling the plug can be surprisingly hard though – it requires admitting failure, which is not easy in government (more on this later). Hence some models stay in production for years, even being retrained every now and then, despite having zero users – just so that no one needs to acknowledge failure. That prevents learning and wastes resources but is quite common.

Handling Risk

Silicon Valley's "fail fast, fail often" motto has not quite taken root in most governments. The higher-ups do not like to hear that the project three highly paid people just spent 6 months working on has led to nothing. You can try to explain to them that that is just how it is – that sometimes you simply do not get the accuracy you need, no matter how many hours you spent tweaking hyperparameters or doing feature engineering. But there is a good chance that they will not understand it.

The root of the problem is partly in the background and incentives of the decision-makers. The higher-ups in big tech companies and startups are often people with STEM backgrounds. At the very least, they understand what linear regression is, even if they have not run one themselves in years. And they know that a lot of ideas fail because they see it happening all the time – Google Plus is an example most readers are probably familiar with. Failure is how you get to success.

In government, on the other hand, the higher-ups are usually people with backgrounds in law or management. They have no clue what a p-value is. And they have a procedural mindset that sees failure as a sign that someone messed up along the way. This is starting to change here and there, but progress is slow and uneven.

Government agencies do not normally make profit. In the absence of market signals, what brightens the day of a Secretary of Education or antitrust commissioner is reading positive news about his or her work. A failed data science project yields no positive news. Besides, how will the Secretary or Minister know that the team did actual work and didn't just sit around all day for 6 months?

One way to deal with this problem is to keep your projects low profile until they are ready to be unveiled. Keeping your project between you and your manager in the initial stages helps avoid unwarranted expectations.

The Way Up

There is usually no "technical track" for data scientists in the government: promotions normally entail taking up managerial work. And taking up managerial work means spending more time dealing with people and less time dealing with data and code. As a manager you will have to arbitrate interpersonal conflicts, fight for budget, and attend pointless meetings. It will be harder for you to keep up with the field – you will have less time, if any, to read arXiv papers, take online courses, and participate in Kaggle competitions.

You may try to have a project or two of your own, so as not to get rusty. But – to put it in Paul Graham's terms – you will find that a manager's schedule and a maker's schedule are not compatible. To *make* something you need uninterrupted blocks of several hours. But as a manager, your phone will ring, you will be asked to participate in last-minute meetings, and you will be interrupted for all sorts of reasons – all the time. The people you will report to will not grant you 4 or 8 hours a week to do technical work; they will be too removed from the technical world to understand your need for that.

If none of that appeals to you, then you will likely have to pass up promotions and stay at the same pay grade.

Working in Government Does Not Make You an Angel

Government-inclined data folks often adopt a condescending tone when talking about the private sector. "I want to do more than maximize clicks," "I want to do more than help people choose a dishwasher model," "I want to do impactful work," and "I want to do something that matters." The underlying sentiment is that using your quantitative skills for public service is inherently more valuable than using them to generate profits.

That sentiment betrays a disturbing self-righteousness. The last few years have seen big tech come under increasing criticism and scrutiny. But it is thanks to Amazon's insanely efficient distribution chain that people can get toothpaste when stores are closed due to a pandemic. It is thanks to Google's search algorithms that people in low-income countries can find educational content that helps them lift themselves up. It is thanks to YouTube's channels that a poor kid in the middle of the Amazon forest can make a living as a videogame live streamer. It is thanks to Tinder's matching algorithms that over a third of married people find their spouses. To believe yourself morally superior because you work in government (or, worse, because you want to) is disrespectful and a display of ignorance.

There are plenty of opportunities to do good by doing quantitative work in government. And it is great that many people are motivated by the desire to improve social outcomes. But the simplistic "public service good, private sector bad" narrative that is popular nowadays is distorted and at times self-serving.

More Resources

If you want to know more about government work before you commit to it, it is worth connecting to "datagov" people on LinkedIn, Twitter, and Clubhouse. That will expose you to a variety of data-centric government projects, and you will also learn about conferences and seminars where these projects get discussed. You can engage in these discussions, contributing your ideas and maybe some original work; because governments are supposed to be transparent, it is a lot easier to learn about and participate in its projects than to learn about and participate in, say, Google's or Facebook's projects.

Working in Quasi-Governmental Research

John Bordeaux

Introduction

You have read about government positions, and you may also have considered consulting work. After all, a Ph.D. earns you respect around a conference table. I've been in Pentagon meetings where someone inevitably asks: "Wait, what does Dr. Bordeaux think of this idea?" No one in the room knew what my degree was in or if my studies were relevant to the question at hand, and yet, there was an unearned respect. (This also reinforced my privilege, as a white man, and I realize this irrational deference stems from more than just my degree.)

In consulting, I was once little more than a prop for a consulting firm trying to win business in China. I have been literally flown halfway across the world as a demonstration that the firm could produce this (white) Ph.D. Prospective clients thanked me for coming, as if I wasn't another consultant trying to win their business. Also in consulting, I joined a project kickoff call with a client in the US legislative branch – who promptly explained that she had worked for a specific government contractor as a consultant and thus "knew all my tricks and would be watching closely for any shenanigans." While this exchange was inappropriate and set a poor tone for the relationship, there is a somewhat deserved reputation regarding contractors just looking to embed themselves and enjoy the billable hours rather than solve problems.

Consulting can be a heady and lucrative business, while government work can be rewarding on its own merits. But there is a category of career missing in this list: welcome to the murky world of the quasi-governmental organizations. What are colloquially referred to as "think tanks" but not to be confused with political or

J. Bordeaux (✉)
RAND Corporation, Arlington, VA, USA
e-mail: bordeaux@rand.org

© The Author(s), under exclusive license to Springer Nature
Switzerland AG 2023
N. Jackson (ed.), *Non-Academic Careers for Quantitative Social Scientists*,
Texts in Quantitative Political Analysis,
https://doi.org/10.1007/978-3-031-35036-8_10

idealogical organizations; these include national labs (NL), university-affiliated research centers (UARCs), and federally funded research and development centers (FFRDCs). These are not consulting shops, but instead provide a valuable continuity of competence across administrations and the inevitable churn across the federal workforce. They are the corporate memory for governmental administration. They employ economists, political scientists, data analysts, social scientists, behavioral psychologists, management scientists, etc. A robust workforce designed to tackle questions that may not be fully formed. In consulting, a government client knows what they want and puts out a request for proposal (RfP) for a specific product or service. For FFRDCs, the government comes to the organization asking questions that are not as easily framed. How do we define and inform the key players who manage the nation's critical infrastructure? What has been the effect of "Don't Ask, Don't Tell" on the military workforce? How prepared is NATO's northern front for a Russian move against the Baltic states? How can agencies comply with congressional mandates ranging from the Evidence-Based Policymaking Act of 2018 to the annual National Defense Authorization Act to topics in education, health research, and social equity?

And so much more. While the work described herein may characterize to a degree life in national labs and UARCs, my personal experience is limited to FFRDCs. My hope is to whet your appetite to consider this pseudo-governmental space as a career option, hopefully convincing you to join a highly trusted organization that partners with government agencies to help understand trends and develop workable solutions to advance the public interest mission.

What Is an FFRDC

Federal Acquisition Regulation (FAR) 35.017–1 provides the defining characteristics for FFRDCs:

FAR 35.017–1 "An FFRDC meets some special long-term research or development need which cannot be met as effectively by existing in-house or contractor resources. FFRDCs enable agencies to use private sector resources to accomplish tasks that are integral to the mission and operation of the sponsoring agency. An FFRDC, in order to discharge its responsibilities to the sponsoring agency, has access, beyond that which is common to the normal contractual relationship, to Government and supplier data, including sensitive and proprietary data, and to employees and installations equipment and real property. The FFRDC is required to conduct its business in a manner befitting its special relationship with the Government, to operate in the public interest with objectivity and independence, to be free from organizational conflicts of interest, and to have full disclosure of its affairs to the sponsoring agency."

An FFRDC presents the opportunity for a long-term relationship with a federal agency, often trusted with researching issues and challenges for which the agency is not staffed. After all, the Executive Branch is first tasked with executing the functions of the federal government. Looking ahead to understand the implications of emerging and predicted trends that may affect these functions is addressed in the nation's research and development investments – and a significant portion of these go to FFRDCs.

In practice, an FFRDC is a federal agency's in-house research and development capability on a contract that is reviewed every 5 years. Rather than the consulting and systems integration firms that pursue individual product and service acquisition opportunities, these are designed to be long-term partnerships with a special understanding of the individual agency's mission and history.

FFRDCs are prohibited from competing against consulting work; they cannot respond to requests for proposals issued through the acquisition lifecycle. They cannot do Systems Engineering and Technical Assistance (SETA) work, often referred to as "butts in seats." This reference can be confusing as there are FFRDCs engaged in actual systems engineering. SETA work is different: these are positions that augment federal staff, often sitting in the same office. Finally, FFRDCs are prohibited from doing inherently government tasks. They cannot represent government decisions in any form, from acquisition to policy.

Pasteur's Quadrant

In understanding what an FFRDC is in practice, beyond what is described in the FAR, it is useful to review the work and subsequent critique of Vannevar Bush, in *Science, The Endless Frontier*.[1] Building on an ancient understanding of science, Bush characterized two very different types of science, necessary different to preserve what he called the "freedom of inquiry." Basic scientific research, Bush wrote, held enormous promise for all mankind, but only if it were freed from the implications of its work. The scientist engaged in basic inquiry cannot, in Bush's view, be concerned or directed by the potential application of benefits derived from his research. That, he argued, was the realm of the other type: applied research. This dichotomy drove federal funding for generations – as President Roosevelt had requested his views to help frame federal investment. The government should simply fund basic scientific research without expectation of specific results, while applying this deliverable expectation to applied scientific research.

In 1999, Donald Stokes () provided the rationale for a new perspective on the relationship between science and technology.[2] Stokes used the example of Louis Pasteur to identify what he called "use-inspired basic research" and placed this in a useful 2x2 matrix.

---

[1] https://www.nsf.gov/about/history/nsf50/vbush1945.jsp

[2] Channell, David F. Technology and Culture, vol. 40, no. 2, 1999, pp. 390–92. JSTOR, http://www.jstor.org/stable/25147317. Accessed 16 Dec. 2022.

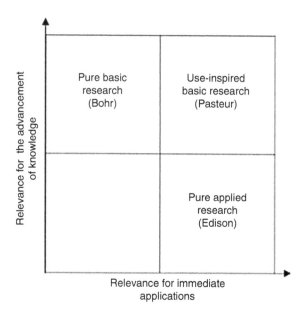

Niels Bohr provides his example of "pure" basic research as envisioned by Vannevar Bush, while Thomas Edison represented "pure" applied research. Pasteur's research, which advanced humanity's understanding of infectious disease, was directly applicable to the design and development of vaccination. FFRDCs and other science and technology government partners can be said to work in Pasteur's quadrant and are actually not permitted to work on tasks that belong in Edison's – perhaps serving as the "consultant's quadrant."

The Observer Monkey

There is a famous explainer of corporate culture that sounds apocryphal, but actually is *very* loosely based on an actual experiment (Stephenson, Gordon R. "Cultural acquisition of a specific learned response among rhesus monkeys." Progress in Primatology. Stuttgart: Gustav Fischer Verlag. p (1967): 76–80). Various consultants and TED talker types have mangled the actual findings, which were nowhere near as interesting as the fable. Nevertheless, I will continue the fable here to make my point.

A behavioral scientist assembled a group of monkeys into an enclosure, with a ladder leading to bananas at one end. Aides stood by with hoses and doused any animal who climbed onto the ladder to get at the food. In fact, they doused them all. One monkey ascended the ladder; they all got wet. It didn't take long for the group to understand the rather cruel pattern, and finally at some point they took matters into their own hands. When one of their number attempted to climb the ladder, the group would remove him or her from the ladder and "explain" that was not a good idea.

This went on for some time, until no water was needed to prevent any animal from attempting the climb.

Then it got interesting. The scientist removed a monkey and brought in a new one who had no experience with the water or the lesson. Sure enough, new guy heads on over to the ladder, only to be rudely introduced to the idea that "we don't climb that ladder here." Fast forward, and each one of the original group is removed and replaced with a new one; the enclosure eventually consisted of five new monkeys – none of which had ever been sprayed with cold water, and none of whom would ever go near the ladder and would punish those who do.

This explains organizational culture better than nearly any story I can imagine. "We just don't do that here." "It was apparently tried years ago, and people got fired." Whatever the tale, there is an oral history of corporate behavior that informs the culture – and is rarely questioned because few were around when the original lesson was learned. And over time, the reasons are likely lost to history; but all just know "that's not how it's done here."

But what if there had been a monkey outside the cage, watching the entire experiment over time. This part wasn't attempted, but consider: if the new population were able to saunter over and ask the observer monkey what was up, she could share "well, the bipeds used to spray everyone when someone climbed the ladder - but they stopped doing that a while ago after the grant money ran out."

One role for the FFRDC is to be this observer monkey. These quasi-governmental organizations are often the corporate memory for the administrative state. General officers often serve no longer than 2 years in a position, senior administration officials often depart at the end of an administration, and the federal workforce experiences churn driven by factors that also affect the private sector economy. It is not unheard of for the sponsor who retains you for a study is replaced by the time the results are briefed. Your job in an FFRDC/UARC/NL is to become the "corporate memory" for the operations of the US federal government.

Daily Life in an FFRDC

As you may expect, the increased trust associated with these organizations leads to specific limitations on who can work there. You will complete an annual declaration regarding personal conflicts of interest and will be expected to recuse yourself from research work in specific topic areas where you have a personal or financial conflict of interest – likely an annual reporting requirement. More than likely, you will be asked to obtain a security clearance, particularly if you are supporting intelligence community or national and domestic security agencies. At the very least, you will be earning a position of "public trust" and can expect some examination of your background before working on government-funded studies.

An advanced degree will serve you well, as these institutions often operate in an academic atmosphere with expectations that your work will be published and available to the public as appropriate.

The studies you work on may be multi-year efforts or you may find yourself supporting several different smaller studies at once. You will have access to data sets not available to the general public or most academic institutions. You may design and develop statistical analyses, analytic models, tabletop "wargames," or visualizations to communicate insights.

While you are not SETA, you may work closely with a program management office to help them develop and track organizational performance metrics that advance the individual mission. Often, FFRDCs are called upon to aid in workforce planning for new or expanding agencies. Quite often, they are brought in to help a government sponsor understand how to resource the newest executive order from the White House or congressional mandate.

Your work could range from the theoretical (increasingly) to practical solutions based on sound theory, while also thinking through the long-term picture, and preferably adding to the canon for that specific topic area. You may provide data analysis to support Army doctrine or econometric models to estimate the implications of doctrine or courses of action.

You will likely need to network, that overused term, in order to get "coverage." You work on billable hours, whether your day is spent supporting a government sponsor, and grantee, or perhaps on an internally funded study. Often, the FFRDC hosting organizations will have modest budgets for you to expand concepts where no external sponsor is willing to underwrite. For example, I am currently leading a study where the work is to consider systemic risks to US critical infrastructure. Some of that work involves expanding our understanding of system risk in ways that are currently beyond our sponsor's intent. Internal funding allows us to explore these other concepts and publish our findings directly to the public.

While organizations may differ, for most, a timesheet will be filed at the end of every pay period. The Defense Contract Audit Agency (DCAA) or similar body conducts random inspections to ensure you are working on studies for which you have been authorized. With little notice, you may find yourself answering their questions about what you are working on, who authorized it, and to demonstrate proof of this authorization. This again goes to the trusted relationship enjoyed by FFRDC personnel and the requirements that accompany it. When someone emails you a charge code authorizing you so many days on a study, save that email as your evidence!

The studies or projects are overseen by a principal investigator. For my employer, there are multiple FFRDCs within the organization, but also other divisions that do similar work funded by grants or municipalities. The work may differ slightly, but the academic use of "principal investigator" remains and is reminiscent of a research university culture. Also, my employer uses a matrix organizational structure, which means my performance reviews and compensation are the responsibility of the Engineering and Applied Science Department – while my work is overseen by the appropriate FFRDC leadership for the study I am supporting. Other organizations may differ.[3]

---

[3] A list of FFRDCs and operating institutions can be found at https://www.nsf.gov/statistics/ffrdclist/.

Studies may begin with a literature review and structured interview methodology. In fact, the proposal that precedes any decision to fund work must include specific methodologies that will be used to conduct the analysis. Interviews are constrained by several considerations – for federal sponsors: the Paperwork Reduction Act of 1980 (https://pra.digital.gov) limits the number of surveys that can be distributed to federal employees. In all cases, an Internal Review Board (IRB) will need to approve the interview protocols to ensure individual privacy is protected throughout. Recall you are working in applied research, the realm of Pasteur. Building on the literature and gleaning insights from policy practitioners and government leaders helps to set the context for what insights may be practical and relevant to the chosen study questions. One criticism of FFRDCs is that research can become far removed from the practice and can result in reports that become "shelfware," rarely read and featuring recommendations that are not considered implementable. In reality the engagement, conversations, and presentations throughout a period of performance are often what the government needs most – and the report reflects our commitment to publicly releasing research results.

In the post-COVID era, organizations that run FFRDCs will likely allow for increased remote work – although collaborative technologies will only partially make up for the in-person experience, and classified work will still require secured office space authorized for the processing of classified information.

Finally, a brief list of research methods and tools you can expect to find within an FFRDC (extracted from the RAND Corporation leadership briefing):

- Cost-benefit analysis
- Econometrics
- Modeling and simulation
- Readiness assessment
- Requirements analysis
- Scalable data analytics
- Social network analysis
- Statistical analysis
- Systems analysis
- Training design and evaluation

Measures of Performance

My performance is measured quite simply: Did the study sponsor value what we delivered, and would they turn to us again for similar research assistance? Reviews are everything to a restaurant and everything to an FFRDC.

The FFRDC funding differs, but generally follows a pattern: There is a maximum revenue number that cannot be exceeded, except at the expense of other FFRDCs. This is referred to as "the pipe," and "filling the pipe" is the measure of performance for an FFRDC. In other words, attracting enough interest in your research capacity indicates its relevance to its home agency. If you have a $100 million dollar "pipe" but only attract $20 million in revenue, you may find yourself disinvited from the recompete when your contract is up. If you consistently fill or nearly fill the pipe, you may get re-awarded the contract without competing. One interesting aspect to this – FFRDCs are all budgeted together by Congress. In order to "increase the pipe" for any one FFRDC, the money will come out of the potential revenue for another!

Because of this, some may argue that the FFRDC's measure of performance is a measure of revenue – and to the extent revenue indicates market interest in what you can do for the sponsor, that may be correct. But I argue that revenue is an indicator of relevance. Every 5 years, the sponsoring agency will either continue the affiliation or choose to compete the contract if the revenue/relevance is unsatisfactory. You are providing an essential function, and if you are not sufficiently relevant to the sponsoring organization's needs, your organization may lose the opportunity to recompete for the FFRDC contract vehicle. Recall the purpose of an FFRDC is to aid the government in areas where they are not resourced to consider long-term strategic research insights – these needs do not go away, but agencies may turn to other less satisfactory options if the FFRDC is not considered a trusted and useful partner.

The individual performance measure is study sponsor satisfaction. Following the end of a study, the sponsor organization will receive a brief survey that asks about satisfaction, did this answer the question, would you return to this organization in the future, etc. Revenue measures may be skewed by several large studies, while the true measure of these organizations is their continued relevance to the supported agencies. A successful FFRDC becomes a trusted partner for solutions that are not amenable to the acquisition of products or services.

Finally, a successful FFRDC/UARC/NL relies on a talented and motivated workforce. Consider a career in public service that begins with entering a think tank.

Acknowledgment The concept that FFRDCs can be understood as working in Pasteur's Quadrant was advanced by my RAND colleague, Dr. Henry Willis. I am indebted to him for this insight, and hope I have done it justice here.

Proudly "Disinterested": Public Administration and Social Science PhD Programs

Daniel Casey and Mark Fletcher

The true test of a good government is its aptitude and tendency to produce a good administration

Hamilton, quoted in Bilmes (2011)

A Road That Weaves In and Out of Academia?

A common assumption in discussions about higher education career pathways (and the central topic of this edited collection) is the road that leads out of academia: we train students to think critically, to write professionally, and to use specialist skills, and then we release the vast majority of them to the private sector. More recent discussion has extended this to questions about PhD training and whether PhD candidates are being adequately trained for a career in academia or a career outside of the university (or some mixture of both) (Casey et al. 2023; Berdahl et al. 2022; Jones 2013). Universities, governments, and students in Australia and internationally are reconsidering the purpose and nature of PhD programs. Previous assumptions that PhD graduates would be able to get a secure, stable, and permanent academic job is a thing of the past. In our own field of political science, there has been a steady decline in new PhD graduates successfully getting tenure-track positions; in the USA, postgraduate placements went down from 38% in 2010–2011 to 26% in 2019–2020 (McGrath and Diaz 2021). This framing means that the conversation is anchored in the perspective of the University: knowledge and skills flow *from* academia *to* the wider community.

D. Casey (✉) · M. Fletcher
School of Politics and International Relations, Australian National University, Canberra, Australia
e-mail: Daniel.Casey@anu.edu.au; Mark.Fletcher@anu.edu.au

87

N. Jackson (ed.), *Non-Academic Careers for Quantitative Social Scientists*,
Texts in Quantitative Political Analysis,
https://doi.org/10.1007/978-3-031-35036-8_11

A richer story is one where the road weaves in and out of academia, a story of push and pull factors that make some decisions more appealing than others, and a story of the relationship between industry and higher education. It is a story where knowledge and skills also flow back into the University, as well as flowing out. The overall picture is of people moving in and out of academia over the career lifecycle, just as they move in and out of other career pathways.

As contrarian as it may seem for a chapter in a book on nonacademic careers for quantitative social scientists, in this chapter, we are going to tell you two stories of moving in the other direction from industry – in our case government and policy – into academia and how our backgrounds enriched our academic work, as well as being able to support the research of those around us. This chapter is critical self-reflection from two authors about our own pathways back into academia and the push and pull factors which will either retain us or move us back into policy. Through this, we develop the picture of the career path that weaves both in and out of academia and how experiences from both domains inform each other. We promote a broader view of the skills that quantitative political scientists bring to work in government and policy, challenging the intuition that former quantitative researchers should first consider roles as departmental "data scientists." We engage with recent "Research Impact and Engagement" policies to show how nonacademic experiences enhance academic skills, particularly in communication and research end-user identification. This chapter is mainly crafted for current PhD candidates, or recent PhD graduates, who are thinking about working in government.

Tertiary Education in Australia and the PhD Pathway

A small amount of context is needed to frame this story: what is the typical Australian PhD experience, and how does it differ from the experience in other countries? The Australian PhD program is based on the UK model, of an "apprentice" learning at the foot of their "master," rather than a structured program of coursework, comprehensive exams, prospectus, and dissertation. The Australian PhD is traditionally undertaken in 3 to 4 years of full-time equivalent study and usually requires the completion of an 80,000-to-100,000-word dissertation. In the social sciences, most universities have no or minimal coursework, and none have comprehensive exams. There is, therefore, a high degree of variance between Australian PhD experiences, with significantly less structure than you might expect in other countries. With this variation comes a high degree of freedom for training. Both authors undertook training in basic empirical research methods (including nonquantitative methods), but specialization in particular methods was tailored by choice of thesis topic.

Both of us had extensive work experience prior to entering a PhD program. Australian PhD candidates are comparatively older than in other countries and more likely to be part-time. Although we are both doing our PhD full-time, Australian PhD candidates are often doing their PhD part-time while continuing to work. This might also influence expectations for postdoctoral career. A recent comparative survey of political science PhD candidates found that while almost three-quarters of Canadian political science PhD candidates were "primarily interested in pursuing an academic career," just under half of Australian survey respondents answered the same way (Casey et al. 2023), and COVID is likely to have significant impacts on career trajectories (Rutledge-Prior and Casey 2023). The key questions that arise are about the nature of the doorway back into academia and who chooses to walk through that door. Is there an expectation that people can walk through the door, undertake a PhD, and then return to their previous careers?

It is not clear what influences a person to continue with academia. Some of the story is linked to how a person enters academia. Daniel and Mark both grew up in Victoria but now study at the Australian National University (ANU) in the Australian Capital Territory (ACT). Daniel went to the elite Melbourne High School, while Mark went to significantly less prestigious high schools in regional Victoria (Bendigo and Gippsland). Following secondary education, Daniel moved to the ACT and went to the ANU for his undergraduate degrees in arts and law; Mark went to the University of Melbourne for his undergraduate degree in arts.

After finishing their undergraduate degrees, why did they not move straight into graduate school? In Daniel's case, he wanted to change the world and do something meaningful. In Mark's case, he was tired of being poor. The Australian Public Service invests significantly in recruiting recent graduates. It is common for the government and large firms to be part of "career fairs" on campus where they promote to students the prospects of employment. Unlike entry into undergraduate study, graduate recruitment tends to be extremely competitive. Following their undergraduate degrees, both authors entered the public service as part of the graduate program: a recruitment scheme to expand the talent pool of the public service especially in policy development areas (rather than in service delivery areas) (Casey 2006). Recent changes to the public service's graduate program have been the emphasis of a "data stream" of graduates: just as law graduates and economics graduates have typically had different pathways through the graduate program, the public service is specifically targeting graduates with skills in data analysis to move into, for example, the Australian Bureau of Statistics. At the end of undergraduate study, there are therefore significant pull factors away from academia, both in terms of the personal circumstances of the individual and in the perception of alternatives.

Daniel's career was more traditional than Mark's: Daniel worked across health policy, Indigenous policy, communications policy, social security policy, and defense policy. He also worked briefly for Mental Health Australia, the peak not-for-profit organization for the mental health sector. Most recently, he was a senior policy manager, responsible for teams of up to eight people managing policy issues such as income support for students, pension payments for older Australians, or family benefits for new parents. Mark, on the other hand, accumulated degrees. After several years of being a public servant and policy adviser, he completed a law degree at the ANU while working in administration and policy. He then went back to the public service as a legal officer and senior policy officer, simultaneously completing his legal practice qualification as well as another specialist law degree. Although the workload is high, this is not an uncommon approach in Australia, where a lot of postgraduate degrees are undertaken alongside outside employment. But that contact with academia is typically not "sticky": a person is likely to continue with their career with the additional qualification being used to obtain promotions or pay rises.

The networks with the university increased our awareness of it as a career option, but the fact both of us had established careers in the public service also reduced the risk of failure. Daniel started his PhD while on extended leave from the public service. This arrangement means that Daniel has a job to return to, if he wishes, when he completes his PhD. Mark resigned from the public service to commence his PhD but maintains his professional networks. For both of us, we feel that these networks, as well as our prior work experiences are likely to make us less sensitive to obstacles and thus less prone to the knocks, failures, and challenges of undertaking a PhD. We also can't ignore other factors common to the authors that made them more likely to enter academia and succeed. We both speak English at home, we are not the first of our families to go to university, and our social networks are comfortably middle class. These factors influence career mobility generally and are particularly relevant when we consider the role that experiences and networks have in career development.

Leveraging Skills and Developing Skills

Our backgrounds not only provide us with structural advantages; our backgrounds also provide us with research advantages. King, Keohane, and Verba (1994, p. 15) argued that there were two components to good research questions. The second component – the specific contribution to an identifiable scholarly literature – is entirely an academic task of understanding the relevant discipline, the literature, and the unresolved tensions that have emerged. But the first component is often overlooked: "a research project should pose a question that is 'important' in the real world." Experiences beyond academia help to identify these questions. We both chose research questions that were connected with our experiences in the public service. Daniel studies citizen correspondence to government ministers following his experiences drafting and clearing responses on behalf of the minister (Casey 2022, 2023); Mark studies the public understanding of law drawing on his experiences in complex areas of law and the law reform process. We do not mean to promulgate the false dichotomy of academia being outside of the "real world," but we do want to say that experiences in public policy helped inform our understandings of what was important, useful, and consequential for people's lives outside of academia.

The explanatory text provided by King, Keohane, and Verba about the first component illustrates our point. "Political scientists have no difficulty," they write (King et al. 1994, pp. 15–16), "finding subject matter that meets our first criterion." They then list wars, famines, and economic catastrophes. Much harder is finding research questions that are equally important but less cinematic; firsthand experience of these "business-as-usual" problems fosters new creative insights for developing questions and theories that can be tested.

The false dichotomy of academia being outside of the "real world" clearly wants to leak into this discussion: that academic studies focus on big, cinematic questions that are not applicable to the "business-as-usual" world, or on entirely too niche issues, that nobody beyond the researcher could possibly care about. We want to challenge this further and argue that it is also the firsthand experience with applying quantitative research methods to problems that helps inform the identification of "business-as-usual" problems. People working in administration, policy, and governance tell themselves stories that explain the world around them. Why is the process this inefficient way rather than some imagined efficient way? Why do we have this policy goal instead of that policy goal? Why are these voices heard over those voices? And often some problems are simply invisible without a quantitative approach.

For a real-world example of this, Mark was working in auditing and talked to people about their key performance indicators: how had they been developed and what did good performance look like? One area wanted their team to have a high degree of accuracy (measured as an error rate) per item processed and a high number of items processed per day. To rank team member's performance, they would multiply these two values together, not realizing that this was mathematically identical to the error rate made per day – team members who processed fewer items also had lower error rates and therefore did disproportionately better than those who processed the vast majority of the work. When the story is presented this way, the team looks foolish, but in busy, high-performing, goal-focused teams, it simply never occurred to them to think about or question what their performance numbers were actually telling them.

The general problem about capacity to undertake evidence-driven policy development and assessment is well-recognized. In 2019, the APS undertook an independent review (known as the "Thodey Review") of its "capability, culture and operating model" (Commonwealth of Australia 2019). The Thodey Review noted the "proliferation of advisory networks available to ministers" with the effect that "some ministers no longer regard the APS as their primary or even preferred source of advice" (Commonwealth of Australia 2019, p. 113). The use of consultants for technical expertise has resulted in a knowledge transfer away from the APS, with the APS now lacking key policy development skills – which are often synonymous with core quantitative research skills. But, without high-quality quantitative skills, some problems are simply invisible to time-poor public servants trying to deliver policy proposals on time. The ability to assess, interpret, and communicate complex numerical data is no longer a generalist skill, with emphasis now being on communicating conclusions rather than on communicating reasoning.

Regularly crossing the bridge between academia and the public service also ensures that the workforces are conversant with each other. Like many Anglophone countries, Australia has become fixated on "research impact and engagement." In 2015, the Australian government undertook a review of the university funding system (known as the "Watt Review") which, among other things, argued that

Australia's research system was very high quality but lacked the ability to measure its impact quantitatively. Australia had already implemented a quality assessment exercise (called "Excellence in Research for Australia"), and it was recommended that an impact assessment exercise should sit alongside it (Commonwealth of Australia 2015, p. iii). Impact was defined consistently with the definition used by the Higher Education Funding Council for England: "an effect on, change or benefit to the economy, society, culture, public policy or services, health, the environment or quality of life, beyond academia" (Commonwealth of Australia 2015, p. 65). One of the key hurdles in getting academic work into public policy is that academic works are frequently not written with public servants in mind as an audience. Academics write for other academics, and the peer review process necessitates this focus. "Translating" research into materials that are accessible to public servants requires expertise and has a time cost, but this cost is significantly reduced when the author knows how to write quickly, accurately, and efficiently for both audiences. The researcher who has worked as a research end-user in government, or other policy roles, obviously has an advantage in being able to communicate to those most likely to engage and use the research.

Increasing the number of people in the workforce who have careers that shift back and forth between academic and the public service results in a workforce that is better skilled and can draw upon a richer array of experiences. In academia, this will lead to research questions that are better informed and research outputs are better targeted; real problems are both made visible and better explored.

The Career Toll Bridge

The final element of our argument is the extent to which crossing the bridge results in a "career penalty." The PhD student is, after all, the bottom rung of the academic career ladder, so both Daniel and Mark had to take a hit (both in terms of salary and career seniority) in order to come to academia. If you use the unrefined measure of considering two jobs being equivalent if they have equal salary, Daniel and Mark are about three rungs lower on the career ladder by shifting career streams.

The different career streams use different indicators for career advancement. Being promoted from a policy officer to the director of a public service section is never going to be influenced by how many academic publications you have authored. Similarly, managing a team of policy officers does not give a good indication of your ability to teach and research. But this framing undervalues the transferability of skills. The first time Daniel did a peer review for a journal, without any detailed guidance about how to do it, or what to look for, unsure how to commence. Yet, he quickly realized that this was a skill that was readily transferred from (or to) public service. In the public service, Daniel was regularly required to comment, critique, and improve the work of others, including making decisions about whether the idea itself, and the writing, is good enough to go forward. He quickly found that writing peer reviews was no different to writing "Exposure Draft comments" on Cabinet submissions – Does it make sense? Is it a good idea? Do the number "add up"? Is it good enough to go forward?

To some extent, moving from a PhD program to the public service is an easier pathway than the return journey: the "road out" is considered more normal than the "road in." One frequent obstacle on the pathway out is that PhD graduates typically struggle to translate their skills to policy settings. During our time in the public service, we would have been on dozens of selection panels to hire new policy officers. There are three skills that we look for when hiring staff: the ability to think, the ability to communicate, and the ability to work as a team. Everything else, including subject matter expertise, you can learn on the job. Candidates who demonstrated the ability to "think" demonstrated that they could systematically engage with the issue, understand what is actually happening, and hypothesize what might lead to improved outcomes – really fairly similar to a standard research design. The key is not going to be their ability to run sophisticated quantitative tests. Similarly, there is no expectation that the candidate will be a subject matter expert. For better or worse, the normal public service career leads across a large variety of subject matters, and (with some exceptions) it is not typical for policy offers to have any formal academic training in those subject matters. So, the fact that your PhD might be in outgroup trust in Balkan states or a quantitative analysis of letters from members of the public to the Australian Prime Minister in the later 1990s and early 2000s should not stop you from applying for a job in health policy or in agriculture policy. What matters is your ability to think logically and sequentially through the issues, know how to get up to speed quickly, know how to develop arguments, and know how to balance the strengths and weaknesses in others' arguments.

Public service managers don't instinctively see a neat alignment of the skills developed through the PhD and the skills needed for policy work. The common perception is that PhD candidates sit alone in a room for 3 years, reading and writing one big paper – that's what Daniel thought before he started his PhD. Outside academia, a PhD is often seen as "just another degree" – sure, it's harder and takes longer, but outsiders often struggle to appreciate that a PhD is not just 3 more years of study. So that misunderstanding is something that new PhD graduates need to combat if they are applying for government jobs. Public service hiring committees do not care about your specific research area, and chances are you'll never use your subject-matter-specific knowledge in the public service. Yet we've seen PhD graduates pitch themselves as experts in some niche subject area. The usual clue that the PhD graduate does not understand the shift in streams is that their CV includes three pages of all the publications they have produced – this is information that is simply not relevant or persuasive for a recruitment process. Instead, focus on how the work you've done demonstrates your ability to think, communicate, and work in a team.

Conversely, being able to transition back to academia is more difficult because recruitment committees are looking for academic outputs and ability to teach. It is difficult to demonstrate a future in which you are a highly cited researcher when your CV has a focus on policy development. The strategic actor who wanted to maintain the ability to move back and forth between academia and policy would be to work in areas that provided opportunities to maintain a steady stream of academic publications. Some universities will permit people to maintain adjunct affiliation, effectively providing access to library collections and the ability to use the institutional affiliation. Subject to some constraints, managers in the public service will not take issue with officers publishing information content. Constraints include that there is no conflict (or perceived conflict) between publishing and the policy work.

In both instances, the fundamental difficulty is in remaining competitive in two different career streams. Addressing this difficulty means diversifying your energy to maintain two different skill sets and to maintain the currency of your knowledge and experiences. But, as we have illustrated, some of this energy is subsidized by the richness of the diversified experience: the skills and knowledge to identify solutions both in policy development and in developing research questions.

Like any career choice, there are individual circumstances at work, opportunities, and risks. We have seen in our own careers how those factors interact and what trade-offs we made along the way. Although it is common to view nonacademic jobs as a second-best option for PhD graduates, a career path that moves between academia and nonacademia can open up more opportunities if done strategically. Push and pull factors will affect people differently, and awareness of those factors might not be immediately apparent. The extent to which careers outside of academia are perceived as real options has a significant role to play in whether or not the option will even be considered. And this is not merely an awareness that there are jobs outside of academia, but that there are jobs where the skills can be meaningfully transferred. Preoccupation with "data scientist" roles means other opportunities are unnecessarily discounted. Through the experiences of others, we can see how we can keep options open, maximize the chance of successful outcomes, and minimize the risks associated with failure. Moving backward and forward between academia and the public service has challenges and difficulties associated with it, but it will always trump getting stuck in a career where options forward are limited (or nonexistent).

What Comes Next? Post-PhD Choices for Daniel and Mark

So, where to now for Daniel and Mark, once they finish their PhDs?

What initially attracted Daniel to policy work was the ability to "make a difference" and to improve the lives of other Australians. But, in the end, Daniel regarded the public service as "a calling" (Schorr 1987) rather than just a job, and while he may not return to the Australian Public Service after he finishes his PhD, he will no doubt seek to contribute to these values of public administration, recognizing that "the true test of a good government is its aptitude and tendency to produce a good administration" (Hamilton, quoted in Bilmes 2011). Daniel thinks that, despite the slowness with which the ship of state moves, he still helped it navigate better pathways: he is particularly proud of improvements he made to payments for Australia's first nations to help ensure they completed high school (DSS 2018). He also sees a high degree of correspondence with his personal values: transparency, efficiency, accountability, impartiality, and respect for public institutions is what drove him and drives what he sees as the ideal public service. These values are becoming increasingly important as the partisan divide in society grows. The fundamental question about career path for him will be whether he can attain that kind of self-actualization and fulfilment in academia or whether stepping back and forth between careers gives him a more well-rounded sense of career satisfaction.

Mark is more likely to have a hybridized career path than Daniel. Reflecting on the push and pull factors described in the main body of the chapter, Mark finds the work environment of the public service to be a significant pull factor: stability, certainty, and hierarchy are workplace attributes that he values. Given his research background in quantitative empirical legal research, he is likely to have ongoing collaborations with academic networks, both research and teaching. The fundamental question for him is whether the "career penalty" of staying in the hybrid space is simply too great a tax – will he still want to be "mid-career" at 40?

Ultimately, the pathways taken will be informed by the ideas explored in this chapter: How do we best position ourselves for the career stream we are currently in, and how do we remain competitive when we want to cross the bridge into the other career stream at some future point? What are the costs of maintaining this competitiveness in both streams and the risk of failure? We all instinctively know that quantitative research skills are an asset both inside the academy and in the public service; the key issues are how we use those skills, how we imagine what career pathways are available with those skills (beyond mere "data science"), and how we communicate the benefits of those skills to outsiders.

References

Berdahl, L., Malloy, J. & Young, L. (2022). Faculty Perceptions of Political Science PhD Career Training. *PS: Political Science & Politics*, 53, 751–756.

Bilmes, L. J. (2011). Federalist Nos. 67–77 How Would Publius Envision the Civil Service Today?. *Public Administration Review*, *71*, supplement 98–104.

Casey, D. (2006). Managing and sustaining the APS workforce: a graduate perspective. *Public Administration Today*, (6), 35–36. https://search.informit.org/doi/10.3316/ielapa.200603788

Casey, D. (2022). "Dear John….": Letters from the public to Prime Minister Howard. *Policy Perspectives*, Issue 2, http://hdl.handle.net/1885/276128

Casey, D. (2023). Punctuated equilibrium and the dynamics of political participation: the case of letter writing. *Policy Studies*, 1–20. https://doi.org/10.1080/01442872.2023.2202385

Casey, D., Rutledge-Prior, S., Young, L., Malloy, J., & Berdahl, L. (2023). Hard Work and You Can't Get it: An International Comparative Analysis of Gender, Career Aspirations, and Preparedness Among Politics and International Relations PhD Students. *PS: Political Science & Politics*, 56(3), 402–410.

Commonwealth of Australia (2015) *Report of the Review of Research Policy and Funding Arrangements)*   https://www.education.gov.au/review-research-policy-and-funding-arrangements/resources/review-research-policy-and-funding-arrangements-report-november-2015 (accessed 13 January 2023)

Commonwealth of Australia (2019) *Our Public Service, Our Future, Independent Review of the Australian Public Service* https://www.pmc.gov.au/sites/default/files/resource/download/independent-review-aps.pdf (accessed 13 January 2023)

DSS (Department of Social Services) (2018) "Student measures – 2018 Budget" https://www.dss.
    gov.au/sites/default/files/documents/05_2018/d18_13650_budget_2018-19_-_factsheet_-_stu-
    dent_measures.pdf (accessed 13 January 2023)
Jones, M. (2013). Issues in Doctoral Studies – Forty Years of Journal Discussion: Where Have We
    Been and Where Are We Going? *International Journal of Doctoral Studies,* 8, 83–104. http://
    ijds.org/Volume8/IJDSv8p083-104JonesFT129.pdf
King, G., Keohane, R. O., & Verba, S. (1994). *Designing Social Inquiry: Scientific Inference in
    Qualitative Research*, Princeton University Press.
McGrath, E., & Diaz, A. (2021). APSA Graduate Placement Report: Analysis of Political Science
    Placements for 2018–2020. *APSA Preprints.* Doi: https://doi.org/10.33774/apsa-2021-jmxt3
Rutledge-Prior, S., & Casey, D. (2023). "An Isolating Experience Aggravated by COVID":
    Exploring Disconnections Between Political Science PhD Candidates and Supervisors. *PS:
    Political Science & Politics, 56*(3), 357–364. https://doi.org/10.1017/S1049096523000161
Schorr, P. (1987). Public service as a calling: An exploration of a concept. *International Journal of
    Public Administration*, 10(5), 465–493. https://doi.org/10.1080/01900698708524575

Applying the Transferable Skill Set of a PhD to Emerging Data Fields

Sarina Rhinehart

As I crafted my academic job market materials in the summer and fall of 2020, in the shadow of the COVID-19 pandemic and prior to any vaccine rollout, I felt my long-held dream of working in academia slipping through my fingers. While I had always dreamed of the shiny tenure-track position, I knew that even under normal circumstances, the number of jobs was fewer than the sum of qualified candidates all pursuing the same goal.

The number of posted open positions shrunk further as the unpredictability of how the pandemic would play out pushed colleges and universities to pause or cancel hiring for the year. In addition to the lack of available academic positions, I was also anxious about the thought of having to move across the country with little control over where I would be relocating and requiring my partner to leave a job he loved. I began to worry about whether the skills and experiences gained through pursuing my PhD in political science had prepared me for success outside of the academic community.

Therefore, in November of my final year of graduate school, I crafted my curriculum vitae into a condensed resume and began searching for and applying to a handful of jobs in my desired geographic area and positions I felt both sounded exciting and would put to use the research and data skills I learned as part of my PhD. In considering an academic position, I had the perfect vision of how I could continue the work I started with my dissertation, which included using Bayesian item response theory and survey experiments to examine the role of gender in politics. However, I had a much foggier idea of how these skills and knowledge could translate into success outside of academia.

As I look back now at my graduate education and reflect on my career thus far outside of academia, I can see clearly how my PhD prepared me for my work in

S. Rhinehart (✉)
EL Education, New York City, NY, USA

© The Author(s), under exclusive license to Springer Nature
Switzerland AG 2023
N. Jackson (ed.), *Non-Academic Careers for Quantitative Social Scientists*,
Texts in Quantitative Political Analysis,
https://doi.org/10.1007/978-3-031-35036-8_12

state government, as well as my current position in a national nonprofit, and has set me up for future career success. If someone would have asked me to define "data governance" a couple years ago, I would not have had a good explanation. However, because of the adaptability of my data and research skills, I was promoted to serve in state government as Executive Director of Data Governance for the Oklahoma State Department of Education.

In this position, I started, implemented, and led the agency's data governance program, including building the structures, roles, and processes to set up long-term success of the program and strengthen an agency-wide culture that embraces the value of high-quality data. During my time in state government, I found tremendous growth opportunities for myself and other social science PhD graduates in these areas.

As state agencies across the country increasingly see a need to invest money, resources, and staff into improving their collection, management, and use of data, state governments are hiring in fields that are not often found as majors in universities' academic catalogs but are areas critical for the long-term success of a state agency's data. In this chapter, I provide tips to understanding how to apply the skills learned during a social science PhD to state government work, especially in emerging fields where the adaptability of a social science PhD serves as an advantage in new positions where few have the degree or specific experience to fit the needs in an emerging data field.

Transferable Skill Set of a PhD

Upon reflection of my alt-academic career, the most critical skill I gained throughout my graduate school experience that has allowed me to be successful in data work in state government is being a flexible problem-solver, who can think creatively from both a technical and business perspective to address data problems or improve data processes.

I often found myself serving as an internal consultant within the agency for the various departments and teams who want or need to collect and use data but need someone with the expertise on data best practices and solutions or considerations that need to be part of the conversation. At times, this work is a combination of communications, technology, legal, process, and policies, in addition to data work.

For example, there are people both within and outside the agency who would like to use our data for decision-making, research, grant applications, communications or presentation materials, and a variety of other reasons. These people will make a request and have an idea in their heads about what data they would like. I will meet with them after they submit a request to walk through exactly what they want and what data can best serve their needs, as well as the necessary context around the data they need to be aware of when using the data to draw conclusions. I often find myself in the role of helping to bridge the gap between the people who want to use data for decision-making but need guidance to ensure the data meets their needs and is used accurately and responsibly.

My data problem-solving skills are also beneficial in evaluating and identifying data quality concerns, finding the source of the data quality issue, and designing and implementing solutions to ensure the agency's data are accurate, complete, and timely. I find working to resolve data quality issues scratches the same itch for why I enjoyed doing research in graduate school because I run through the familiar process of identifying a key question and using data to test the potential causal story.

A common situation that arises is a staff member identifies a weird trend in the data. My team members and I first try and identify if the data may be a true outlier or, more likely, a data quality issue. After we have identified the problem, we next dig into the why. A data quality issue could stem from a number of sources, including a lack of awareness or knowledge among those who enter the data, it could be data is entered correctly but is not translating correctly as it is processed and moved into the state's data structures, or it could be a whole host of other issues resulting in poor data quality.

In graduate school, I was always curious about measurement and survey methods papers, including the best ways to measure people's attitudes and beliefs. That knowledge is now put to use to examine how measurement issues may be the root of data quality issues. An example from my work in a state educational agency is that we may collect a binary indicator of if a student is in an alternative education program or not in a given school year, but the reality is that a student may move in and out of an alternative education program throughout a school year. Therefore, that variable needs to be collected with a start and end date rather than a simple binary indicator.

Specifically working in state government, resolving data quality issues often requires critical thinking for how to navigate systems that are sometimes outdated or clunky to work with. I ran into several instances where I saw an opportunity to make a small change in how we collected a data element; however, once I dig into the issue, it is often much more complicated than originally envisioned because there are a number of people and teams involved who often have different needs for the data, and changes take managing people, business, and technology needs simultaneously.

Beyond helping the agency and staff collect, manage, and use our data, I also collaborated with third parties who want to use the agency's data including researchers, nonprofits, and the media. My experience of working on my own research helps me better serve others to provide them with the correct data to address their research questions and ensure the data are high quality and can reliably be used for research.

In addition to problem-solving, another skill from my PhD experience that is essential in state government data work has been my ability to be a quick learner who can more easily adapt to new and changing situations. A perfect example of this was when I first interviewed to work at the Oklahoma State Department of Education and learning to code in a new program. During my PhD, I learned to code in R and Stata; however, central to much data work in state government is SQL. SQL, which stands for structured query language, is a programming language used to manage relational databases. We use SQL to access our data and manipulate it to look at subgroups or calculate aggregates, among other functions. If you are interested in government work, I would recommend you check out SQL and familiarize yourself with some of its uses.

Something that I was not fully prepared for in applying to nonacademic data jobs was the various methods the interview panel will use to gauge your data knowledge and skills. One panel gave me a data set a couple days in advance of the interview and had me run some analysis and craft a 5-min presentation to present to the panel. Another had me submit some R code I previously wrote and write a brief narrative explaining my coding process.

However, for my state government position, there were multiple steps to evaluate my data skills. First, I received two exercises where I could use my preferred programming language to evaluate data sets and write up a narrative of my findings. Additionally, because the position would require me to work heavily with SQL, they assigned me a timed exam where I had to write sample SQL code. As someone who at that point had almost no knowledge of what SQL even was, I jumped on Linkedin Learning the weekend prior to my interview to take a 3-h video course on SQL basics. I was pleasantly surprised that because of my coding background in other software, learning a new language was not that much of a leap, as many share similar functions.

A background with any coding language makes the learning curve less steep for learning new software, and I encourage job seekers to be open to learning new coding languages and to apply to positions, even if you do not know the specific programming language the position is asking for. Even now, although I prefer using R, I strive to use SQL for my work as it is the common language my coworkers use, and I want to write code my colleagues can use in the future.

I emphasized both of the skills I have highlighted, problem-solving and quick learning, in my resume and cover letter when applying to nonacademic data jobs. Below I will highlight some of the additional skills I gained through my graduate school program which I mentioned in my application materials and have proven to be advantageous in state government work:

- Survey research and methodology skills – Basic principles around how to structure survey questions to ensure the data collected are useful and address the questions at hand are valuable as state governments seek to gain insight on how they can best serve their customers. For example, I helped craft a survey the agency sent to school districts to find out their concerns and highest priorities in addressing student data privacy and security.
- Verbal and written communications skills – Attending conferences and teaching courses during my PhD gave me practice in being able to clearly and concisely present data and information, including the ability to communicate to a nontechnical audience. In my current role, I still attend conferences and give various presentations, but I also find this skill useful in my daily work as I communicate with my colleagues and those outside the agency. In interviews, I highlighted my teaching experience as effectively translating complicated concepts while spotlighting the central question and key findings to those who know less on the topic than I do.

- Project management – In graduate school, one must balance multiple large-scale projects simultaneously including writing their dissertation, teaching courses, collaborating with co-authors on other research, and all the other projects graduate students find themselves engaged in. The ability to independently design and execute multiple large-scale projects from start to finish demonstrates the organizational and detail-oriented skills needed to be successful in the, at times, chaotic environment, of the daily work in state government.
- Data visualizations – Presenting data as a simple visualization is often the best way to communicate complex ideas to an audience. Being able to create clear and useful visualizations is pivotal to making sure data are used and interpreted correctly. It is a bonus to have some experience with interactive data visualization tools, such as Power BI or Tableau, that allow state agencies to connect their data to a dashboard where others can explore the data themselves. State agencies are increasingly seeking out the use of these tools to communicate out data to various audiences.
- Data quality and analysis – Being able to manage large data sets, collect original data, assess data quality, clean up a messy data set, and how to effectively analyze and interpret complex data are all skills state governments need. Those who are interviewing candidates may be unaware of the amount of data work and training one receives as part of a social science PhD program. In interviews, I often walked through examples of handling messy data, working with large data sets, and explaining how I used data to answer my research questions.

Overall, in reviewing and applying for state government jobs, not many promoted that they were specifically looking for a PhD. Most listed they were looking for someone with at least a master's degree. However, in my experience in a state agency, there are many individuals with a PhD across many fields including history, psychology, music education, political science, education, and statistics. In particular, I have seen those with a PhD promoted quickly within their agency or across state agencies.

One key consideration in applying for state government jobs is to be aware of the politics of some positions. States have varied rules around whether leadership positions are appointed or elected. In some agencies, where leadership is elected, some positions may not be guaranteed under a new elected leader or the culture or priorities of the agency may shift, so I encourage asking during interviews about the transition process and how that impacts employment and the agency, as a whole.

Emerging Data Fields

Since graduating and leaving academia, I have seen success for myself and other social science PhDs who possess the skills outlined above, particularly in new and growing data positions, as state agencies have realized the importance of collecting and using high-quality data to drive decision-making. State governments have a need to employ highly skilled staff who can grow into new and changing positions. Below I outline some data fields that I believe social science PhD graduates are well suited to pursue in state government.

Data Quality

Data quality is an essential value to the function of all areas of a state agency. Policy makers within an agency and state legislators use the data an agency manages to determine funding, establish goals and priorities, and set their legislative agenda for the creation of new policy. Any research or decision-making using data is only as reliable as the quality of the data. For example, if data quality issues have stifled the correct identification of students who drop out of high school, the data may under-count dropout rates, which has the consequence of policy makers being less likely to invest time and resources to improve the issue.

My first position within the Oklahoma State Department of Education was in data quality. The agency receives data from more than 500 school districts on students, teachers, and more that is used for decision-making, in addition to numerous required state and federal reports. While most data sent in by districts are high quality, I found myself investing significant time into identifying data quality issues and potential solutions to improve data quality.

The agency is in the process of investing into creating automated processes to assess data quality, moving away from the old, time-intensive manual processes that sometimes lead to problems. In speaking with other state agencies, there are many others undergoing similar large-scale projects to address data quality issues through improved technology, policies, tooling, and processes, making this an area where state governments will increasingly be hiring for.

Data quality is especially important and challenging in the rollout of a new data collection. For example, if the agency has a new data collection due to a new federal requirement, we have to create and communicate training to our school districts so they know how to collect and report the data, we have to establish the technology needed to collect and use the data, we create business rules for how the data can be used, and we develop best practices to assess the accuracy and completeness of the data. Overall, state government agencies are increasingly seeing the value of having and using high-quality data and are investing resources and time into the technology and staffing to meet these needs.

Data Governance

After about a year into my position in state government, my agency made the decision to create its first ever position in data governance as they recognized the need for an enterprise-wide data management strategy. While I was hesitant to take a position where I lacked direct experience, I found this work fulfilling and using many of the skills I developed in my PhD.

Data governance is broadly about how an organization manages its data including the policies, processes, and stakeholder roles that structure how the agency collects, manages, reports, and releases data. As I built the foundation of our agency's data governance program, I drafted our data governance mission and charter, as well as started up our agency's data governance board and additional subcommittees to support this work to enable discussion and decision-making around all things data. The overarching goal of a data governance program is to improve the efficiency, availability, quality, and privacy of an organization's data to improve the capacity to use information for data-driven decision-making. I also worked to make sure internal and external stakeholders who want to use the agency's data do so responsibly and in a way that maintains data privacy and security.

In a large state agency, each division tends toward being siloed, such that each team has detailed knowledge of their own work but not much knowledge about what other teams are doing and how it might align with their work. In my role, I was a generalist who could bring an enterprise-wide focus to data management and help teams understand the role of their data within the larger system and reduce redundancies in data collections and make sure the data we collect and report are meaningful and timely to stakeholders.

Another crucial role of data governance is knowledge management for the agency, which includes ensuring the documentation of all policies, processes, and business rules. Documentation protects an agency against loss of knowledge due to staff turnover and ensures staff have the information they need when they need it. A crucial part of documentation work is crafting, managing, and updating data dictionaries or data catalogs, often documenting historical metadata on data elements or data collections.

Data Literacy

State data are used by various stakeholders including internal employees, state legislators, federal agencies, media, researchers, nonprofits, businesses, and marketers. However, those seeking to use state data might not always have the best understanding of what data to ask for or how to use the data. Data literacy is all about teaching and making sure these various stakeholders properly understand and use data. Additionally, data literacy is concerned with how the agency can improve its communication of data including through visualizations, methods for presenting data, and how to contextualize complex data.

For example, we could publish a simple statistic, and five different parties might interpret that statistic in five distinct ways if we do not effectively and strategically communicate the data. Another concern is data users taking data out of context. For example, a media outlet might take our data and compare it with data from surrounding states, but each state may measure that data point differently, making

comparisons not useful. Another misuse of data could be external organizations trying to tell causal stories with state data without understanding the full picture. For
example, a nonprofit could use data on school math test scores to show their math
tutoring program was successful without considering how other factors, including
the school's population of economically disadvantaged students, might impact math
testing scores. Overall, data literacy serves to take complex processes and data and
make it accessible to diverse audiences.

Data Analysis

Of the data fields presented in this chapter, data analysis is probably the most familiar to those coming from a social science PhD program, and it is a high-demand
field in many state agencies. Data analysts are essential in state government for
helping with mandated reporting, pulling and evaluating data for internal and external stakeholders, and assessing and identifying data quality issues. Analysts are
detail-oriented problem-solvers, who must logically think through the root cause of
data issues and develop solutions.

However, one challenge with seeking out data analyst positions is that many
organizations use this job title to mean diverse things and at different levels of organizational leadership. In evaluating job postings for data analysts, I would recommend reading the description closely to ensure it aligns with your expectations.

Data Privacy

As an extension of my position in data governance, I increasingly found myself
working on data privacy and security issues as the agency works to protect its data
by reducing risk and maturing its overall security and privacy functions. While
some data privacy positions are more technology focused, some may be ideal for
those with a data background. For example, state agencies often have a cybersecu-
rity team that invests time and resources into protecting state data and devices from
outside threats, but risk also comes from internal practices around how data are
managed and shared. State agencies increasingly need data privacy staff as they
shift toward a more proactive approach to protecting data. Additionally, there is
increasing public interest in how states are protecting data, and states are making
efforts to be more transparent about their practices.

Work in data privacy in state government involves balancing the needs to reduce
risk of unauthorized disclosure of data and giving people access to data to use for
essential research and decision-making. A background in data can be useful in crafting policies around data privacy best practices and training staff on how they can use
data in a secure way. A significant part of my job was sharing data with third parties,

and I needed to be responsible with ensuring all data sharing follows federal and state law and promotes data privacy best practices to protect the agency's data.

Conclusion

While I once dreamed, as many PhD students do, of working as a professor, I do not see myself ever attempting to get back into academia. When I made the decision to accept a position in state government, it was a hard decision that I was uncertain about at the time, but I now feel like I made the best decision for myself and the people in my life. My position has allowed me to continue exercising many of the data and research skills I learned in graduate school while also learning and growing in new areas that are preparing me for whatever lies ahead in my career.

Especially as state governments seek to increase their capacity to collect and use data, there is a need for highly skilled individuals with a data background who can provide leadership in new and emerging data fields. State government is a ripe industry for social science PhD graduates as they consider how they might translate their graduate school experiences and knowledge into a successful alt-academic career.

Part II
Advice for Non-academic Job Success

How to Market Yourself for Careers Beyond the Professoriate

Laura Schram

Many social science doctoral students will explore career opportunities beyond the professoriate. Traditional doctoral training prepares students to articulate the knowledge and abilities that they could bring to a faculty position, but rarely provides guidance for how to market oneself for other career paths. For example, many well-meaning faculty mentors use terms like "the job market" to describe the *tenure-track faculty* job market, assuming that political science faculty jobs are the only jobs that their students are exploring. After 5 or more years as a doctoral student developing esoteric knowledge and learning jargon in order to speak the language of their discipline, it is a challenging act of translation for social science Ph.D. students to clearly and persuasively communicate their value to other career fields. In this chapter, I share three principles that will help you to market yourself effectively for careers beyond the professoriate.

Principle 1: Reflect on Your Career Interests, Values, and Skills Before Job Searching

As an undergraduate, I fell in love with the concept of institutions. I vividly remember my first comparative politics class when the professor invited students to take sides in a debate about which system offered superior governance, parliamentary or presidential democracy. I was the lone voice in a class full of American undergraduates arguing for the efficiencies that a parliamentary system can provide for forming governing coalitions and passing legislation. I declared my major in international

L. Schram (✉)
University of Michigan, Ann Arbor, MI, USA
e-mail: lnschram@umich.edu

N. Jackson (ed.), *Non-Academic Careers for Quantitative Social Scientists*,
Texts in Quantitative Political Analysis,
https://doi.org/10.1007/978-3-031-35036-8_13

studies with a focus in international politics and economics shortly thereafter. After several years in the workforce following my college graduation, I decided to pursue doctoral studies because I wanted to delve more deeply into my interests in the relationship between institutions and political outcomes and because I believed I would thrive being a professor and creating the kind of active learning environment I had loved so much as an undergraduate. I developed new skills both as an instructor and a researcher as a doctoral student and my professional interests evolved.

As I neared the end of my doctoral studies, my interests were not the same as when I started my program. Did I want to be a faculty member, balancing the demands of teaching, research, and service? If so, I knew I was only interested in a career at a teaching-intensive institution. Or did I want to focus exclusively on teaching and learning? Prior to graduate school, I hadn't even heard of career fields like educational development. Other than academia, what career fields valued instructional skills? In addition to these questions about the evolution of my professional interests and skills, I had other considerations with which I was wrestling. When I started doctoral studies, I was singularly focused on my scholarly career and interests. In my final year of my doctoral studies, I was married and pregnant and my life priorities had changed. What kind of work-life integration did I want, and what professions would support the kind of integration I was seeking? I had many questions I needed to answer related to my professional interests, skills, and values.

As someone whose job is now to support doctoral students in their career and professional development, I know that before you jump into a job search, you must first start with some deep examination of yourself. There are three lenses that I would suggest you use for that self-examination. First, what are your professional interests? Think of your interests as the professional activities that put you in a "flow" state. In positive psychology, flow is defined as "the state in which people are so involved in an activity that nothing else seems to matter; the experience itself is so enjoyable that people will do it even at a great cost, for the sheer sake of doing it" (Csikszentmihalyi 1990, p. 4). Many of us can easily call to mind our hobbies that put us in flow, whether it's playing an instrument or distance running. A good way to discern what professional activities put you in flow is to reflect on which tasks you enjoy most in your day-to-day life as a graduate student. What activities put you in a zone where you are completely absorbed in those tasks and yet you still leave your work energized? What are you doing when you're at your best? This could include more traditional doctoral student activities, as well as volunteer or other complementary experiences. As a doctoral student, I most enjoyed teaching and mentoring others, and I once commented to my partner that I couldn't believe I got paid for my part-time job at the campus teaching center because I loved the work so much that I would have done it for free. What are the activities that you enjoy so much that doing them every day would leave you thriving, not just surviving, at work?

The second task in your self-examination process is to identify your skills. These are the talents and abilities that you have developed as a scholar and professional and can include skills developed in roles you held prior to graduate school. Prior to graduate school, you likely had jobs during or after your undergraduate studies.

What were those jobs, and what skills did you develop through those experiences? Many graduate students have significant work experience between undergraduate and graduate studies where they gained workforce experience and marketable skills. In graduate school, you have worked hard to develop many skills that are highly valued in the workforce, from quantitative or qualitative methodological skills to the ability to communicate complex ideas to lay audiences (a skill you surely developed if you ever taught an introductory social science course). Skills such as these that are applicable to a wide array of fields are often referred to as "transferable skills," because you can apply these skills in a wide range of settings. Many graduate students assume that they don't have marketable skills because they've been taught to think of themselves as highly specialized in a very narrow subfield of their discipline. Other graduate students think they don't have transferable skills because they've been so steeped in the culture of criticism in academia that they think they will never be good enough in these areas to claim them as skills. I assure you that if you completed a doctoral degree in social science, you have many skills that are valued by employers. You just need to take the time to reflect on your abilities and talk about your skills without using jargon. Later in this chapter, I will go deeper into the importance of identifying your skills to pitch yourself to jobs beyond the professoriate.

Lastly, what values are important to you as a professional and a scholar? Social psychologist Daphna Oyserman defines values as "internalized cognitive structures that guide choices by evoking a sense of basic principles of right and wrong (e.g., moral values), a sense of priorities (e.g., personal achievement vs. group good) and that create a willingness to make meaning and see patterns" (2015, p. 36). Values are your priorities that guide your choices and help you to make meaning of your experiences. Knowing your values in addition to your interests and skills will enable you to identify career fields and organizational cultures that align with your deeper priorities and what matters most to you.

There are several resources designed to support doctoral students in identifying their professional interests, skills, and values. First, ImaginePhD (https://www.imaginephd.com) is a free online career exploration and planning tool for Ph.D. students and postdoctoral scholars in social sciences and the humanities. The tool was created by the Graduate Career Consortium, an international professional organization of university administrators who provide professional and career development for Ph.D. students at their institutions. Using ImaginePhD, you can take assessments designed for doctoral students to identify your interests, skills, and values and then engage in intentional career exploration and planning. This self-reflection is a critical first step in helping you to focus your job search on fields and organizations that will be a good fit for you. Second, take advantage of the resources on your campus for career exploration and coaching. Most research universities now have professional staff (many with Ph.D.s themselves) who can support you through career exploration workshops and one-on-one coaching services. Depending on your campus context, these professionals may be in your career center, your graduate school, or your home department. Coaching is particularly helpful because an effective coach will help you mine your self-assessments for deeper insights and work with you to identify action steps for your job search. Finally, there are several excellent books that have well-designed self-assessment activities for career exploration, including *Next Gen PhD: A Guide to Career Paths in Science* (Sinche 2016) and *Designing Your Life: How to Build a Well-Lived and Joyful Life* (Burnett and Evans 2016).

Principle 2: When You Are Ready for Your Job Search, Get to Know Your Audience and Tailor Your Pitch to Them

While a small number of employers (e.g., policy think tanks, education-related foundations, universities, etc.) will understand the value of a Ph.D. in social science, most will not. Therefore, once you've honed in on your career interests and feel ready to begin job searching, it is critical to tailor your materials to the jobs and the organizations to which you are applying. Do not just blindly send out job applications. An important first step is to learn the language of your audience. In order to learn a new professional language, you need to immerse yourself in conversations with folks who are fluent in that language. This means you need to build your professional network in the fields that interest you. Just like you learned social science terminology through reading scholarship in your field, discussing concepts in graduate seminars and research meetings with your faculty mentors and at disciplinary conferences, talking with professionals in the fields that interest you will help you to learn their language and what matters to them when they are hiring. Such conversations are typically referred to as informational interviews. Many graduate students cringe when they are encouraged to network, but just like it is critical to connect with social science scholars in your subfield at disciplinary organization conferences if you want to pursue a faculty career path, it is critical to connect similarly with professionals in whatever career field you want to pursue. The goal of these conversations is *not* to get a job. Rather, the goal is to learn about your interviewees' career journeys and gain insights on their professions. You can ask interviewees what their day-to-day work life is like, test assumptions you might have about jobs in their fields, and learn what they are seeking when they hire folks. Through these discussions, you will begin to learn the lingo of their field, as well as the nuances of their roles. Additionally, your interviewees may be willing to share their networks with you or suggest potential companies and organizations that might be a good fit for your skills. To that end, you should be prepared to share a bit about yourself and your skillset so they can make those connections. There are many helpful online resources on how to conduct informational interviews (including on the ImaginePhD platform mentioned earlier), if you are new to having career conversations and are seeking sample questions you can use for these conversations.

In your informational interviews, avoid jargon and narrow focus on your esoteric scholarly interests. In my time as a political science Ph.D. student, I spent several years mastering previously unfamiliar terminology and methods of the discipline. In fact, my family could not understand what my dissertation was about when I told them it was entitled, "Conditional Extremism - When Do Exclusionary National Identities Spur Hostility to Immigrants & Radical Right Support?" I had mastered the jargon of my narrow subfield of comparative political psychology. Unfortunately, none of that jargon was legible in the career field that I was most interested in as I was applying for educational development jobs in my final months of graduate school. My faculty mentors at a research-intensive university drove home to me that I would be primarily evaluated on my research when applying to faculty jobs at institutions like my own. Unfortunately, despite the immense amount of time we spend on our dissertations, when applying to jobs beyond the professoriate, hiring managers will almost never be interested in the finer details of your dissertation scholarship. They are also very unlikely to be familiar with the jargon of your field. Rather, they will be interested in your skills and experiences and how those can be leveraged within their organization (see Principle 3).

In addition to having informational interviews, there are several other ways to connect to professional conversations in your fields of interest in order to learn the language of those fields. Follow professional conversations through reading press articles, white papers, or journal articles – whatever information sources are the norm for dissemination of information in that profession. Follow thought leaders on social media, and attend webinars or conferences by professional organizations or employers in the fields that interest you. Update your own online presence (e.g., your LinkedIn profile, your personal website, etc.) to align your public professional brand with the kinds of jobs and career fields that interest you. Recruiters in many career fields use LinkedIn to identify potential candidates for open positions, and hiring managers may Google you if they are looking to learn more about you as a potential candidate for their open position. You want to ensure that your public presence reflects your career interests.

Once you've begun to learn the language and priorities of the field you're interested in and you are ready to apply to jobs, carefully look at position descriptions for jobs that interest you to assist you in tailoring your job materials. Having served as a hiring manager myself now for many years, I can quickly identify candidates who have not read the job description and are just applying to any job that they are remotely qualified for. These applications are almost never compelling and often require me to carefully decode the application materials to discern whether the candidate is worth considering. On the other hand, I can just as readily identify which candidates have carefully read the job description and taken the time to cogently explain how they are an excellent fit for the job and my organization. These applications always make it to the "let's consider this person" pile for the hiring committee to discuss and very frequently make it to the first round of interviews. In other words, it is very hard to stand out in a large pool of candidates when you're sending the exact same materials to each job you apply for, especially when many candidates are taking the extra time to tailor their pitch to the hiring manager.

It might sound daunting to tailor your materials to each job, but if you've done the careful self-reflection work outlined above, you should be applying to a manageable number of clearly defined career fields and job families that are similar enough such that you can make tweaks to a master résumé and cover letter. Note that for most industries, you will want a one-to-two page résumé, not a curriculum vitae (CV). Sending out an academic CV to jobs beyond the professoriate (with a few exceptions, such as jobs in higher education administration) will signal that you have not read the job description and don't understand the norms of the field. Similarly, many organizations no longer request cover letters and rely purely on the résumé to assess candidates. Submit only the application materials requested by the organization to demonstrate that you understand the field.

Job postings always list required and desired qualifications for the job. Ensure that your résumé and cover letter (if requested) clearly demonstrate that you meet these basic requirements. You don't have to meet all of the requirements, but make sure that you make it easy for the reader to understand which qualifications you do have. In addition to the job qualifications, position descriptions typically outline the primary job responsibilities. Make it clear how you have the skills required to take on those responsibilities and use the language in the job description so that your audience does not have to read between the lines or do translation to understand how you will be able to do the day-to-day tasks of the job. Spotlight any past experiences where you successfully managed similar responsibilities.

Finally, do your research on the organizations that interest you. When organizations say that they assess candidates on "fit," they often mean that they want to hire folks that are on board with their organizational mission, vision, and values. While these are often explicitly stated on organizations' websites, you can also use your informational interviews to learn about organizational culture and climate. How does the organization align with your own professional values, and how can you see yourself uniquely contributing to the organization's mission? Your cover letter is a suitable place to spend just a few sentences clearly articulating how you see yourself helping to further the organization's mission. It shows that you've done your homework on the organization and that you understand their vision for the future and how you can help them achieve that vision.

Principle 3: Articulate the Skills and Experiences You Bring That the Organization Needs

When doctoral students are trained to be a future faculty member, they are encouraged to think of themselves in terms of their narrow area of specialization. With the exception of perhaps quantitative methodologists, social science doctoral students often do not think of their assets in terms of the skills that they bring to their professional work. When pitching yourself for jobs beyond the professoriate, employers will typically be interested in those skills rather than your dissertation findings. For example, if you are applying to be a data scientist at a large social technology company, recruiters and hiring managers will be interested in your statistical analysis and coding skills. If you are applying for jobs in management consulting, you will want to pitch your ability to do in-depth research and analysis and to communicate persuasively to deliver strategic advice.

Many Ph.D.s struggle to identify their skills, as they've been taught to think of themselves instead in terms of content expertise. But if you've completed a doctoral degree in social science, you've developed many valuable skills through your research and teaching. Break down the skills that you've gained in those experiences. For example, in your social science research, you certainly comprehended, synthesized, and interpreted large bodies of information and formed persuasive arguments. Depending on your research, you may have also conducted complex quantitative and qualitative analyses, facilitated focus groups or interviews, translated languages, written code, performed experiments, or designed and conducted surveys. In your teaching, you communicated complex information to lay audiences, prepared and delivered effective presentations, designed lesson plans, managed discussions, and provided constructive feedback to facilitate learning. These skills – and many more that you developed during your time as a doctoral student – are assets to many organizations. As noted earlier, consider the additional skills you gained in previous professional experiences, too. If you would like resources to help you identify your skills, ImaginePhD and the Individual Development Plan tool available through the American Academy of Arts and Sciences (https://myidp.sciencecareers.org/) offer skills assessments designed specifically for doctoral students. Additionally, once you identify your skills, be sure to add them in the skills section of LinkedIn, as employers often search for potential candidates based on skillsets.

By the end of your doctoral program, you've likely thought about yourself for several years as a student. Most graduate students don't think of themselves as professionals with jobs. However, your résumé should not say that your job title for the last 4 to 6 years is "Doctoral Student." As a scholar in training, you've actually had many job experiences. You most likely have been an instructor and a research assistant. Most doctoral students have many other job experiences, including unpaid ones, that can be listed on their résumés. The kinds of experiences that I thought of as "side hustles" or "gigs" during graduate school were actually all critical job experiences that directly led to me getting my first job in educational development. I was a graduate student mentor to other instructors in my department, had a part-time job as a graduate student instructional consultant at my campus teaching center, and worked as one of the instructors in our campus' summer pedagogy course for international student instructors. I learned through informational interviews and decoding job postings that these are precisely the kinds of job experiences that hiring managers in educational development are looking for. Make a list of all the part-time jobs you've had during your career as a graduate student, and I suspect that like me, you will find you've worn many professional hats during your doctoral training. Many social science graduate students also perform volunteer work during their doctoral studies. Did you volunteer at a local organization that aligns with your interests, engage in social or political advocacy work, lead a graduate student organization, or take a leadership role on a department or disciplinary organization committee? All of these are professional experiences that you can put on your résumé.

As noted earlier, curate your many experiences during and before graduate school to align with the jobs you are interested in applying for. When I applied for educational development jobs, I didn't list every single research assistantship that I held. I did, on the other hand, list every job experience I had related to instruction, mentoring, and pedagogy.

When I ask graduate students how many futures they can imagine for themselves when they finish their degree, the most common answer that I get is two. The reality is that there are many more than two job possibilities for you. Looking at career outcomes of Ph.D.s in social science from the last decade at the institution where I got my doctorate alone, there are folks in dozens of different interesting jobs beyond the professoriate in diverse fields such as consulting, government, data science, nonprofits, and higher education. To effectively pitch yourself to career fields such as these that interest you beyond the professoriate, you need to spend time doing intentional career exploration and self-reflection, tailor how you pitch yourself using the language of the career fields that interest you, avoid defining yourself in narrow terms of your dissertation topic, and emphasize your skills and job experiences.

References

Burnett, B. & Evans, D. (2016). *Designing Your Life: How to Build a Well-Lived and Joyful Life*. Alfred A. Knopf.
Csikszentmihalyi, M. (1990). *Flow: The psychology of optimal experience*. Harper & Row.
Oyserman, D. (2015). "Values, Psychology of." In: James D. Wright (ed.), *International Encyclopedia of the Social & Behavioral Sciences*, 2nd edition, Vol 25. Oxford: Elsevier. pp. 36–40.
Sinche, M. (2016). *Next Gen PhD: A Guide to Career Paths in Science*. Harvard University Press.

Beyond Visa Sponsorship: Navigating the Job Market as an (Non)Immigrant

Analía Gómez Vidal

It was my fourth year in graduate school. I had joined my program with a very pragmatic view about career development. I was not set on going into academia after graduation, but rather exploring options. Earning a doctorate, I thought, was less about becoming a professor in the tenure track and more about raising the ceiling of the opportunities I could aspire to. It made sense. After all, I was the first one in my family to graduate from college, let alone move across the Americas on my own to pursue graduate school.

So, I did what felt more logical at that time, halfway through my program: explore my options. I have always been drawn to career development. Not just for myself. I have been the informal advisor for many of my friends, and friends of friends, over the years. I have also worked professionally at it right before moving to the United States. But during my time as a graduate student, I had come to realize that there were not as many options for international students. Intuitively, I knew this. Adding the sponsorship requirement to hiring decision-making adds an extra layer of bureaucracy and risk to potential employers. But I signed up for graduate school not fully knowing that my experience would be fundamentally different to that of my US peers. I was restricted by the inability to pursue research assistantship overloads that could turn into co-authorships and experienced attending panels where senior faculty members would say "get citizenship" as the one viable option to access most of the external funding for fieldwork and dissertation writing. Job searching would not be the exception.

I went through placement records to see where others in my situation had landed. I Googled a lot. I reached out to our graduate school administrator. At the time I was searching for this information, there was only one international student who

A. Gómez Vidal (✉)
Stanford University, Washington, DC, USA
e-mail: agv@terpmail.umd.edu; https://agomezvidal.com/

© The Author(s), under exclusive license to Springer Nature
Switzerland AG 2023
N. Jackson (ed.), *Non-Academic Careers for Quantitative Social Scientists*,
Texts in Quantitative Political Analysis,
https://doi.org/10.1007/978-3-031-35036-8_14

successfully stayed in academia in the United States in the previous 12 years. Only one international alum from my department had successfully graduated and landed a tenure track job, changing her immigration status from F-1 (student) to H1-B (worker) and eventually resident. For those who had decided to transition into non-academic jobs, I was disheartened to hear that they had gotten married before going into the market. Nobody else in my network had succeeded in following this path as an international student/worker.

The message was clear: It would be hard, and I would have to be prepared for whatever came my way. Spoiler alert: it was hard. But it was not impossible. Most importantly, it was the type of transformational process that helped me refocus on what matters most to me and empowered me to make decisions that others did not always understand, at least initially. My goal at this stage did not change. I wanted to raise the ceiling of the opportunities I could aspire to. I wanted to find my own path, equipped with all the skills, experiences, and insights I had gained throughout my career so far.

That is how I started a soft search that lasted most of my time in graduate school, learning by trial and error what worked and what did not. I would browse around to identify organizations and jobs I was interested in. I would attend panels and webinars and happy hours in the Washington, D.C. metro area that caught my attention. Sometimes I made friends in these places. Sometimes I realized that maybe those were not good options for me. I continued this process until my fifth and last year of guaranteed funding.

The summer of 2019 was not the busiest of my time in graduate school, but it was the most stressful. Without a finished dissertation or any publications waiting to come out, I needed to go into the job market and get a job. My advisor warned me at the time that the academic job market would not be gentle and let me know that it would not reflect my value as a scholar, but rather the way the market was at the time. I felt I had no choice. But again, I was not set on an academic position, so I decided to pursue a dual search: in academia and outside of it. It was one of the few summers in which I did not work, thanks to an external fellowship that provided some income. I divided my time in two: Mornings would be my dissertation work time. Afternoons would be all about interviews and job searching.

The process itself was exhausting. The emotional journey was the most difficult part. Navigating the uncertainty and fears as an international graduate student was not a walk in the park. But I learned a lot in the process, and I identified several traits and resources that I benefited from while going through this stage. They were invaluable in helping me navigate this time while connecting with myself and what I envisioned longer term. With them, I landed my first job post-graduation in the United States. And my second one, too.

In this chapter, I explore some of these traits and resources through the lens of my own experience as a white Latin American immigrant who came to the United States through an approved student visa to pursue postgraduate education. I recognize that there is an enormous amount of privilege informing my experience and that much of it and the resulting advice may not resonate with other international students based on their own identities. I also acknowledge that international students and workers are a very heterogeneous group, and our experiences and opportunities in the United States may differ greatly. Yet I write this chapter in the hopes that this discussion can spark a much bigger debate and that it helps others expand on it to improve the lives and experiences of all international students.

What We Bring to the Table

When it comes to understanding the experience of international students, it is very easy to get caught up in the barriers that we face. Truth be told, these barriers are not small in any way. They start with leaving our families and what we know behind. Endless paperwork and deadlines follow. Through it all, there is a clear sense of dread and conditionality to our lives. Adding to the scarcity mindset, graduate school contributes to a paradox. As graduate students we develop a "never enough" mindset that keeps us expecting more from ourselves, continuing to feel like students who never fully become experts. At the same time, because of all our training, we gain invaluable skills and develop expertise in a set of subjects and methodologies. The paradox then arises as our inadequacy feeling clashes with our newly honed skills. In the job searching process, this manifests often as graduate students who cannot fully identify how much they can bring to the table. In many cases, this also translates in fear of not being competitive or appealing enough for a job in industry. Adding to that the insecurities and fears that arise from consistently facing messages of rejection, conditionality, and continuous paperwork make this combination particularly difficult to navigate. It is understandable then that many international students dread this process and have a hard time being optimistic about their future.

At the same time, finding ourselves caught in the midst of these struggles often prevents us from recognizing and truly seeing ourselves and what we have to offer. Succeeding as international students and workers requires certain traits that make us more likely to succeed in the workplace. First, someone who decides to become an international student has in them a fair amount of courage to push outside of their comfort zone and to build a new stage in their lives somewhere else. For many, including myself, that means arriving to a new place that they have never been and without any friends or family around. International students learn to use their skills and resources to create opportunities, and a life, from the ground up.

Another trait often present in international students is adaptability. Because they often encounter scenarios that are new and challenging, international students are also more likely to use their toolkit and figure out ways of solving the situation at hand. This goes hand in hand with the third trait, which is resilience. In the path forward, an international student is required to figure out how to make the most out of very stressful situations, many of them out of their control. To successfully navigate these experiences, they develop their agency and resilience, which then becomes a key pillar to their success. From a cultural perspective, many international students have learned English as a second language. While many of us have had complicated journeys with our English proficiency and our accents, there is no doubt that our ability to carry our lives in a second language and to succeed professionally using it is also related to our adaptability and our communication skills. More broadly, our experiences living in a very different culture from the one we were brought up in also inform our cultural sensitivity when interacting in everyday life.

One last trait that I find important to highlight is our ability to navigate complicated legal systems. From the very beginning of our experience, we are faced with a significant number of requirements, forms, and legal documents. Keeping up with every single aspect of our immigration status also helps us become more attuned and aware of all the moving pieces in this fundamental aspect of our everyday life. At the same time, this makes us more resourceful and aware when the job searching time comes.

Thinking Outside the Borders

It has been my own experience that while navigating the uncertainty of what's next in my career, I often disregarded the many resources and opportunities that were in front of me, let alone my own traits and skills. Sometimes, we get so lost and so attached to the outcome that we do not give ourselves the chance to take a step back, inquire about our motivations, understand our goals and vision, and fantasize about an alternative that could be as satisfying, if not more. If these words resonate with you, I invite you to take some time for yourself, maybe grab a pen and a piece of paper, and give yourself permission to explore what you see for yourself. In Box A, I share with you a set of questions to help you reflect.

One essential aspect of our experience as graduate students is that often dealing with the immigration system and the job market structure in the United States can end up affecting how we see ourselves. It is important to recognize and rethink that as we pursue our careers longer term. While international students are great in many, many ways (see previous section), we also tend to suffer from tunnel vision and often internalize a lot of the external barriers we face. Granted, not all international students face the same barriers. Many cannot afford to go back to their home countries for a wide range of reasons, or they consider alternative host countries for their next step. Just like the US immigration system can be difficult to navigate, any other country where we are not citizens will also represent a new set of barriers and learning curves.

But there is something to be said about being intentional. What incentivizes you to pursue the next career move? Is it a location, is it a job title, is it the financial opportunities? In many cases, we are often stuck thinking about how we want to make it work in the United States. We have gone through a process of uprooting when we left our home countries, and many of us might have reasons to avoid that feeling of uprooting again. Maybe that is your situation. Or maybe you are more interested in exploring opportunities and traveling to other places. Reflecting on these questions and making room for imagining alternatives can help you move away from hyper-focusing on the obstacles and considering the opportunities. Whether that is the case, or not, self-reflection can still become a powerful tool for reassessing and recommitting to the life and goals you want to pursue.

Box A: Reflections for Strategy and Planning

Whether you are a student years from going into the job market, just getting started, or in the thick of it, reflecting on what you have to offer and what you envision for your life can be extremely helpful. Taking some time and space to reflect on this vision will be grounding, so as you navigate the ups and downs of the process, you can go back to this vision as a force to guide you to your next action.

Here I share some of the questions I have explored in my own process as a way of guiding and shaping my vision. I suggest you read through them and keep them in mind. When you have some time for quiet and reflection, grab pen and paper and use these questions as guidelines to jot down your thoughts. But don't overthink it! There are no right or perfect answers. Every one of them is a starting point for your exploration, and you will consistently add or update what you have thought about and written down.

There are two sets of questions below. The first group is focused on your self-assessment. These questions aim at exploring what you would like to do next, what skills to use, what context draws your attention, and how you see yourself in that context. They are a starting point for digging deeper into how you see yourself and what you want to pursue next. The second group of questions aims at identifying action items. There is some overlap between the two groups for a reason. Questions in the second group help you find concrete ways to get moving toward your goal. They can give you some of the key pillars, so you design your own road map through the job search.

Self-assessment

What skills do you want to use/expand on as part of your next job?
What areas/topics are you most interested in? Why?
How do you see yourself contributing to these areas or topics?

Discovering action items

List the main skills or subjects you want to guide your job search. Are there similarities/overlaps? Are they very different?
List the key sectors, industries, or titles you are interested in. Are these roles/sectors you are already familiar with? What other information do you think is important for you to gather?
Through these questions, you will identify some of the information gaps you currently have about roles, sectors, or even organizations you might be interested in. Plan for networking, informational interviews, LinkedIn searches, or other strategies that can help you narrow these gaps you have found.

Defining Success in Our Own Terms

One of the hardest aspects of going through the job market as a graduate student is that we are traditionally trained and expected to follow a certain path. This has been changing over time, with faculty and mentors being more open to and aware of the alternative options to academic careers. But unfortunately, many have never gone through that experience, and their knowledge about it is extremely limited or non-existent. This puts students in a difficult spot: we are told that we can pursue whatever path we want, but we are only taught about one of them. Alternatives to academia then become a void that can be daunting, and the process of learning about it and exploring can feel isolating.

My own experience required me to confront and challenge external expectations, but also my own narratives about what success looks like. As I was starting my job searches in the summer of 2019, I was also experiencing my first encounter with professional coaching. Through a few free workshops and resources, I started to learn more about some of the beliefs and habits that kept me from validating my own voice. Coaching, along with therapy, helped me envision the life that I wanted to lead. Through this exploration and self-awareness, I realized that I wanted to prioritize specific aspects of my personal and professional life when making career decisions. For example, I realized that I loved teaching and mentoring, but I would rather prioritize research as a driving force of my next career move and explore alternative ways of teaching and mentoring.

But when the time came to make a decision, that clarity did not take away from the conflicting feelings. Specifically, I found myself in front of two options: an offer to be a researcher at an international organization in the area I had lived for years or to fly-out for a campus interview for a teaching position cross-country. Intellectually, I knew the first option was the one that aligned more closely with what I envisioned for myself. But I spent at least a week in anguish, crying and wondering about whether to take that job or not and whether to complete the fly-out interview or not. I felt the burden of my training and expectations. Who was I failing if I made this decision? Who was I disappointing? Could I live with that? Would I regret this decision later? For the previous 5 years, I had heard endlessly about how difficult the market was, how very few truly make it, and what a privilege it was for those few who even had a shot at it. Here I was, after a few months in the academic market, and the privilege of going through multiple interviews and landing a fly-out, only to potentially leave that behind. Academia offered another benefit that was particularly enticing for international students: sponsorship. According to many of the international scholars I had met with and discussed job searching with, landing a tenure track job meant being sponsored by the university for a work visa and soon after for residency. Rejecting a fly out meant also rejecting the possibility of the path of least resistance to stay in the United States.

It was not an easy decision when all these factors were considered. But I made it, and I decided to craft my own path, pursuing a research-oriented role outside of academia while exploring ways of mentoring and teaching outside a 9-to-5 job. The good news is I have not regretted it since, and while most of my support system held space for me to make my own decision, some also wondered why. Many might have wondered where my entitlement came from, closing a door that so many work really hard for, myself included. But ultimately, that is the misconception academia often fuels: it was not entitlement; it was a vision for the life I wanted to pursue. We all have one. Some are more aware of it than others. In the best possible scenario, this vision comes from what we want for ourselves, and what we can make happen, rather than what others want for us.

Job Searching: Some Practical Tips

Having clarity on what you want for yourself is a big part of the process, but not the only factor. In addition to this vision, and the positive traits international students have and hone as part of their lived experiences, there are other resources that can shape your success in searching for your next career move. To a certain extent, they are all intertwined, as you will notice reading through this section. This list is not exhaustive, but I believe it is fundamental. The four factors I highlight are community, networking, options, and self-awareness. As I describe each of them, I also include a few tips based on my own experience.

Community

The first and most important resource that an international student can rely on as part of their job search is their community. You might be the first one in your family to pursue this path altogether. Hopefully, along the way, you have also expanded your community personally and professionally. You will need all of them in different ways. Your family and friends, especially those outside of the academic environment, will be invaluable for support, perspective, and hopefully laughter. Your graduate student peers will also be a great source of validation and commiseration as you all share the struggles of job searching. In many cases, your professional acquaintances and networking peers might become essential in your quest for informational interviews and potential opportunities. If there is one piece of advice that you take from this chapter, let it be this: invest in and cherish your communities because regardless of the outcome they will help you navigate life. No matter how isolating it can feel at times, you are not alone.

   Where can you get started? Hobbies might be one answer. Less than 2 years into my graduate program, I realized I was in a difficult spot. I had moved to the area for my program, and I did not know anyone outside of campus life. Soon after, my burnout was clear. There was no aspect of my life that did not relate directly to my program, my assistantship, or my research. I did not have a space or activity to disconnect for a while and recharge. While going through the many emotions that I felt at that time, from the stress and the loneliness, I came up with a New Year's Resolution for 2016: I would start a new hobby and make friends outside of my program. That is how I started doing improvisational theater at Washington Improv Theater (WIT), in Washington, D.C. It has been over 7 years since the first time I attended a free workshop, and it has undoubtedly changed my life. But that is the subject of another chapter. For now, make sure to explore your creativity and make friends outside of campus. It will prove beneficial in many, many ways. Building community might be one of them.

Networking

Networking does not come easily for many. International students need networking more than any other group of job searchers. Two reasons why networking plays such a big role are information gaps and referrals. Networking can be thought of as methodology in the project of job searching. For example, if you're interested in an industry that you have little knowledge about, informational interviews become more valuable for you to gain information about a certain industry role or company. Networking is part of this research project. Pick the methodology that feels more authentic to you and go gather the data.

At the same time, because of the additional layer of investment that sponsoring represents, international students benefit tremendously from having an extensive network that can vouch for them in specific job searches. The likelihood of any international student making it far into a job interviewing process increases significantly when they have an internal source that can refer them. That being said, every sector and industry has its own idiosyncrasy. For example, there is a lot of variation across and within industries regarding using referrals and recruiters. Addressing the informational gaps I mentioned earlier through networking can also help you identify what works best when it is time to get referred.

Here are several practical tips to consider for your networking strategies. First, your campus initiatives, professional organizations, and communities are some of your biggest allies. They can make networking much easier by providing smaller environments where you can get to know about other colleagues and their experiences, interact with them, and learn from what they share. You can even continue the conversation afterward! These professional environments provide the space for you to learn what you are interested in and what you are not. Make the most out of them as part of your exploration, and you will likely discover new paths to choose from. In many cases, colleagues you meet through these initiatives and organizations can become long-term peers, coworkers, and even friends.

The second tip is universal: know your audience. In academia, we are trained to introduce ourselves by sharing what our research is about. Among graduate students, your dissertation is your elevator pitch. That is not a good approach when meeting nonacademic professionals, unless they happen to work directly on the topic you work on. Even then, I would not recommend it. Instead, do your homework by identifying what the other person works on and is interested in. Make sure that you introduce yourself by sharing what you can do and connect it with what they do. For example, chances are you are going to connect more with the other person by sharing what type of methodologies you have used, picking their brain about a subject they work on, or simply sharing what stood out about their trajectory and you want to learn more about.

Lastly, do not expect people to refer you without them getting to know you first. In my experience, no matter how much I am rooting for you, it is very unlikely I will vouch for you, or refer you for an opportunity, without knowing about you and your work. I have been in multiple awkward conversations in which students have requested, point blank, to be referred during our first conversation. Sometimes, even before sharing their work. Do not do that. Ultimately, networking is about building and nurturing relationships. Focus on that first, and the rest will evolve from there.

On that same topic, remember: LinkedIn and social media are your best friends... if you use them right! When you approach someone online, make sure to be respectful and to lead from a place of connection. Job searching might be thought of as a numbers game, but networking is not. When you connect with someone on LinkedIn, make sure to always send a message beforehand. Many users, myself included, do not feel comfortable adding connections without meeting them first. At the very least, let them know what made you want to reach out and connect with them and what you are seeking by sending them this invite. Extra points if you do not add them until they explicitly agree to connect! On the flip side, you may not always receive a reply to your message. That is normal and may have nothing to do with you sending it. Life happens to all of us at the same time, with its ups and downs. No matter what people's good intentions are, their bandwidth might be narrow, and LinkedIn messages may fall through the cracks. Don't let that discourage you.

Options

This factor does not entirely depend on you. But it is important that you keep it in mind, as I have mentioned earlier in the chapter. Why? Because we are all likely to develop tunnel vision, focusing on the scarcity mindset of graduate students, internalizing the external barriers we encounter as international students, and feeling stuck in only one option or path. When we fall into that trap, we operate less from a place of possibilities and resourcefulness and more from a place of fear and constraint. Our lived experiences and external barriers are real. But so are our skills, resources, experiences, and traits to move us forward. As you keep going on this path, remind yourself that you are more than a degree, a visa status, or a job title. You are a human being with wants, needs, dreams, and options. Explore them. Learn about them. Consider them. Most importantly, reflect on them: what options align with, and nurture, the life you want to lead? When you give yourself permission to wonder, you may encounter aha moments that will help you get unstuck and reassess.

A fundamental aspect of considering your options is learning about your legal standing. As you navigate this process, make sure you can learn as much as possible about your immigration status, what options are available to you, and what you need to move forward. Legal consultations can be expensive, but if you have the chance to talk to an immigration lawyer, do it! They will help you understand what you need individually and what the available paths forward are. While universities have international students and scholars' units, these units primarily focus on overseeing and advising you on your current status as an international student or scholar. Legal counseling will help you understand the bigger picture. This information will allow you to make informed decisions about what you need to get for your next career move and what might be the best alternative if it is not possible. In some cases, being aware of these alternatives and knowing who to contact for questions can also be an asset in the job searching process and afterward.

Self-Awareness

Probably the biggest resource that has helped me navigate this path, especially the emotional aspect of job searching as an international student, has been the support tools like therapy and coaching. Through the self-awareness and exploration of my vision for my personal and professional life, I felt empowered to make decisions that aligned with this vision, regardless of what others might think. After all, success is never guaranteed. But you will gain, and grow, a lot more from the process if you find your grounding force within yourself. For me, it meant walking away from the traditional academic path and accepting trade-offs that have shaped my life and career since. At the same time, it has also opened the doors to experiences and lessons I had not foreseen. Becoming a certified professional coach was one of them. Today, I write these pages as part of my own journey in growth and alignment, seeking to support other international students the way I wish I had been supported back then. Use some of the questions posed throughout this chapter to get started if you have not already.

Make sure to reach out to existing resources on campus for mental health. Some of the more toxic traits of academia is the inability to speak openly and bluntly about the toll graduate school takes on us. This is even more impactful among international students, considering the additional layers of conditionality, isolation, limited resources, and microaggressions (among other factors). Finding balance and support for yourself as part of your journey, whether you are already job searching or not, will help you navigate it while keeping an eye on your well-being and taking care of yourself. Here is where hobbies also can play a significant role since they contribute to a sense of balance and wholeness that you can hold on to throughout the ups and downs of graduate school and job searching. Just as you are more than your productivity, you are more than a job interview, and a rejection (or an offer!) does not determine your value as a person.

Concluding Remarks

Navigating the job market as an international student is a different experience than what most domestic students go through. Namely, international candidates may be highly qualified for a job and yet encounter disappointment when organizations are not willing to sponsor them. The external barriers to securing a job opportunity are often internalized, as a fundamental part of who we are is also linked to the legal barriers that get in the way from getting hired. The path forward is hard, and it requires strategy and planning that differs from your domestic peers. But it is not impossible.

More importantly, there are two important reminders that we often fail to make explicit for international students. The first one is that as an international student, you have a lot more to offer than what you might perceive as you navigate the immigration system and its barriers. The second one is that, whether you want to secure a full-time job post-graduation in the United States or elsewhere, you have the power to make decisions that get you closer to the life that you envision for yourself. You are capable and equipped to navigate the obstacles that arise as a result, too.

The road can feel incredibly isolating, and frustrating, as you navigate it. In many cases, programs might have few international students. Campus resources do not always facilitate community building among international students, and it can be hard for coordination among students by themselves. But as you go through your career development exploration and later on your job searching, make sure to invest in and lean into your community. Meet other international students on campus and alumni. Network with colleagues and mentors across fields. Share your job search with domestic colleagues, friends, and loved ones outside of academia. Connect with members of professional organizations you are part of. You will soon feel less alone in this process, and you may be opening doors you did not know existed.

Job searching is like a research project. You identify what you want to go for, you plan for it, you gather all the data, and you do not know what the final answer to your question will be. It takes time and energy, and you must be proactive. But eventually, you will have your answers. Just like a research project, you also need to pick a methodology that aligns with your skills and addresses the question at hand. In job searching, you need to choose an approach that feels authentic to you. Once you learn more about the industries and roles you are interested in, you will also have to adjust your strategy to your potential employers and their best practices. This process is iterative and always adjusting. Until you get that one job offer.

Getting that one job offer can be difficult and take a lot of time and energy. Success is never fully guaranteed, and you may find yourself going back to the drawing board multiple times. But no matter how disappointing it can feel at times, you can still make the most out of it. Every process leaves lessons and new information behind. You may be honing your interviewing experience. You may be identifying companies, roles, or sectors that feel aligned (or not). No matter what you face next, remember: your vision is your anchor, your experience is your guide. Navigate this process by prioritizing what you envision for yourself, learning from your experiences along the way, and adjusting so you can get closer to your own version of success. I hope you do, and once you look back, you feel proud of whom you become as part of this process.

So You Want to Work in Tech: How Do You Make the Leap?

Matthew Barnes

"I want to work with data in tech, but where do I begin?" If you have started or if you are thinking of starting down the road of moving from academia to the tech industry, this chapter is for you. I will provide a practical guide to making the leap from social science PhD to a career in the tech sector, but prior to that, setting expectations is paramount. I argue that there are two primary shifts in mindset required to make the leap and be successful. These are:

1. *You need to shift from ideation to execution*: The name of the game now is execution, not searching for a counterintuitive finding or a novel identification strategy. Projects will occur at a quicker cadence – think in quarters and months, not years. The focus of your performance reviews will be on how much impact you had, how much value you created.
2. *Your core function is now engineering*: Data work is engineering work. You will work inside of a system with many moving parts. You will clean data, move data from one database to another, ensure that machine learning (ML) models are reproducible, build an experimentation platform that is accessible to others, optimize queries, and/or automate data reports, among other tasks.

Whether your desired position is as a data scientist, data analyst, machine learning engineer, analytics engineer, or data engineer, the majority of your work will be building a solution to deliver value to the business. The tools and models you will build to answer critical questions will enable others and guide decision-making by the senior leadership team.

This focus on engineering and execution (and its corresponding impact) will guide my advice on which skills, tools, or languages to learn, how to build a portfolio, how to edit your résumé, and how to prepare for interviews. But with this focus

M. Barnes (✉)
SoFi, Seattle, WA, USA

© The Author(s), under exclusive license to Springer Nature
Switzerland AG 2023
N. Jackson (ed.), *Non-Academic Careers for Quantitative Social Scientists*,
Texts in Quantitative Political Analysis,
https://doi.org/10.1007/978-3-031-35036-8_15

on breadth, I will sacrifice depth; however, I will direct you to other resources to explore. One I recommend in particular is "Build a Career in Data Science" (Robinson and Nolis 2020) for more details.

Given that the audience of this book is quantitative social science PhDs with a wide array of backgrounds, skills, and interests, I will focus on tech more broadly and outline the different paths available to you and how to best set yourself up for success.

Why listen to me though? I received my PhD in political science from Princeton University in 2015, and I was an Assistant Professor of Public Administration at West Virginia University from 2014 to 2017. During that time, I taught applied statistics to MPA students, where I realized that I was more interested in the practical applications of statistics and data science I was seeing in both the public and private sectors. I also enjoyed the more collaborative and fast-paced aspects of certain projects, so data science seemed like a natural fit. I joined the Insight Data Science Fellows program (unfortunately no longer offering new sessions) which helped PhDs make the transition to data science careers. Since that fellowship, I have been a data scientist and machine learning engineer at both small startups and large corporations.

In my data science career to date, the work has become more engineering-focused. Yes, communication is important. Being able to present your results with the right language and appropriate level of rigor and detail for the audience is a crucial skill, but it will not be your day-to-day work (although it may be eventually). In my first job for 84.51 (the analytics arm of Kroger), I built a machine learning model that predicted whether a customer was likely to shop at a competitor. Most of my time on that project was spent debugging Spark and figuring out how to process data and train a model on a distributed system. At Finn AI, a small startup, I worked on the deployment process of natural language models and built a pipeline for data analytics. For Microsoft, I built a model to predict whether a Stream video would be viewed or not, and I also worked with software developers for building out the telemetry for the new Photos application. Currently at SoFi, my work lately is migrating a pricing model to a workflow using Snowflake, AWS, Docker, and Airflow. Making tweaks to the model was quick and easy; the hard work is getting all these systems to talk to each other so the model can run and score data daily.

With Expectations Set, Let Us Take the First Step

Different Paths and Titles

Before you can write a résumé or start preparing for interviews, you need to know what you want and what you are marketing yourself as. Do you want to be a generalist data scientist who can meet many needs (reporting, modeling, some data engineering)? Are you a specialist in experimentation and causal inference and want to continue that work? Or do you want to focus on building predictive models and putting them into production? The answer to these questions will shape how you craft your résumé, which jobs you apply to, and how you prepare for interviews. So what paths and titles are available to you?

At a high level, the most common roles are:

Data Engineer – develops and maintains data architecture and pipelines, maintains data in databases, and builds pipelines to ensure that people can get the data they need.

Analytics Engineer – to oversimplify, this is a cross between a data engineer and data analyst. An analytics engineer cleans, transforms, tests, deploys, and documents data to enable ease of data use across the organization.

Data Analyst – queries data to answer business-critical questions, creates dashboards, and delivers insights.

Data Scientist – can include some or all of the following: develop and productionize machine learning models to predict outcomes, communicate product metrics and progress, and design experiments (A/B testing) to test new products, features, or models.

Machine Learning Engineer (MLE) – develops machine learning models and puts them into production, where they run on a set schedule.

Research Scientist – a research scientist is more removed from product and the "bottom line." A research scientist develops and implements new tools, algorithms, and models, which will be used by data scientists, analysts, and engineers across the company.

Some general observations about the data landscape:

The data science hierarchy of needs (Rogati 2017), first written in 2017 but just as accurate, generally aligns with the number and types of jobs available. For many companies, data science is a "nice to have," not a "need to have." If you want to maximize your chances of getting employed, you need to develop software engineering skills so that you can quickly and effectively log data, move data, clean data, and ensure these processes are reliable and reproducible. You also need to be able to query and interpret data, and communicate the findings, to enable decision-makers.

Even as a data scientist in a company with dedicated data engineers and analysts, most of my day-to-day work involves the above tasks at the lower levels of the pyramid. Boykis (2019) succinctly depicts the landscape of data science today: "data science is and has always been primarily about getting clean data in a single place to be used for interpolation." The Anaconda 2022 State of Data Science Report (Anaconda 2022) also reflects this reality: respondents indicated that about 38 percent of their time is spent on data preparation and cleaning and 29 percent of their time is spent on data visualization and interpreting and reporting results.

Developing Skills and Tools

So now you have an idea about which paths are available. Which skills, tools, and languages should you learn? I have included a list of books, tutorials, and blog posts at the end of this chapter that I found helpful when making the leap, as well as recent resources that have advanced my skill sets. To address tools first, my experience mirrors that of Boykis (2022): the three fundamental tools you need in your toolbox are SQL, git, and CLI. You will encounter all of these (or some version of them) in every role at every tech company.

SQL (Structured Query Language)
You will not be able to do anything until you can retrieve data from a database. SQL will allow you to do that. It is quick and easy to learn, and once you develop an understanding of how queries work, you can move on to optimizing queries and designing and building your data architecture.

Git
Contrary to most academic projects, in the tech industry, you will be working with others on already established projects. In order to track changes in files and work collaboratively, you will use git for version control. Whether you use GitHub or GitLab as your platform of choice, you will need to learn how to create new branches, commit code, pull down newer code from others, create a pull request (in GitHub), or merge request (in GitLab), how to review others' pull requests, and how to fix errors and walk back changes.

CLI (Command-Line Interface)
Your company will use either a cloud provider (most likely) or an on-premises solution (increasingly rare) for storage and compute. Regardless of the platform, be it AWS, GCP, or Azure, you will need to be able to ssh (Secure Shell Protocol) into those machines in order to navigate the file structure and execute your code.

But what about *Python* versus *R*? The general advice is to know at least one extremely well. As a social science PhD, you most likely know R and/or Stata. However, I recommend learning and using Python. I used R during my academic career and during my Insight fellowship, but I have used Python in every data science and machine learning engineering position since moving to industry. It is more widespread and common within data science: 58 percent of respondents to the Anaconda survey indicated they "Always" or "Frequently" use Python, compared to 26 percent for R (Anaconda 2022). Python is a must for data engineering, analytics engineering, and machine learning engineering. That said, a new language or tool could displace Python in the next few years. Or maybe you will join a company that codes in Java and you should learn that instead. Other tools like this you can learn on the job. SQL, git, and the command line will have you prepared to hit the ground running.

With those tools in your toolbelt, what about skills? According to respondents in the Anaconda 2022 State of Data Science Report (Anaconda 2022), the top five most important skills or areas of expertise missing in data science and machine learning within their organizations are:

– Engineering skills (38.2%)
– Probability and statistics (33.3%)
– Business knowledge (32.2%)
– Communication skills (30.6%)
– Big data management (29.2%)

As a quantitative social scientist, I will assume your probability and statistics knowledge is on point. Machine learning (ML) knowledge and practice is essential and your experience with it may vary, so I have included resources below.

The communication skills you have developed during your PhD can now be utilized to help you execute and deliver your work to the organization. If you have presented your research to a broad audience (technical and nontechnical) or if you have taught statistics and quantitative methods to undergraduates or master's students, then you have the skills to succeed. How should you frame your requests to engineers and data scientists? They will want and appreciate more technical answers. What level of detail needs to be put into a slide that is intended for the leaders of a business unit? They will focus on the "so what?" question. There you can communicate how your model impacts the bottom line: "the improved precision of our customer churn model allows for better targeting of users to incentivize them to stay, and thus will lead to a $10 million gain in revenue per month." As you progress in your career, communication skills will become even more crucial, whether you proceed along an individual contributor (IC) path or a manager path.

Developing business knowledge will mostly come from experience and will depend on the domain of the particular company and organization you join. But to get started, listen to company quarterly earnings calls and read company financial reports. How do they make money? What do their balance sheets and income statements look like?

Developing "big data" skills will also come from on the job experience. With so much else to learn, I would move this down the list of priorities. Learn Python and SQL on a single machine first. Spark and Snowflake can come later. But if you are interested in a data engineering role, this skill is more important, so I have included resources below to check out.

That leaves engineering skills. Again, the majority of your work, whether as a data scientist, machine learning engineer, or data engineer, will be focused on developing scripts and/or entire systems to move, manipulate, clean, train, and score data, which is why this chapter emphasizes the skills and tools to accomplish these goals. So how does one develop engineering skills? Reading, but more importantly, doing. Learning the tools mentioned above is part of it. Building a side project or two, which you can include in your portfolio, is crucial. Contributing to an open-source project is another way to get started. Learning how to ask good questions on stack overflow will further hone your abilities.

Building a Portfolio

Building a portfolio will help you develop and demonstrate the needed tools and skills. Can you take a broad question, refine it, obtain data to answer the question, employ a suitable method or model to answer the question, possibly automate the process, and then communicate your findings?

Having a portfolio project hosted on GitHub that you can point to will demonstrate those skills, and the process of building it will give you material for your resume and points to discuss in interviews. You will be able to talk about what you learned, what works, what did not, how you adapted, and what other approaches or methods you would try if you were to continue the project or begin again.

So what sorts of projects should you consider? Well, it depends on which type of role you are interested in. Data analysts and insights-focused data scientists will want to focus more toward doing an analysis, building a report or dashboard, and communicating findings. Those interested more in data engineering and machine learning engineering (and those aspects of data science) will want to focus on projects that build pipelines or deploy a machine learning model to production.

Ideally, the question should drive the choice of data. The question and the data should be interesting to you and a hiring manager. Yet another ML model on the Titanic or Iris datasets will have your application thrown into the nearest garbage can.

The project can and should be iterative. You can add more steps at the bottom of the data science pyramid (data collection and ETL) or at the top (deployed machine learning models). You could start the project on your local machine and then move the workflow to the cloud provider of your choice (AWS, GCP, or Azure). You could then increase the complexity at any of these steps.

The continuum of a project can follow something like:

- Scrape data from a website.
- Store it in a database.
- Query your database and export it as a dataframe (or start here by loading a csv or hitting an API).
- Perform data cleaning and exploratory data analysis (EDA).
- Train and evaluate a machine learning model.
- Deploy a machine learning model accessible via a simple web app and REST API.
- Build a dashboard that monitors metrics, and/or create a slide deck that showcases your project and findings.
- Write a blog post explaining the project and process in more detail.

The next iteration of your project could add steps from above or make some enhancements like:

- Schedule a job to scrape a website that updates daily and ingest that data into a database, either as a simple cron job or in Airflow.
- Add unit tests to your Python scripts for data work and/or modeling.
- Explore a more complex statistical, machine learning, or deep learning model.

- Containerize your work with Docker.
- Integrate continuous integration and continuous delivery (CI/CD).

Once your project is at a sufficient stopping point, the last step is to write about it. I recommend writing both a blog and creating a slide deck that would be presented to a business leadership team. I can offer the materials I created as part of my Insight Fellowship (Barnes 2017), which had a somewhat more technical blog post and the linked deck I presented to the Vice President of the company I partnered with on the project. Is it perfect? Far from it. Being unable to discuss either the domain or specific topic I worked on due to a nondisclosure agreement was one major hindrance. But flaws aside, it was something I could link to in a résumé and an example and experience I could discuss in interviews, showcasing both technical skills and communication skills.

Résumé

The single most important thing to remember about your résumé is that it is a sales and marketing document whose goal is to get you an interview. To do that, you have to demonstrate execution and impact. The résumé gets you an interview; it is up to you to get yourself the job. So how do you turn your academic CV into a résumé?

Unless you are applying to a research scientist position where evidence of publications is asked for, limit your résumé to one page. That is it. One. Not two. It is not a CV. If your résumé makes it past the automated applicant tracking system and into human hands, the hiring manager may only glance at it for 10 to 20 seconds. Like I said, it is a sales and marketing document. Make it count.

To structure your résumé, you will generally have three main sections: Experience, Education, and Skills.

Experience

This is the most important section of your résumé and where you show off the skills you have that qualify you for the job. That portfolio project you worked on? List it here (alternatively, you could have a separate "Projects" section). Your dissertation is probably the meatiest experience you have available, so break it down into chunks. Highlight the functions you performed that align to data science, data engineering, and data analytics skill sets. Did you field your own survey? Conduct text analysis on a large corpora? Build an R package? You want to take these experiences and turn them into quantifiable and action-driven bullet points that demonstrate you have the skills for a tech job. Importantly, you want to quantify the impact you had.

The same applies for any teaching you have done. Replace something like "Taught classes on quantitative methods to undergraduates" with "Organized and taught three 15-week courses in applied statistics in R to 135 undergraduates, earning an average score of 4.8/5 in student evaluations, with 95 percent of students electing to take the next course in the methods sequence." Here you demonstrate what you did, the scale of it, and the impact it had.

Education

Here you list your education experience, degrees, and, at this early stage of your career, any relevant coursework or specializations, like Bayesian statistics or causal inference.

Skills

Key tools, languages, and methods you have that you would be able to discuss in detail if asked. Avoid keyword stuffing, and ensure that if you list "causal inference" or "C++" here, there is a corresponding entry in the Experience section that mentions that tool or method.

Check out "Build a Career in Data Science" (Robinson and Nolis 2020) for more details about crafting a résumé. The authors also discuss how to write a cover letter, which I do not cover here. Generally, in tech, cover letters are optional; I have only written a cover letter if the job advertisement explicitly asks for one.

Interviews

So now you have one or more side projects under your belt and a crisp résumé, and you have started to apply for jobs. Next up is the interview. The interview process for tech roles is complex at best, broken at worst. No one interview process is alike, you will be assessed on skills you will not use in your day-to-day role, and you will have to either do live coding or complete an extensive take-home project that could occupy an entire weekend. That said, there is a general pattern that interviews follow.

Initial Chat with Recruiter

A 30-minute phone call with a technical recruiter whose goal is to assess whether you meet the qualifications and if you would be a good fit for the role. You will be asked high-level questions like "Tell me about yourself" and "Why are you interested in this position?" If the job description mentions a particular tool or language, the recruiter will probably ask if you have experience with that technology. The key as a candidate is to show enthusiasm and curiosity and have clear, concise answers.

Discussion with Hiring Manager

After the initial screen, you most likely will have a call with the hiring manager. This will feature the sort of high-level questions like in the initial call, but you will also receive some behavioral questions, which begin like "Tell me about a time when…" or "Give me an example of…." You may also receive some technical questions or be asked to walk through a case study relevant to the role and team you would work on.

Technical Screen

After the call with the hiring manager, you will proceed to a technical screen to assess your skills with SQL, Python, data structures and algorithms, statistics and probability, machine learning, systems design, and/or a business case study. If the interview is in person (more common before a global pandemic), you will be coding on a whiteboard. If the interview is virtual, you will use anything from CoderPad (a live coding and development platform for interviewing) to a blank Google document to write your code.

For SQL, you will be provided a prompt and an example table or tables, along with their columns and data types, like "Using the 'Employees' table, find the second highest salary of employees." Key techniques to know for these sorts of questions include aggregation, joins, subqueries, and common table expressions (CTEs), along with window functions. StrataScratch is a great resource for SQL interview questions encountered in the wild.

For Python, you will either receive prompts similar to the SQL questions (e.g., "using the pandas library, calculate each user's average session time") or data structures and algorithms questions. LeetCode is the primary resource for these sorts of questions. An example is the Two Sum problem: "Given an array of integers, return indices of the two numbers such that they add up to a specific target. Assume that there exists exactly one solution, and that you may not use the same element twice." Here you can solve the problem using a naive solution by iterating over the list twice to find a pair of integers that add up to the target, which would have $O(n^2)$ runtime. Using a hash table or dictionary is the faster $O(n)$ runtime approach.

For probability and statistics, you could face questions on anything typically included in the first methods course encountered in your PhD program, so brush up on the usual suspects like independent events, probability distributions, measures of central tendency, hypothesis testing, and confidence intervals. The type of questions could require calculating the answers by hand, like "A discount coupon is given to N customers. The probability of using a coupon is P. What is the probability that one of the coupons will be used?" Or it could focus on your understanding and communication skills, like "How would you explain a p-value to a product manager?"

For machine learning, you may be asked to complete a take-home assignment that takes 4–8 h to complete. This could replace other elements of the technical interview or be in addition to a technical round. Given that these are time-consuming and that you may be interviewing with several companies, ask the recruiter or hiring manager if you can be assessed via another method if you are unable to fit this into your schedule.

During the technical round for ML, you could be asked to explain high-level basics or to explain a particular algorithm in-depth. In past interviews, I have received both a rapid fire round with questions like "What's the difference between bagging and boosting?" and an in-depth discussion of XGBoost with the question "How does XGBoost perform tree pruning and how is that different from a Random Forest?"

Also common for machine learning interview questions are deep dives on past projects you have worked on, as well as hypothetical case studies and how you would solve the questions with machine learning. Typical questions include "Why did you choose the modeling approach you did?," "What tradeoffs did you encounter?," and "How would you continue the analysis if you had more time?" You will also want to connect the methods to the business use case. Who is requesting the analysis and who is the intended audience of the end product? Does the use case dictate what type of model you would choose or the appropriate evaluation metric (e.g., precision versus recall)? How would you convey this to a business lead?

System design interviews are more common for engineering-heavy roles. You will be given a vague prompt and will be expected to gather requirements and produce a technically sound solution. Possible questions include "How would you build this ML pipeline?," "Do you ingest the data in a streaming format or batch format?," "Why?," "What are the pros/cons of each?," and "Does your approach meet business needs?"

Behavioral Interviews

Last, there may be one or more dedicated behavioral interviews. These will test your interpersonal and communication skills and show off your past experience. You will already have answered a few in your first couple of calls, but now you will face more extensive questioning. The key here is to frame your answers via the classic STAR method: situation, task, action, result.

Some questions may be generic, like "Tell me about a time when you encountered failure." Others may blend in technical elements, like "Tell me about a technical project where you faced pushback. How did you convince others to adopt your approach?"

There are enough resources on the web about behavioral interviews that you can consult, but I will call out two questions for which you need to have a great answer, because you will get them:

– Why are you [leaving academia, transitioning to data science]?
– Why do you want to work for [company]?

In these questions, show excitement, knowledge about the company, and, above all, your skills and your ability to do the job.

Final Thoughts

The transition from academia to the tech industry will be difficult and you will experience a bumpy road at times. I shared what I believe are the most important practical tips to making the transition smoother, from developing skills and tools, crafting a résumé, and preparing for interviews. Along each step of the journey, remember the shifts in mindset required to make the leap and be successful: execution and engineering.

One topic I did not cover here is networking. Search social media (Twitter, LinkedIn) to find the data community and reach out to others who have or are currently moving from academia to tech. This could lead to a referral for a job now or in the future. Robinson and Nolis (2020) discuss this approach further in their chapter on résumés, cover letters, and referrals.

Last but not least, take a deep breath, and have fun learning and building!

Resources

SQL

pgexercises https://pgexercises.com/
SQL Zoo https://sqlzoo.net/wiki/SQL_Tutorial
Mode SQL tutorial: https://mode.com/sql-tutorial/
Stratascratch https://www.stratascratch.com/

Git

Pro Git https://git-scm.com/book/en/v2
Dangit Git!?! https://dangitgit.com/en

CLI

The Linux Command Line https://linuxcommand.org/tlcl.php

Python

Google's Python Class https://developers.google.com/edu/python

Automate the Boring Stuff with Python: Practical Programming for Total Beginners by Al Sweigart
Effective Python: 90 Specific Ways to Write Better Python, 2nd ed. By Brett Slatkin

Machine Learning

Hands-On Machine Learning with Scikit-Learn, Keras, and TensorFlow: Concepts, Tools, and Techniques to Build Intelligent Systems 3rd ed. by Aurélien Géron
An Introduction to Statistical Learning: with Applications in R, 2nd ed. by Gareth James, Daniela Witten, Trevor Hastie, and Robert Tibshirani
Elements of Statistical Learning: Data Mining, Inference, and Prediction, 2nd ed. by Trevor Hastie, Robert Tibshirani, and Jerome Friedman
Machine Learning: A Probabilistic Perspective by Kevin P. Murphy

Big Data

Designing Data-Intensive Applications: The Big Ideas Behind Reliable, Scalable, and Maintainable Systems by Martin Kleppmann
Learning Spark: Lightning-Fast Data Analytics. 2nd ed. By Jules S. Damji, Brooke Wenig, Tathagata Das, and Denny Lee

Additional Resources The Missing Semester of Your CS Education https://missing.csail.mit.edu/

Quastor https://www.quastor.org/
Stack Overflow https://stackoverflow.com/
Julia Evans's Wizardzines https://wizardzines.com/

References

Anaconda (2022). *State of Data Science 2022: Paving the Way for Innovation.* https://www.ana-conda.com/state-of-data-science-report-2022

Barnes, M. (2017, June 28). "Don't Miss a Step: Predicting Late Consumer Behavior." Medium. Retrieved December 14, 2022, from https://medium.com/@matthew.barnes16/dont-miss-a-step-predicting-late-consumer-behavior-19cd657939e3

Boykis, V. (2019, February 13). "Data Science Is Different Now." Retrieved December 14, 2022, from https://vickiboykis.com/2019/02/13/data-science-is-different-now/

Boykis, V. (2022, January 9). "Git, SQL, CLI." Retrieved December 14, 2022, from https://vicki-boykis.com/2022/01/09/git-sql-cli/

Robinson, E., & Nolis, J. (2020). *Build a Career in Data Science.* Manning.

Rogati, M. (2017, June 12). "The AI Hierarchy of Needs." Hackernoon. Retrieved December 14, 2022, from https://hackernoon.com/the-ai-hierarchy-of-needs-18f111fcc007

So You're Thinking of Leaving Grad School: Setting Yourself Up for Success

Elisa Rapadas

It's 2 AM. A 23-year-old graduate student sits in her bed, in the dark, listening to hectic jazz music at the lowest volume in her hand-me-down earphones. The glow from her 2012 MacBook Pro nearly illuminates the entirety of the 500-square-foot studio, which is embarrassingly furnished with dorm room rugs and a broken sofa bed. The only thing she wants is to close her eyes and finally rest, but she knows she can't. She is frantically writing analysis code for her research project that she has to present virtually in a few days. Her laptop fan hums needily, and she worries that she will wake her sleeping partner who works a 9–5 job. She feels nothing but exhaustion and an inhuman sense of being driven by a motor to try to finish this work, but her fingers barely type. She's listening to music but cannot focus. Her head is buzzing with anxiety, but also a light calm, the only calm she's felt today (tonight?). The calm of it being 2 AM and not having to worry about an email from her PI (the professor who leads the lab she works in), which she has already seen many of this week. She writes a few lines of code, makes one chart, and turns in, understanding that her PI will probably ask her about this later.

One thought occurs to her. *Isn't this what I wanted? Wasn't this my dream—to be doing science at a top tier university? So why am I having anxiety attacks? Why am I miserable every day?*

This student is real, and she is the author of this chapter. Maybe you know someone like me. Maybe you feel like me. I am a part of the nearly half of PhD students who will not finish their PhD (Cassuto 2013). Leaving was not what I planned, but it was the right decision for me after really looking at all the factors in front of me: my experiences in my short time in graduate school, the realities of the academic job market, the skills I gained in grad school being applicable elsewhere, and, overall, the fact that an academic lifestyle is not the life I want to live. I was deep into a

E. Rapadas (✉)
Former PhD Student, Chicago, IL, USA

N. Jackson (ed.), *Non-Academic Careers for Quantitative Social Scientists*,
Texts in Quantitative Political Analysis,
https://doi.org/10.1007/978-3-031-35036-8_16

graduate program, and it was so easy to get tunnel vision and keep working toward the next thing: the next talk, the project, the next publication, without stepping back and reevaluating what the real end goal is.

Of the people who do finish their PhDs, only around a quarter of them receive tenure-track positions (Carey 2020). You are probably familiar with the academic job crisis, and that is why you are here reading this book. Now is as good of a time as any to start working on your exit plan.

This chapter is aimed toward people who are currently in their PhD programs and simultaneously weighing their career options and whether to leave their programs. I want to put out the obligatory disclaimer that my experiences are my own and that my path will not work for everyone. But one of the reasons why I wanted to write this chapter is to normalize talking about "mastering out" and leaving graduate programs with a master's degree instead of a PhD and to put into publication the feelings and pain I went through as I made this tough decision. I also provide practical tips for seeking out industry jobs while still enrolled in your program and deciding to leave.

Identity Foreclosure

At 22 years old, I entered graduate school at a R1 institution after 4 years of undergrad in which I committed myself to academia. In between going to basketball games (I sat in with the pep band) and rushing to the dining hall for late-night tater tots, I spent summers in research programs and semesters running experiments. Like most people who commit their early 20s to science, I am a highly neurotic, overly conscientious nerd who dreamed of being a professor just like professors I knew and liked so well. I loved going to office hours, learning new psychology concepts, and wrapping my brain around experimental methods and statistics.

I went to a small liberal arts college (SLAC) and I was unfamiliar with norms at large R1 institutions, but I did my best to pave my path to graduate school. My university was awarded a grant to support STEM education for marginalized students, and I saw this as my opportunity to learn more about going to conferences, conducting research, and networking. Through this grant program, I had access to resources and opportunities that I had no idea existed. I spent almost all of my time in undergrad working to get into a top PhD program. I was so single-minded in my pursuit that I never even thought to consider anything else. I lived and breathed research with the single goal of going to graduate school to become a professor at a small liberal arts college, and nothing was going to stop me.

Clearly, something did stop me, or I would not be writing this chapter. Maybe you are reading this story and seeing some red flags. Forgive me for this, but a Psychology 101 concept came back and haunted me as I recalled my story: Erik Erikson's identity foreclosure (maybe my psychology degree was good for something!). Identity foreclosure is when an individual prematurely commits to an identity, role, value, or goal that others have chosen for them, before exploring alternative roles (Erikson 1963). My role my entire life was "smart girl." When I got to college and was hearing about and exploring career paths, the thought of doing more school to eventually work at school sounded perfect for me, and I never even considered anything else.

My family and my friends were so proud. I was so proud. I had something lined up after undergrad, at my dream program where I already knew my PI because I had done summer research with her lab. I entered my program in Fall 2019. By this point, your "oh no" senses may have started tingling, as the world was just months away from plunging into chaos from the COVID pandemic.

It Turns Out I've Had ADHD My Whole Life

After one and a half quarters of in-person activities, in March 2020, everything moved online, and the world was chaotic. I had a difficult time focusing in my classes, which everyone did. I had a difficult time doing research, which everyone did. My paternal grandmother in Guam died in June 2020, and I could not go back to her funeral. I gave a research talk a few days after my grandma died. It was a complete blur. Then, my maternal grandmother died a few months later in August 2020. I had to withdraw from a class in my winter quarter, and eventually my PI became frustrated with my performance. The year 2020 was a disaster, and 2021 was not looking much better.

Something felt wrong to me. I was not absorbing anything in my classes for months and months, and I genuinely was having trouble getting research off the ground, due to a mixture of grief and mental health issues and a mentor mismatch. Although I had known my PI before entering the program, in working more closely together, I realized I needed a type of mentorship she could not provide. Suddenly my "smart girl" identity felt off. Every day I felt like a failure. I had to be pushed to the brink to put out original research for my end-of-the-year brown bag presentation, and it was not enough progress. And I dreaded the next step: having to take my comprehensive exams. More than 100 readings to absorb and take notes on over the next 2 months. Every single day, I was breaking out into hives and crying out of frustration. I wanted it all to end. Every day was a slog through comps readings and taking notes.

In July 2021, I received my annual evaluation. After a "heads up" from my PI that it was going to be less than positive, I braced myself. When I received the letter, there was a soft ask to reevaluate what I really wanted out of my career and my life. I cried for days after receiving this letter, but there was nothing else to do. Time marched on, I needed to finish comps, and I needed to keep going even though my body desperately wanted a break.

In August 2021, right in the middle of my comps, I got an appointment with a clinical psychologist—a spot opened after a few months of waiting. My difficulties during online learning in 2020 had me suspecting that something was different about me from my cohort of grad students. And I had always felt that underneath my "smart girl" identity was a real imposter—I thought back to how I took a long time to complete tests, how I nearly failed high school music class because I did not read directions, how I procrastinated basically every paper and assignment but still got good grades (then reinforcing the procrastination), how I got a debate scholarship but was a poor debater because I could not process the other team's arguments in real time, how I literally withdrew from a college course because I genuinely forgot I was enrolled in it, how I never calmed down because I felt like I was always in crisis mode, how my mother constantly told me to stop shaking my legs at the dinner table, how I was doing something with my hands constantly, etc.

Despite excelling, despite graduating with a college degree, despite getting into an R1 PhD program, I felt like I was always trying to outrun my "bad brain." How could I have never suspected? I had a whole degree in psychology but never even considered it. The clinical psychologist diagnosed me with ADHD-C in August 2021.

This diagnosis was one answer to questions I had about myself for decades. And I now had a report in hand showing that many of my difficulties were related to this thing inside my head. Now, I know there are academics out there who have ADHD. However, from my own personal experience, academia is a rather ADHD-unfriendly occupation. Much of the tasks that academics do on a daily basis are self-motivated and ambiguous. Lovers of academia might see this as flexibility, but I saw it as an extremely detrimental lack of structure.

I got my diagnosis in time to receive 1.5× time accommodations on my comps. At this point I started to worry that my administration thought I was lazy or making things up. I did not sleep for days. I worked through my new health issues to complete this exam. I developed eczema, which is common in my family, but not for me, until that moment. I barely ate. I had earphones in at all hours of the day slogging to finish this exam.

Finally, after 7 days, I did. When I finished, I felt no sense of accomplishment. A few weeks later, I found out that I passed comps and was a step closer to candidacy. I should have been joyful—I had gone through the academic ringer and made it out alive—but I did not even feel a sense of relief. Just complete and utter numbness, with a hint of defeat.

This is when I knew something had to change. Maybe I should consider the soft reevaluation of my career like my evaluation letter suggested. It's cliche, but the opposite of love is not hate, right? It's apathy. I felt nothing when I thought about my research. Just a vague sense of exhaustion, and after this comprehensive exam, I felt like I had been thrown in a washing machine put on spin cycle. Why did everything have to be so hard for me?

And here's the messed-up thing: I had no idea whether what I was going through was "normal" grad school mental health issues or something else, something worse. I know graduate students are often neurotic people. Everyone told me that graduate school was going to be hard. That it was a marathon, not a sprint. I tried so desperately to calmly keep my head above water, all while I felt like I was drowning. On top of the difficult time I was having in graduate school, I was existentially terrified of my job prospects. Even though I was at a top program, I was one of its worst performers, the least productive, and the least willing to move to a location I was not happy with. The thought of moving from city to city for postdocs until I received an academic job made me sick. But again, all of these qualms felt relatively "normal" for the average academic, and I had no reason to think that what I was going through was different.

But I just couldn't take it anymore. Something had to give. Graduate school was hard, but it should not have been not break-out-in-rashes hard. And everyone who spoke of their graduate school struggles also spoke of reward: Of the reward of doing research they were passionate about, about being able to pursue interesting questions—things I loved about doing research before graduate school. But I was no longer feeling a sense of reward, not even a vague sense that things would get better eventually. Everything felt wrong, and I had to do something, anything.

Now On to Practical Advice…

Now that I have outlined my thoughts and feelings as I made the difficult decision to leave, I want to highlight practical tips that helped me secure a job after I left my program. While there is a burgeoning online community of former academics in many different industries, which I am truly grateful for, I have found that there are fewer resources for individuals who are thinking about leaving in the middle of their program.

Truthfully, leaving your program is still stigmatized in academia, so I am grateful for the opportunity to share my story and to share resources. It is still somewhat shameful to talk about leaving a program, and I know that even though most people have been nothing but kind to me, there will always be individuals in academia who view mastering out as being a quitter who couldn't hack it. I am not disputing that that's what I am—I *did* quit my program. I couldn't hack it. But the important thing is *the worst thing I thought could happen to me happened to me, and I am okay.* I am gainfully employed in a job I love, and maybe I don't have a PhD, maybe I am a quitter, but I am finally happy, and that is much more than I can say for when I was supposedly following my dream of being a scientist at a top university. Without further ado, here are what I feel are the most pivotal steps in my journey.

1. *I went on medical mental health leave.*

My therapist helped me apply for an MLOA (medical leave of absence) from my university with my new ADHD diagnosis as well as some other diagnoses I received. I would get two quarters to be treated for my mental and physical health issues and still receive my stipend. Of course, each university is different and not all of them offer paid medical leave. From my personal experience, I didn't even *know* my university offered paid medical mental health leave until my therapist (who is not affiliated with my university) told me about it. For individuals who see themselves in my story, it is worth it to examine medical and mental health leave options at universities, because those options are often not publicized. I didn't even know where to start, so something as simple as searching "Medical Leave Policy [your university]" online to get necessary phone numbers and policies might get you to where you need to be.

I was on medical and mental health leave for two quarters, Fall 2021 and Winter 2022, and it was a necessary and important step for my personal and career development. I was not allowed to take classes or work on my thesis during my leave (thankfully), but I still had access to a variety of resources from my university, including career services.

As I mentioned before, I have ADHD, so having structureless days, even more structureless than being in graduate school, felt daunting. But I had just gone straight through school, even summers, without so much as even considering a day off. So going on leave was entirely necessary for me even though I had to contend with scheduling things myself. I had wonderful support systems. I was able to visit my family and friends often. I rode my bike along the Chicago lakefront. I read more books than I had ever read, slept well, went to concerts, listened to a lot of music, got engaged to my partner, and overall tried to get my sense of self back—a sense of self that had been conditioned out of me during graduate school.

The lack of structure was an obstacle, but it was one that I had tools to help. I had my wonderful therapist who I saw once a week to give me structure, I had a project to work on for a virtual conference, I had a virtual language class I was attending, I kept in touch with my diversity committee and attended meetings, I was spending my day working on my resume and LinkedIn page, I was reaching out to friends and friends of friends to ask about different career paths, and importantly, I was making time for myself to do things I love. I felt like a person again.

2. *I frequently visited my university's career services with the intention to edit my resume and LinkedIn page.*

Again, this is not something that is available at every university, but if you have career services at your university, know that graduate students can use these services too. I had the added benefit of having a career advisor specifically for PhD students who had a PhD herself. She was familiar with the fact that I was stuck in an academic mindset, and she was familiar with common mistakes that PhD students make when trying to write a resume, and she helped me fix them.

Even if you do not have a PhD-specific career advisor at your university career services, career services resources geared toward undergrads are *still* incredibly helpful for graduate students, *especially* those who have been in academia for their entire lives and have never so much as even considered writing a one-page resume instead of a CV. Outside perspectives are valuable. There is this concept in cognitive science, the curse of knowledge, and it's exactly what it sounds like: being too knowledgeable in a subject renders us unable to explain it to novices (Camerer et al. 1989). Being stuck in the PhD world can make us so tunnel-visioned that we can't even fathom anything else or explain what we do to a nonacademic person. It is so important to keep a circle of nonacademic friends and colleagues.

3. *I networked by reaching out to old friends and friends of friends—without an underlying career motivation.*

Networking can be intimidating, but I tried to see it as catching up with old friends, which it really is when you think about it. I organically followed up with folks I had not spoken to in a while who I had known were leaving academia or thinking of leaving. One of the first people I reached out to was a graduate student of my former PI's friend, who had received an internship in tech. Another person I reached out to was a friend of a friend from a lab that I had worked in who was working a part-time internship while in her PhD program.

Connections likely exist all around you, and it is important to know where to look. I would prioritize reaching out to existing connections before cold-emailing or cold-LinkedIn connecting with people who are "big" on non-ac or alt-ac social media, although I have also had good experience with cold-connecting. But I think viewing networking as a fun thing I wanted to do (catching up with old friends) helped me greatly and made me a better communicator when I was cold-emailing folks. However, I do understand that even being exposed to a network of academics who left was part of the privilege of being at a top university. I will say, though, your old friends, your cohort mates, and people around you in graduate school, no matter what type of program you are in, likely have something to offer, and you likely have something to offer them too. Getting to know your equals and contemporaries (in other graduate students and postdocs) around you is incredibly valuable and can be even more valuable than networking with higher-ups. I have had a lot of success and learned a lot by wanting to catch up and talk to them about their careers, but also catch up with them as friends.

4. *I attended free conferences and found social media groups that showcased non-academic paths.*

I learned so much by attending the free <u>Beyond Academia</u> conference hosted by the University of California at Berkeley. I attended panels with former academics who were now in different industries, and they provided their contact information to follow up with them. I learned a lot about career paths like science communication. Another helpful resource has been The Professor Is Out as well as LinkedIn and Twitter communities.

5. *I and applied to a variety of jobs and internships.*

I used my newfound resume and cover letter skills that I learned with my career advisor to apply for a variety of internships and full-time jobs while on leave. Transparently, I was rejected from every full-time job I applied to, but honestly, it did not sting as much as academic rejection stung. Academic rejection feels very high stakes—there are so few jobs out there that one rejection can mean the end of your entire search for this cycle. Outside of academia, there are so many jobs in so many industries that the rejections I was receiving felt like a drop in the bucket. Finally, I received an interview for an internship at the market research company where I now have a full-time job. This is pretty general advice, but it just takes one yes in order for you to move forward with a career change. That is what happened to me. Once I got the internship, I performed well and was hired back full time. That was also the case for a few other people I know who received internships during or after graduate school.

I don't have a N of very many people, but it seems like when you receive an internship, you simply have a higher likelihood of the company getting to know you better and seeing you shine than when you cold-apply for a full-time role. This is a strength of still being in graduate school while searching for an exit plan—you can still apply for internships, and there are even internships that exist out there at huge companies that are specifically for PhD students. This is another area where I will say to please take caution with your university policies. I had an internship, but I had to declare it to my university and not receive my stipend that summer because I was getting paid for a full-time job.

A note and tip regarding the fact that not everyone can go on leave: Find your "optional" tasks and replace them with career and professional development tasks. I acknowledge that going on leave is not an option for everyone, so this is what I would say to someone who feels like having an exit plan is necessary but cannot go on leave: Consider following the tips above while in graduate school, treating it like another research project or task. Add career and professional development to your to-do list and prioritize it accordingly. Academia is rife with tasks that seem big and obligatory in the moment, but when they are really examined, *you* don't have to be the person who does them. Maybe it is a review that you can say no to (even though that can be incredibly difficult). Maybe it is committee work that you can collaborate on rather than lead. Take the time to find the "optionals," the things that are not technically necessary for you to do to complete graduate school.

CV to Resume Practical Tips

Before I close out this chapter, I wanted to provide some practical examples of resume writing compared to CV writing. It can be hard to visualize, so I've included examples from my own CV and resume.

1. *Split up your many jobs as a graduate student and focus on your skills rather than research outcomes.*

As many of us know, CVs are long documents that focus on our research and research experience. On my CV, I described my research projects, what I found, and what I did, like this. Not everyone does it like this, of course, but this is one example of how my research took front and center in my resume.

Research Experience
PERCEPTIONS OF ASIAN AMERICANS FEB 2020-PRESENT
Primary Investigators (PI): ████████████ ████████████
- Set up and collected 400 participants through Amazon's Mechanical Turk and conducted study in Qualtrics; analyzed data and created plots using R Studio
- Collected norming data for foreignness, warmth, and competence
- Findings (2020): Participants select similar stereotypically Asian, positively valenced, and high status traits for Asian-Americans as they do for Japanese-Americans (an East Asian group). Participants chose significantly *fewer* stereotypically Asian, positively valenced, and high status traits for Filipino-Americans (a Southeast Asian group). These data show that Filipino-Americans are not typically viewed as "Asian" by the general American population and that this group is often invisibilized.
- Findings (2021): Results of Asianness from 2020 replicated, and valence results did not replicate. New participants selected more competent and high status traits for Asian Americans and Japanese Americans than they did for Filipino Americans.

While all that was necessary for when I was in academia, it was not necessary when applying for nonacademic jobs. In the resume that got me an internship in market research, here is how I characterized my graduate school experience. I broke research, teaching, and committee work into three different "jobs" (because we all know that they *are*) and had separate bullet points for all three, which focused on the *skills* I possessed, rather than the findings of my research.

GRADUATE RESEARCHER SEPT 2019-PRESENT
████████████
- Designed and spearheaded survey research on Qualtrics with over 400 Amazon Mechanical Turk participants to investigate perceptions and stereotypes of Asian Americans
- Programmed reproducible R code to generate quantitative insights and produce data visualizations for over 10 independent and dependent variables, which has been standardized and modified for future projects
- Publicized findings through research presentations at major conferences like the Society for Personality and Social Psychology (SPSP) Annual Convention, which generated discussion from scholars at different institutions

STUDENT DIVERSITY AND INCLUSION COMMITTEE MEMBER AUG 2020-PRESENT
████████████
- Collaborated with team members to analyze and present internal data on department climate to faculty members from the annual Diversity and Inclusion survey which led to direct departmental policy changes, including improving teaching assistant scheduling and addition of accessibility signage in department buildings
- Created marketing materials and promoted the Sneak Peek program, which recruits historically marginalized prospective students to preview Northwestern's psychology graduate program

GRADUATE TEACHING ASSISTANT JAN 2020-PRESENT
████████████
- Taught an online classroom of 20 students in a Developmental Psychology discussion section; developed lectures, group discussions and collaborative activities; received an average student evaluation of 5.57/6.00
- Compiled resources and research opportunities for students who were interested in developing research skills

In my resume, I used action words and focused on the skills I gained, and I also took verbiage directly from the job posting and used that verbiage in my resume. Do not sell yourself short by "just" characterizing yourself as a graduate student. You are so much more, and graduate students do many different jobs. When writing a resume for industry, showcase those unique skills from all those different jobs. Even if you are "just" a PhD candidate, you are a scientist, a researcher, a teacher, a committee member, and a leader—and it is important that all those roles come across in your resume.

2. *Do not view writing a resume as "converting" your CV. It is writing an entirely new document.*

The objective of a CV (to showcase every single academic and research accomplishment) and the objective of a one-page resume (getting a specific job) are pretty different. Look at the difference in verbiage between my CV and resume example. Get in the mindset of crafting a story out of many roles you play as a graduate student—a story where you gained many skills, like data analysis, people management, leadership, and others, and a story that is *specific* to each job.

If you are applying for a research or data job, highlight your research skills. If you are applying for a job in higher education but not a teaching job, highlight your people skills and committee work. Based on the job, make judgments on which of your positions to highlight and which to cut or not highlight.

3. *Get feedback from many sources, including those who have made the transition out of academia to people who have never been in academia at all.*

I previously mentioned the utility of going to my university's career services. They gave me great feedback on my resume and documents. In addition, I had some friends of mine who had transitioned out of academia take a peek at my resume. Most importantly, I had friends who had *never* been in academia look at my resume. Sometimes even our best efforts to make our academic skills legible can be *too* academic. Outside perspectives will be utterly valuable during a transition out.

Conclusion

Leaving your graduate program is a deeply personal decision that only you can make. I came to the decision after struggling in graduate school during COVID, discovering I had ADHD, and realizing it was time to cut my losses. When reading this chapter, I hope you reflect on what brought you to graduate school. When I reflected, I realized my path to graduate school was prolonged identity foreclosure and that I had not really examined any other paths. You might realize something similar, or you might also realize that the reward of doing your research and your drive to stay in academia is your strongest motivation.

Ultimately, I want people to choose what works best for them. And, for some people, what is best for them is leaving, which we don't talk about enough in academia. I hope that this chapter helps destigmatize leaving your program and that I have provided practical tips for exploring other paths beyond academia while still enrolled in a PhD program. Cheers!

If you want to chat more with me, follow me on Twitter. Frankly, I don't really post (I'm not much of a content creator) but I'm always happy to chat with people about my journey.

References

Camerer, C., Loewenstein, G., & Weber, M. (1989). The Curse of Knowledge in Economic Settings: An Experimental Analysis. *The Journal of Political Economy*, 97(5), 1232–1254.

Carey, K. (2020, March 5). The Bleak Job Landscape of Adjunctopia for Ph.D.s. *The New York Times*. https://www.nytimes.com/2020/03/05/upshot/academic-job-crisis-phd.html

Cassuto, L. (2013, July 1). Ph.D. Attrition: How Much is Too Much? *The Chronicle of Higher Education*. https://www.chronicle.com/article/ph-d-attrition-how-much-is-too-much/

Erikson, E. H. (1963). *Youth: Change and challenge*. New York: Basic books.

Kill, Pivot, Continue: Tips and Tricks for Career Transition Away from Academe

Robert L. Oprisko

Introduction

When an idea is being assessed for investment, the decision tree is limited to kill, pivot, or continue. Killing is a decision to immediately eliminate investment of time, money, and effort in that direction as it's determined to hold a nonviable value proposition. Continuing is the opposite of a decision to kill – successful progress toward a return or expected return with a reasonable calculus to the investment is either experienced or projected. Pivoting is harder to execute; it requires looking objectively at what worked in the initial investment and ruthlessly altering course away from the originally intended destination toward one that shows promise; it sacrifices an untenable vision for a viable path forward, and it's what we're going to explore here.

Odds are your time in the academy has an expiration date. You can either prepare for the inevitable blow to your identity and bend it to your benefit or you can allow the shift to break you. (It almost broke me.) If you find yourself less confident on *how* to pivot rather than that you *should* or *need* to pivot away from academe, this is probably the right chapter for you.[1]

I was always good at school, so I kept at it. I kept at it as the future burned from the Global Financial Crisis of 2008, turning the reality that brought me to grad

---

[1] Congratulations to all of you lucky Ivy League graduates who get to continue living the dream. To those who must kill the past to create the future, I am truly sorry.

R. L. Oprisko (✉)
Allstate, Asheville, NC, USA

© The Author(s), under exclusive license to Springer Nature
Switzerland AG 2023
N. Jackson (ed.), *Non-Academic Careers for Quantitative Social Scientists*,
Texts in Quantitative Political Analysis,
https://doi.org/10.1007/978-3-031-35036-8_17

school to ashes. In 1 year, 54% of academic jobs were cut; funding was cut.[2] By 2014 the downward trend continued until some disciplines saw only 5% of graduates enter the tenure-track employment pipeline, almost all of whom came from the most prestigious graduate programs.[3] The economic reality of postgraduate investment shifted. This trend has recently worsened with the COVID-19 pandemic; the academic job market has been met with systemic hiring freezes[4] accounting for a single-year decline of 80% of job openings.[5] The public perception of college as a worthwhile investment is in decline,[6] and some employers have been publicly fostering that sentiment due to a tight labor market.[7] It is presently estimated that 34% of PhD graduates are retained in higher education, less than half of which are tenure-track, of which 80% of those hail from the top 20% of PhD-granting programs.[8] There are individuals from non-elite universities that overperform and land great jobs at great schools, but a single data point does not a bell-curve make.[9]

I worked five jobs simultaneously to get through my PhD, with the first often starting at 7 am and the last ending between 1 and 3 am. Grinding and perseverance were necessary skills to develop in order to complete the program. When I graduated, I leveraged a friend of a friend to get an interview for a 1-year contract at a regionally prestigious school. I got the job and had an opportunity to set a strategy

[2] Emily Lu, "Economic Crisis Affects Academic Job Market," *Association of Writers Job List* (2008).

[3] Robert J. Speakman et al., "Market Share and Recent Hiring Trends in Anthropology Faculty Positions," *PLoS One* 13, no. 9 (2018).

[4] Colleen Flaherty, "Frozen Searches: Scores of Institutions Announce Hiring Freezes in Response to the Coronavirus," *Inside Higher Ed*, April 1, 20,220 2020.

[5] Chemjobber, "Want a Faculty Position? Get Ready to Wait.," *C&EN* 98, no. 18 (2020).

[6] Emma Whitford, "Not All Americans Think College Is Worth It," *Inside Higher Ed* 2021.

[7] Susan Milligan and Lauren Camera, "Ditch the Degree? Many Employers Are Just Fine with That," *U.S. News and World Report* 2023.

[8] PabloAMC, "Estimation of Probabilities to Get Tenure Track in Academia: Baseline and Publications During the Phd," *Effective Altruism* (2020).

[9] I've written ad nauseum on academic hiring practices, which has been reinforced by subsequent publishing across disciplines and geography. Long story short – where you get your degree from is the single greatest indicator of success in academic job hunting, where you work is the single greatest indicator of research publication success in top locations, and where you publish is the single greatest indicator of success in senior-level academic career transition. It's a prestige-by-association chase all the way through. See the following: Robert L. Oprisko, *Honor: A Phenomenology*, Routledge Innovations in Political Theory (New York, NY: Routledge, 2012); "Academic Prestige in Political Science: 2012–2013 Snapshot" (Inter-university Consortium for Political and Social Research: University of Michigan, 2014); Robert L. Oprisko, Kirstie L. Dobbs, and Joseph DiGrazia, "Pushing up Ivies: Institutional Prestige and the Academic Caste System," *The Georgetown Public Policy Review* (2013); "Placement Efficiency: An Alternative Ranking Metric for Graduate Schools," *Georgetown Public Policy Review* (2013); Robert L. Oprisko and Natalie Jackson, "Superpowers: The American Academic Elite," *The Georgetown Public Policy Review* (2012), http://gppreview.com/2012/12/03/superpowers-the-american-academic-elite/; Robert L. Oprisko, "Honor, Prestige, and the Academy: A Portrait of Political Science Tenured and Tenure-Track Faculty in Phd-Granting Institutions (2012–2013)," in *American Political Science Association* (Washington, DC2013).

for my professional academic career. Being at a disadvantage by not attending a top PhD-granting program, I opted to chart a path adjacent to the typical line. Instead of focusing on elite affiliation (the standard), I leaned in on impact. In 4 years, I produced five books and dozens of articles, expanded my network to hundreds of people around the globe, took leadership of a nonprofit publisher, served as a product owner for emerging education technology, and coached up my students such that they were publishing as undergraduates.

It didn't work. I had to pivot.

I turned a variety of hustles into an insanely successful few years of academic professional life. That's the only way to do it when you don't graduate from an Ivy League institution,[10] can't convince your PhD advisor to co-publish with you (even if it's all your writing) so as to leverage coat-tails to get into a top-tier journal more interested in the imprimatur of its authors than in the quality or innovation of the writing,[11] or are bankrolled by an outside source where you can show for quality of institution and not worry about a paycheck.[12]

There are no tears in business, so I let my academic dreams fade and accepted that I would rely more heavily on my external graduate minor in organizational leadership and alt-academic and nonacademic consulting experience. I worked practically for free for 2 years, getting enough experience with an opportunity to spin it into a greater one.[13] I've survived reductions in force (RIFs) and kept focused on how what I produce today influences what opportunities the future may bear, as only an ex-academic can.[14]

Kill

If you're still in graduate school while you're reading this and have decided it's time for you to kill the academic dream, assess what your institution can provide for cheap or free to aid your transition before exiting. Some programs may have courses that include formal professional certification from an external third party. These are worth their weight for a new grad as it's an effective CV line that transfers to a

---

[10] Oprisko, Dobbs, and DiGrazia, "Placement Efficiency: An Alternative Ranking Metric for Graduate Schools"; "Pushing up Ivies: Institutional Prestige and the Academic Caste System"; Robert L. Oprisko and Natalie Jackson, "Superpowers: The American Academic Elite," ibid. (2012), http://gppreview.com/2012/12/03/superpowers-the-american-academic-elite/

[11] Jean F. Lienard et al., "Intellectual Synthesis in Mentorship Determines Success in Academic Careers," *Nature Communications* 9, no. 4840 (2018).

[12] Anthony P. Carnevale et al., "Born to Win, Schooled to Lose," (Washington, D: Georgetown University Center on Education and the Workforce, 2019).

[13] Many thanks to Stephen McGlinchey and E-International Relations where I moved from a contributing author to editor of *International Political Theory* to sitting on the board, to directing it.

[14] Layoffs. You'll find that the corporate world has a *lot* of neutral language for harsh actions.

professional resume. Having your university vouch for you by way of degree is essential for many roles and is only strengthened by reinforcement.

Diversifying your experience here is critical. In order to transition out of academe, it's much easier if you have experience you can discuss in interviews that isn't directly related to your education or path. Most corporate recruiters and managers won't be versed in the nuances of academic prestige building and may not be as impressed by your accomplishments in this area if this is all you have.

In this vein, it's worth strongly considering an external minor in something corporate for non-quants in non-STEM fields.[15] This introduction moved me to get a certificate as a Certified Scrum Master, effectively a facilitator for a team tasked with developing a new or refining an existing product or service. This external experience has added benefits; you expand your professional network with academics who are more likely to have strong corporate networks of their own, it opens opportunities to teach courses outside of your primary area, and it helps you construct a narrative for transition.

If you aren't able to leverage a paying job in your external area, you may wish to consider a part-time job not connected to academe. It's critical to learn how to compartmentalize your identity and voice between academe and other areas to succeed in your pivot; starting early can only help. There may be opportunities at your university for you to pursue. While in graduate school, I held assistantships or instructorships in political science, in women's studies, and at the library. I also held a Faculty Fellowship,[16] facilitated high and low ropes courses, worked security for the police department, worked in maintenance, and prepared cigar and liquor tastings for corporate officers for a restaurant's private event clients.

Understandably, many of you are scoffing at splitting your time and attention away from the holy pursuit of your singular academic focus. How can you possibly succeed doing this?

You can't.

If you are going to continue in your academic career, this chapter isn't for you.

If you happen to find yourself in the position that you are finishing in the next year, have no real hope of attaining an academic position, and need to pivot hard and fast immediately upon graduation, you may wish to consider a taking out a business loan from the US government. If you aren't already taking out loans, you may want to consider doing so in your final year for the purpose of bankrolling your transition. Please note that student loans are onerous and difficult to impossible to eliminate

---

[15] I paired my PhD in political theory with an external minor in organizational leadership. My original intention was to add a voice that could cut through the politics of the Purdue Political Science Department, alleviating some of the nastier voices from the room. When I took the courses, I was horribly unimpressed as the content seemed simple. Looking back, I think I was experiencing a true fit and missed it. I love political science, but progress in the field can be a fight. Maybe I was a better fit for this new area even if I didn't love it?

[16] At Purdue University a faculty fellow is a mentor for a Residence Hall floor. One of the key benefits of this position was a meal card which drastically saved expenses and time (I could stay on campus as opposed to returning home for meals), which was of increased importance considering the number of roles I held on campus and the amount of time I spent in them all.

even through bankruptcy, so this approach is not one to approach lightly. If you do decide to take out loans, ensure that you know what you are going to do with the money ahead of time. This isn't for living expenses, it isn't for getting by while you figure it out, and it isn't for continuing your academic pursuits. It's an investment in necessary certifications, tools (computer/hardware, software, etc.), training in STEM or STEM-like tools,[17] or professional attire to increase your competitiveness on the job market in your chosen area.

Pivot

Should you already be in the academic world as a professional and need to exit, I endorse as much from the previous section as possible, but recognize that your ability to reinvest in more education is not a viable proposition. You find yourself at the point of pivot and there are actions that you can take to ease your transition. Time is of the essence here because you're likely on a clock with your contract and your next semester or year is not guaranteed.

First things first – you need to produce. If all you do is teach, you don't understand the academic game and need to exit as it is. One of the most useful tools you can leverage in your career transition is your publication record. Rather than wading in a sea of sharks where having published is a norm rather than the exception, transitioning out of academe reverses this truth – you become a unicorn. Similarly, the prioritization of production is changed as monographs[18] and single-authored articles[19] tend to be less valuable than organizing the chaos of group projects.

The publishing activities at which academe scoffs are prized more highly outside than in:

- Co-authored articles[20] show not only the size and depth of your network but also your ability to work with others and broaden the range of your research.

---

[17] I opted for an immersion into SQL as the easiest path to claiming some coding expertise. Having gone to graduate school, you may have experience in this, R, or Python. If that's the case, feel free to celebrate as you're ahead of the game. This being said, if you actually have qualitative methodological experience, you can leverage it very well, especially in user experience, customer support, etc. TLDR: build a skillset for research and analyzing data.

[18] Oprisko, *Honor: A Phenomenology*.

[19] "The Rebel as Sovereign: The Political Theology of Dignity," *Revista Pleyade*, no. 9 (2012).

[20] Robert L. Oprisko and Josh Caplan, "Beyond the Cake Model: Critical Intersectionality and the Relative Advantage of Disadvantage," *Epiphany* 2 (2014); Robert L. Oprisko and Kristopher Kaliher, "The State as a Person? Anthropomorphic Personification V. Concrete Durational Being," *Journal of International and Global Studies* 6, no. 1 (2014); Robert L. Oprisko and Olivia Wolfe, "Resisting Tyranny: Human Rights Organizations, International Organizations, and Promotion of the Rule of Law in Argentina," *Politics, Bureaucracy, and Justice* 4, no. 2 (2014).

- Editing a collection (either chapters for a book volume[21] or articles for a journal special issue[22]) translates into product and program management.
- Organizing a Festschrift[23] translates into leveraging a close-knit network to highlight and explore a unified value proposition from multiple angles.
- Book reviews[24] highlight your ability to distill a lot of complex information into an approachable size and to assess it objectively.
- Textbooks show that you can craft training material.
- Public blogs and articles show that you know how to write at various levels of sophistication for nonspecialist audiences.[25]

Publishing takes time, so if you're looking to transition, it's important to consider destinations that are not as attractive to academics: open access, online, nonprestigious outlets. Nonacademics are less likely to know the difference and may not care if they do. What these provide you with is *speed*. It's easier to talk about a publication record if you have one that you can show and that they can find.

Odds are, however, that you won't have everything in your pipeline out by the time you hit a hard deadline to exit your academic position. Preparing for this eventuality is straightforward. Begin by contacting someone in your network who understands what you're doing and is game to be supportive. A friend who is a department chair can prove very handy here. You may get this offer from your former institution or your PhD institution, which is an option that you can take, but I believe that showing *progression* is better than *regression*. You will need to ask your contact for a zero-time appointment as a "research fellow." This is a quid pro quo relationship and is often limited to a year or 2 just for these purposes. In exchange for no money, but an institutional e-mail, formal affiliation, and access to cheap or free tools/software, you agree to name them as your primary institutional affiliation for research in progress to be published. In other words, they get to claim *your* output as *their* output for little to no investment.[26]

Now that we've covered the end of your academic output, it's time to focus on the pivot toward industry rather than away from academe. Attaching yourself to a

[21] Tim Poirson and Robert L. Oprisko, eds., *Caliphates and Islamic Global Politics* (Bristol, UK: E-International Relations, 2014).

[22] Martin Coward, Kyle Grayson, and Robert L. Oprisko, "Ressurecting Ir Theory: Editor's Introduction to a Special Section," *Politics* 36, no. 4 (2016).

[23] Robert L. Oprisko and Diane Rubenstein, eds., *Michael A. Weinstein: Action, Contemplation, Vitalism*, Innovations in Political Theory (New York, NY: Routledge, 2015).

[24] Robert L. Oprisko, "From Nothing, Everything," *Contemporary Political Theory* 14 (2015); "Failure as the Real: A Review of Slavoj Zizek's Less Than Nothing: Hegel and the Shadow of Dialectical Materialism," *Theoria & Praxis* 1, no. 2 (2014).

[25] Robert L. Oprisko "Entropy V. Thought Traditions: I.R. Theory Isn't Dead Yet," *e-International Relations* (2014); "I.R. Theory's twenty-first Century Experiential Evolution," *e-International Relations* (2013), http://www.e-ir.info/2013/05/25/the-fall-of-the-state-and-the-rise-of-the-individuals-ir-theorys-21st-century-experiential-evolution/

[26] You may find this distasteful. It is. However, this is a way of evading being openly unemployed and gives academic credibility to your in-flight output, which is more important than it should be.

quasi-academic industry such as publishing, reporting, or assessment is intuitive. A rung higher would be educational technology firms, corporate training, or content writers for influencers. The goal on this point of the pivot is to begin to share your professional identity with a nonacademic institution, solidifying the point in your personal narrative which you can identify in interviews to alleviate the concern that you will pivot back to academe if given an opportunity.

Once you have your first alt-ac or non-ac experience, it becomes easier to get the next one. It may even prove useful to set up an LLC for consulting purposes, especially for individuals in high cost of living areas.[27]

When I was transitioning, I hit a wall in academic publishing – the initiatives I had launched when I was in the game were maturing, and I found myself in over my head with projects, demands to commit to national and international travel, and requests to teach, present, publish, and edit. For free, of course; paying for work is something that isn't normalized as it should be in academe. I was also enjoying some opportunities to stay in the game, but not in the Western Hemisphere. I had to choose between were 1) a suboptimal version of my dream or 2) my family. I chose the latter and I dropped a *lot* of projects.[28] Several of my colleagues have killed our relationship over this period; they couldn't understand where I was or how hard it is to create knowledge when you can't show your spouse that it'll pay the bills. The blow to my ego and identity was such that I harbored resentment for not being able to stay in the game longer than I was able. I was offered ghost-writing contracts from very prominent academics at obscenely low rates that they would put their names on to command very high salaries, a part of academe I didn't know existed.

The wall and the absolute lack of interest in my well-being, future, or transition from academe helped force me to embrace the pivot. The effort I had poured into research and writing was now leveraged for finding and winning consulting jobs where I would provide strategic and operational expertise for firms, universities, corporations, and nonprofits that had money but no hunger.

In consulting, I found that the act of writing and publishing is highly sought – by professional consulting firms. There is a hierarchy of these with increasing revenue by class. Here is a rough approximation in ascending order:

1. Staff augmentation level 1 – throw bodies at the problem.

---

[27] Some opportunities will only pay "corp-to-corp" which allows them to drop a contract without notice and is only available to incorporated individual consultants or firms. This can be draining, but if you are in a large city may be worthwhile if you look like you'll hit $50 k in earnings annually or more.

[28] I had to let go of both E-International Relations textbooks that I had crowdsourced from my network and for which I still don't get credit. I couldn't finish two monographs in contract with university presses, couldn't find time for an invited article in the *Journal of Critical Higher Education and Student Affairs* that a former student requested, couldn't afford to go to Switzerland for an invited conference, and couldn't afford to go to Oslo for an invited conference on my own book! I once often thought about how close I had to be to making it in the tenure game, but I now know that I wasn't close at all – success is premised on structural affiliation and prestige, which I would never have.

2. Staff augmentation level 2 – fulfill a need and then automate/optimize your job away.
3. Staff augmentation level 3 – provide a skillset that is not held by the hiring company for a critical project that requires it.
4. Operational effectiveness – evaluate how something is done as an expert and provide a path forward.
5. Strategic effectiveness – evaluate a company's path to achieve objectives and optimize.
6. Thought leader – set a new path to position a firm above its present tranche.[29]

As an academic, you should be able to live into the higher levels of this hierarchy and may be able to leverage your research and evaluation tool kit to live in the top-half exclusively. My work with consulting firms was designed to provide thought leadership and strategic consulting to improve their reputation from a lower level of staff augmentation to a higher level.

When entering a consulting position, I like to present an idea of our relationship before the firm has the opportunity to do so.[30] My preference is to set it as a series of phases with milestone gates where the nature of the relationship changes. The first phase is an hourly remuneration for a set minimum period in order to accomplish something tangible. Second, is either an outcome-based or delivery-based obligation as a transition period. Finally, I put in a long tail of consulting on the work delivered for a period of roughly twice as long as the employment lasted with a minimum of 1 year. This is your residual income phase where you do relatively little work and you enjoy decent pay. The more of these you can string together, the more wealth you build.

Continue

At some point, you may wish to dive fully into the corporate or industrial world rather than merely skating across it as a consultant. This may require you to leverage a favor from someone in your network. If you're like me, you'll have to move to the job (though in a post-COVID world, that may no longer be required) and to take a pay cut from consulting for the added possibility of paid time-off and benefits. Do

---

[29] The money, however, is made in staff augmentation. While a firm will seek to position itself in a higher class to demand higher rates, the volume of work is as important … unless you're a very small or sole proprietor-operator firm. This is where an academic may be at advantage running a one-woman operation or even a pod of specialists.

[30] I hold a minority position on this advice. Most consultants will suggest that you allow the other party to put a price forward to determine your value as it may be much higher than you want. I think that's a good path forward if you truly have no idea of your value or of the market, but that's a great way to look unprofessional long term. In my view, the best idea is to establish your worth by setting a price you prefer and a relationship paradigm you desire. If nothing else, it presents you as something higher than staff augmentation in the eyes of your interlocutors.

it. Six months to a year in a full-time position is enough to erase thoughts that you'll be back in academe in the fall. Depending on your company and manager, it's worth requesting that your academic professional experience be counted as time in grade, thus giving you more PTO and benefits just for asking. I was able to get 10 years credited for my PhD and academic experience.

When in your new role, you may be presented opportunities. It's important to consider how they may improve not only your performance in your present role but also your personal capital moving forward. You may need to do the former, but you should actively seek out the latter. It's important to balance preparation for the future with effective work performance in the present. Some professional development opportunities you may not know exist include:

- Professional certification training delivered by specialists within your organization, but granted by an external third party. This is a great way of taking one of your original certifications and deepening your investment by getting an advanced or master/trainer level.
- Professional organization membership and conference participation. Similar to academe, some parts of industry value investment in a formal community of practice.
- Formal mentoring and management cohort participation. Some organizations hire this out to programs like Torch, while others do it in-house.
- Internal Talent Shares are programs where you can take a structured hiatus from your present job to work in another area for a predetermined period. This is an excellent way to expand your network, broaden your skillset, reposition your value proposition within the organization, and try a perceived new direction in your career.

If you should find yourself in a horrible position where your direct manager is not aligned to your desired path forward, you may need to put your future plans aside in order to escape a potentially untenable situation. The best escape route can often be merely forcing a positive review of your work as it prevents fully blocking your ability to move on internally within the organization.[31] If you can focus your hate, rage, frustration, or anger, you should be able to sidestep a bad manager by building relationships with their peers and superiors (without undermining your manager) and exceeding all reasonable expectations in a way that is irrefutable. Make this person look good because of you and then bow out. If you can't find an acceptable promotional path out, sometimes a lateral transfer is a necessary intermediary step to better things.

Most importantly, by the time you are wrestling with problems like strategically managing your professional development to navigate middle management and enter corporate officer positions, you can conclude that your move out of academe is

---

[31] Intuitive or not, many organizations have a minimum score on your annual evaluation in order to be considered for new opportunities inside the broader enterprise. Always nurture your score.

complete and that you have successfully navigated a pivot into a new career. Congratulations!

Postmortem

Practical guides for difficult moments in life can be depressing to read.[32] Some books will suggest that you write a eulogy or an obituary for your former life so that you can say "Goodbye!" to your former self and gain closure. I disagree; you wouldn't be nearly as competitive on the open market without your doctorate. In fact, you get to find yourself in the upper 1% of society in terms of education, and don't diminish the importance of that separation in terms of awe you may enjoy when not surrounded by peers who have the same.

Your life is yours alone, a path only you get to experience in its completeness or for the duration.[33] Along the way, you're bound to have found just how useful your academic experience is outside of academe – how it has opened doors or, at the very least, made certain that some doors wouldn't be locked when you found them. I wouldn't advise in looking at your academic years with undue fondness or without a critical lens. Academe is, in many ways a backward, feudal hierarchy premised on people who had it far easier in terms of job hunting, promotion, tenure, home purchasing, funding, etc. than you enjoyed. These same people put increasingly unrealistic to impossible impediments in front of your progress out of some sick, twisted desire to leverage a tiny, but potent, power where possible.

Instead, I strongly advocate for you finding an acceptable path for you regardless of what your job function, title, or industry happens to be. Ultimately, a career is something that is constantly under construction even when in use. Today I wear a number of hats: I'm a strategic management consultant to CEOs and COOs in companies that are looking to leverage expertise to separate themselves and their firms into a stronger position vis-à-vis the field, I'm an Enterprise Agile Strategist for Allstate where I work across the 50,000 strong company to operationalize strategic changes and to ensure that tactical work rolls up to desired outcomes rather than working for work's sake, I serve on a number of corporate and nonprofit boards, and I volunteer as a consultant for minority- and women-owned start-ups.

All of these roles are me and I am all of these roles. I do what I do because they each fulfill a desire that I have. I no longer get to be an academic nor do I have academic pretensions. I do have a few books that I want to write before I can't, but that's not about being an academic so much as why I became one. Happily, nobody

---

[32] And just as painful to write! I can't even begin to tell you how many drafts of this I threw away because it was far too bleak to see the light of day.

[33] Hilariously, this is something I wrote about a lot as an academic. My best points can be found here: Oprisko, *Honor: A Phenomenology*; "The Rebel as Sovereign: The Political Theology of Dignity."; "Strings: A Political Theory of Multi-Dimensional Reality," *Theoria & Praxis* 2, no. 2 (2014); Oprisko and Kaliher.

can take away my PhD or other degrees. Nobody can take away my time teaching in colleges and universities. Nobody can take away my publications, refute my progress and success after leaving academe, or argue that I haven't made it financially.[34]

Life hasn't gone how I envisioned it, but it's not bad. I strongly urge you to consider the vast opportunities that life has for you in its wide realms rather than to narrowly focus on a single path forward. Ultimately, you have to live with yourself for the rest of your life; you may as well do so on your terms than anyone else's.

Good luck.
God bless.
Kick ass.
Take names.
Regret nothing.

Bibliography

Carnevale, Anthony P., Megan L. Fasules, Michael C. Quinn, and Kathryn Peltier Campbell. Born to Win, Schooled to Lose. Washington, D: Georgetown University Center on Education and the Workforce, 2019.

Chemjobber. Want a Faculty Position? Get Ready to Wait. *C&EN* 98, no. 18 (2020).

Coward, Martin, Kyle Grayson, and Robert L. Oprisko. Resurrecting Ir Theory: Editor's Introduction to a Special Section. *Politics* 36, no. 4 (2016): 383-84.

Flaherty, Colleen. Frozen Searches: Scores of Institutions Announce Hiring Freezes in Response to the Coronavirus. *Inside Higher Ed*, April 1, 20220 2020.

Lienard, Jean F., Titipat Achakulvisut, Daniel E. Acuna, and Stephen V. David. Intellectual Synthesis in Mentorship Determines Success in Academic Careers. *Nature Communications* 9, no. 4840 (2018).

Lu, Emily. Economic Crisis Affects Academic Job Market. *Association of Writers Job List* (2008).

Milligan, Susan, and Lauren Camera. Ditch the Degree? Many Employers Are Just Fine with That. *U.S. News and World Report*, 2023.

Oprisko, Robert L. Academic Prestige in Political Science: 2012-2013 Snapshot. Inter-university Consortium for Political and Social Research: University of Michigan, 2014a.

Oprisko, Robert L. Entropy V. Thought Traditions: I.R. Theory Isn't Dead Yet. *e-International Relations* (2014). Published electronically June 16, 2014b.

Oprisko, Robert L. Failure as the Real: A Review of Slavoj Zizek's Less Than Nothing: Hegel and the Shadow of Dialectical Materialism. *Theoria & Praxis* 1, no. 2 (2014c): 1–4.

Oprisko, Robert L. From Nothing, Everything. *Contemporary Political Theory* 14 (2015): 32-36.

Oprisko, Robert L. Honor, Prestige, and the Academy: A Portrait of Political Science Tenured and Tenure-Track Faculty in Phd-Granting Institutions (2012–2013). In *American Political Science Association*. Washington, DC, 2013a.

Oprisko, Robert L. *Honor: A Phenomenology*. Routledge Innovations in Political Theory. New York, NY: Routledge, 2012a.

---

[34] I suppose they could, but it would be sound and fury signifying nothing and easily refuted with data.

Oprisko, Robert L. I.R. Theory's 21st Century Experiential Evolution. *e-International Relations* (2013b). Published electronically May 25, 2013. http://www.e-ir.info/2013/05/25/the-fall-of-the-state-and-the-rise-of-the-individuals-ir-theorys-21st-century-experiential-evolution/.

Oprisko, Robert L. The Rebel as Sovereign: The Political Theology of Dignity. *Revista Pleyade*, no. 9 (June 2012b): 119–36.

Oprisko, Robert L. Strings: A Political Theory of Multi-Dimensional Reality. *Theoria & Praxis* 2, no. 2 (2014d): 2–23.

Oprisko, Robert L., and Josh Caplan. Beyond the Cake Model: Critical Intersectionality and the Relative Advantage of Disadvantage. *Epiphany* 2 (2014): 35–54.

Oprisko, Robert L., Kirstie L. Dobbs, and Joseph DiGrazia. Placement Efficiency: An Alternative Ranking Metric for Graduate Schools. *Georgetown Public Policy Review* (2013). Published electronically September 15, 2013.

Oprisko, Robert L. Pushing up Ivies: Institutional Prestige and the Academic Caste System. *The Georgetown Public Policy Review* (2013c).

Oprisko, Robert L., and Natalie Jackson. Superpowers: The American Academic Elite. *The Georgetown Public Policy Review* (2012). Published electronically 12/03/2012. http://gppreview.com/2012/12/03/superpowers-the-american-academic-elite/.

Oprisko, Robert L., and Kristopher Kaliher. The State as a Person? Anthropomorphic Personification V. Concrete Durational Being. *Journal of International and Global Studies* 6, no. 1 (2014): 30–49.

Oprisko, Robert L., and Diane Rubenstein, eds. *Michael A. Weinstein: Action, Contemplation, Vitalism*, Innovations in Political Theory. New York, NY: Routledge, 2015.

Oprisko, Robert L., and Olivia Wolfe. Resisting Tyranny: Human Rights Organizations, International Organizations, and Promotion of the Rule of Law in Argentina. *Politics, Bureaucracy, and Justice* 4, no. 2 (2014): 13–26.

PabloAMC. Estimation of Probabilities to Get Tenure Track in Academia: Baseline and Publications During the Phd. *Effective Altruism* (2020). Published electronically September 20, 2020.

Poirson, Tim, and Robert L. Oprisko, eds. *Caliphates and Islamic Global Politics*. Bristol, UK: E-International Relations, 2014.

Speakman, Robert J., Carla S. Hadden, Matthew H. Colvin, Justin Cramb, K. C. Jones, Travis W. Jones, Isabelle Lulewicz, *et al.* Market Share and Recent Hiring Trends in Anthropology Faculty Positions. *PLoS One* 13, no. 9 (2018).

Whitford, Emma. Not All Americans Think College Is Worth It. *Inside Higher Ed*, 2021.

Presenting Academic Research in the Interview Process and Beyond: A Conversation Between Colleagues

Matt Bernius, Laurel Eckhouse, Amelia Hoover Green, and Kerry Rodden

Introductions and "Origin Stories"

Matt Bernius I'm excited to facilitate this conversation about transitioning from academic to alternative careers for folks with a quantitative research and data science background. Joining me are three of my Code for America (CfA) data science colleagues: Laurel Eckhouse, Amelia Hoover Green, and Kerry Rodden. CfA is a national nonprofit working to improve the delivery of government services at the state and federal levels. We currently have three major focus areas: helping people get and stay on social safety net benefits, helping people file their taxes and get refunds, and automatically clearing criminal records. CfA operates in multidisciplinary teams that include product and program managers, software and solution engineers, designers, qualitative researchers (like myself), and quantitative researchers (like Amelia, Kerry, and Laurel).

To start this conversation, let's share a bit about our respective paths from academia to CfA. As the odd person out here, the qualitative rather than quantitative researcher in this discussion, I'll kick things off.

Over the last two-plus decades, I've had a number of careers. I started in web design and then went back to school to get a master's in qualitative social sciences. I spent a few years teaching at the Rochester Institute of Technology before pursuing a Ph.D. in cultural anthropology at Cornell in 2008. Those studies didn't go very well. Beyond not being a great match for the department's strengths and my advisor leaving at the end of my first semester, I also was really worried about what would happen after finishing school. People were already talking about academic precarity and the lack of tenure-track positions. All of those stresses eventually caused a

M. Bernius (✉) · L. Eckhouse · A. H. Green · K. Rodden
Code for America, San Francisco, CA, USA

N. Jackson (ed.), *Non-Academic Careers for Quantitative Social Scientists*,
Texts in Quantitative Political Analysis,
https://doi.org/10.1007/978-3-031-35036-8_18

mental and emotional breakdown that led me to leave the program. It took a few years of recovery and then a *lot* of interviews, but I eventually got a contract gig at a user experience firm as a design researcher. I transitioned to a full-time position and continued to work at that firm until they closed their office in my city. Then I got a job at Measures for Justice, a nonprofit focused on improving the transparency of criminal legal system data. That was my introduction to civic tech, a path that eventually led me to CfA.

Laurel Eckhouse Well, my short story is that I had a baby and immediately announced "I need to move back to California!"

I'm told I said that the day I had a baby. I have a lot of other memories from that day but don't remember saying that. Admittedly, I was a bit busy at the time. My partner, however, swears I announced that we were moving back to California that night in the hospital. She replied that "we're a little busy with some other things right now, but we can figure that out." I was an assistant professor at the University of Denver. Growing our family helped me decide that other aspects of my life were a higher priority than "being an academic" or even "doing the kind of work that I wanted to do" (though I'm very happy with the kind of work that I'm doing at CfA). So my decision to shift my career came from deciding that I wanted the flexibility that I couldn't have as an academic.

Matt I am so impressed by your clarity in making that decision. Part of what caused my breakdown was my inability to reconcile my attachment to the idea of "being an academic" with the reality of my experience and my concerns about there not being a stable career for me.

Laurel Yeah! I think you can get into a situation where you think there's only one path. It's easy to fall into the trap of thinking "I just need to get to the next stage of this path and see if I like it before I can make a decision about alternatives." But there's always a next stage and I had all these other things I wanted to do, like have children. I realized that I couldn't wait until I had tenure to see if I was actually happy. So I started my job search. I was lucky in that I saw a job on CfA's criminal justice team that was a perfect fit for my research interests and I applied.

Amelia Hoover Green In my case, I got sort of unceremoniously pushed out of academia (although I think my former colleagues might not view it that way). Because I'm sort of naive, I took a Diversity Equity and Inclusion (DEI) job at my university on top of being an associate professor. The DEI work ate up all of my time and energy. It also showed me some really sad facts about institutional priorities. Ultimately, after what Lemony Snicket might label a "series of unfortunate events" that I still don't fully understand, I ended up getting fired from the DEI job. I retained the tenured-professor part of my job, but I realized that, despite having tenure, this was no longer a place where I could continue to work. And that led me to weigh my options.

Between raising a family, teaching, and my DEI work, I hadn't had the time to publish a lot. The job market at the associate level in political science, and in particular my niche of conflict studies, is really, really small. I also had to think about my family. I have little kids and I didn't want to move my family to any random location.

Laurel Right! There were some jobs in places like Chicago, which were all perfectly great places, but not where we wanted to live.

Amelia Really, the only job in my little niche last year was at MIT. And beyond not wanting to move, I knew I wasn't going to get that one. I realized, "You know what, getting another academic job just isn't going to happen." So I spent a couple of months "quiet quitting," so to speak, before I quit out loud. I spent much of that time converting my C.V. into a resume and starting to look for and apply to a lot of data science jobs. The geography aspect was huge – I wanted to find ways to stay here in Philly without necessarily having to yoke myself to a particular institution. Right in the middle of the process, I saw that CfA was hiring for remote positions. Laurel and I are friends and she had already told me that CfA was a nice place to work. I put in my application and here I am.

Matt That speaks to the importance of reaching out to your network during the transition. Now that I think about it, I've found most of my jobs through networking. I think CfA was the first job I ever applied to where I didn't have any direct connections. It's so important to reach out to folks you know and ask for help.

Amelia I'm really aware of the tangible value of networking. It was so important and helpful for me to have Laurel as an advocate and ally throughout this process. And I'm also suspicious of networking as it can also become an engine of inequality in ways that make me uncomfortable. I worry about who gets shut out by it if they don't have the connections (or the confidence to connect). So I try to own that I benefited from it and think about how I can pay that back to my broader communities.

Matt There is definitely that, too. I believe that those of us who have made the transition from academia have a responsibility, for lack of a better word, to help make that jump easier for those coming after us. One way I try to do this is by reserving a few hours a week to meet with people who have questions about how to make that transition.

Back on the topic of transitions, Kerry, if I remember correctly, you went more or less directly from your Ph.D. program to industry. Is that right?

Kerry Rodden Yes, my experience is a little different than the rest of yours. I did a computer science Ph.D. in human-computer interaction. I never seriously considered staying in academia. I was pretty exhausted by the end of my Ph.D. And I was also the kind of person that just got really tired of my research topic. I didn't want to know any more about it for a while.

At that time, there was a fairly standard path in computer science research to go work at one of the industrial research labs, like Xerox PARC. Unfortunately, when I finished up my Ph.D., there was an economic downturn, and none of those labs were hiring full-time researchers. I was able to get brought on as an external consultant by Microsoft Research, and I was there for a little while at their lab in Cambridge, UK.

After a while, the economy started improving and I saw that Google was hiring. I wanted to do applied research and go beyond being cited to having a direct impact on products. I was especially interested in Google because my Ph.D. work involved the topic of search, and what they were doing at the time was just so far in advance of any academic research in information retrieval. I knew that if I wanted to be where it all was happening, I had to be there. I looked across their jobs for what seemed to be the closest fit for the skill set that I had. That role turned out to be a "usability analyst," what we would now call a "user experience researcher." So, I became a usability analyst.

Going from in-depth research and writing to running quick, scrappy usability tests to try to evaluate something that's imminently launching was a big contrast and was very exciting to me. My Ph.D. work felt distant from influencing things that people actually used. Working directly on a product felt much more interesting to me. From there I started to explore bringing my quantitative skills to UX research, doing analysis of large-scale product usage data. I helped create the field of quantitative UX research – I literally wrote the job description for the first quantitative UX research role at Google. I also began to explore data visualization as well, to present quantitative results in a more engaging way.

Ultimately, I became really interested in applying my skills to problems that felt more meaningful to me. That was what brought me to CfA. I had done a consulting data visualization project for CfA, and when an opportunity came up to join full-time, I took it.

Presenting Work During the Hiring Process

Matt Let's talk about the hiring process. CfA follows a hiring process similar to most tech companies. When we're interested in a candidate for a position, the first step is a call with a technical recruiter. The recruiter is an expert in the hiring process, not necessarily an expert in a given discipline. They will ask some general questions to confirm that you meet the general qualifications for the position and that you feel like a good fit for CfA. If everything goes well, your next interview will be with the hiring manager for the position. Usually, that's someone who is from your discipline and maybe the person the position ultimately reports to. The hiring manager conversation is a chance for you to "talk shop," share past relevant experiences, and show off what you know. From there, some disciplines will ask you to share case studies, and others, like data science, will ask you to complete a take-home assignment (sometimes the take-home may come before the hiring manager interview). Assuming your work looks good, you'll advance to a series of short interviews with members of your discipline team as well as folks from the other disciplines you'll be working with.

Laurel and Amelia, you both joined CfA in the last year and a half. Could you talk a little bit about the approaches you took to presenting your wealth of academic experience across the interviewing process?

Laurel You know, I feel like I cheated. I don't necessarily have a lot of advice because this was in some ways the perfect job for me. As I was starting to look for jobs, I went to idealist.org to see what kinds of data science jobs exist in the non-profit world. I wasn't really expecting to immediately apply to anything I saw there, but there was a senior quantitative criminal justice researcher position open at CfA. And I just happened to be a tenure-track professor doing quantitative research on criminal justice issues. It felt like they were looking for me. It was relatively straightforward for me to present my work because CfA was specifically looking for someone in my subject area.

Amelia I had the opposite experience. My research area was civil wars, so when I applied for a position working with social safety net data, I didn't have a huge amount of expertise in that area. In fact, I had more-or-less zero safety net experience. So instead, I focused on some consulting work I had done in the past to demonstrate my ability to pick up new tools really easily. A phrase that I used with Eric, our director of data science, during the final interview phase was that I'm "a curious generalist." Framing myself as somebody who is good at solving problems with numbers, as opposed to somebody who knows a lot about a specific knowledge domain (like conflict studies and civil wars in my case), was key.

Matt You raise such an important point, Amelia. Sometimes folks coming out of Ph.D. programs can spend a lot of interview time talking about the research subject matter area they've become an expert in. And that can be interesting to learn about. But the problem is that they often forget that what we're really interested in learning about is *them*: how they think and approach problems and what they are like to work with. It's good to remember that in industry interviews you need to use your research as a way to talk about yourself.

Kerry, you're typically on the other side of the table during interviews. I was wondering if you could share what types of things you've looked for in the past when you're evaluating a potential new hire.

Kerry One fairly classic mistake I've seen is with research presentations. People are often so familiar with their own material and assume that the audience is going to keep up with all the details of the data. I've seen candidates trying to be as impressive as possible and just flash up some equations and move on, assuming that the audience is going to follow – and instead, they immediately lose everyone. You have to do the opposite in an industrial setting, especially because there could be people on the interview panel who know very little about statistics.

Matt People like me – I have some very basic grounding in statistics, but the moment someone mentions a chi-squared test, I know I'm going to be out of my depth.

Kerry Yes, statistics is not something people outside of data science are interacting with all the time. You can't just reuse your thesis or dissertation defense slides. You have to think about how to explain what you did and why it matters. Generally speaking, during a presentation like that, the audience is not there to grill you on statistics. We're listening to see how well you can communicate your work, which is a very, very different thing.

Matt That is such an important point! Your thesis and dissertation work can be the foundation of a great case study, provided it's presented in a way that resonates with your audience. What I heard you say is that candidates should focus on illustrating why what they are showing is relevant to the position they are interviewing for. When working with folks coming out of anthropology and other qualitative Ph.D. programs, I always remind them that the presentation should be focused on giving your audience insight into the researcher. That's what Amelia did by using her past work to show how she was a "curious generalist who wasn't tied to specific tools." Doing that gave interviewers a strong sense of who she is and the approach she takes to research. Using this approach also helps demonstrate how good a candidate is at communicating with somebody who's not necessarily a data scientist, which is an essential skill in places like CfA where you're often working in cross-disciplinary teams.

Kerry And there's one more thing about presentations to think about: candidates also tend to overestimate the amount of attention that the interview panel is paying to their presentation. As I mentioned, it's common for folks to explain something really important pretty quickly at the beginning, when they're nervous, and miss that the audience might still be on their laptops or distracted by something that just popped up. This is especially true in a remote situation when you never know whether or not someone is looking at another window on their screen. When you start presenting, your audience is often still settling into the presentation, and you can lose people at the beginning very easily and they never catch up – especially if you jump right into technical details. You really have to overfocus on making sure that people understand you because it's otherwise just a waste of everybody's time. Nothing feels worse than trying to explain all this complicated statistical detail when the audience is just completely lost.

It's important to make sure that the audience is with you all the time and keep repeating the main things that you want them to understand. I think this is a fairly standard piece of advice, but it's so important, especially because our instincts often go the opposite way – trying to cram as much stuff as possible into a presentation and avoiding repetition. In fact, following my own advice, to keep repeating yourself, let me say "keep repeating yourself." You can use phrases like "I think this is something important enough that it's worth saying over and over again."

Matt Returning to and emphasizing key points is key! (See, I just did it too!) I know it can feel artificial at times, but it's so helpful for the audience. I also think I heard another great piece of advice in what you said: don't try to pack too much into a presentation or an example. Sometimes it's better to think smaller in terms of the amount of content you are presenting. Don't try to cover something so large that you're going to have to rush through the details and trust that people are going to keep up. Make sure you've got space to breathe and check the audience is with you.

Kerry Yes!

Approaching Take-Home Assignments

Matt Laurel, since you joined CfA, you've transitioned from being interviewed to being the person interviewing others. Given that new perspective, what other advice do you have for people going through the hiring process?

Laurel I feel like the academic candidates we had in our most recent round of hiring have done really well when presenting their work. A different place in the hiring process I've seen people struggle with is the take-home assignment. For example, if there was some kind of major omission in their code or they missed an important step in their analysis.

When I was interviewing, I thought the take-home assignment I was given was relatively straightforward. Of course, it was also focused on criminal justice data, which is something I'm more or less familiar with. What I felt I worked harder on than I normally would with that assignment was commenting. I assumed that reviewers would want to have lots of comments to help them understand what I was doing in my code. Now that I'm a reviewer, that's something I appreciate – I think it gets back to the point about always explaining *why* you are doing something.

Amelia I agree with that. The way you present code can be really important. The assignment is a great place to show that you understand how to do applied research. It's a way to show that you can handle abstraction, write well-commented code, and produce code that can run on somebody else's machine and directory structure. Important stuff like that.

That can be a shift from academic research. In academia, replication often means you share the final data set, with all of the cleaning and transformations already done, and a short .R (or .do or whatever) script that runs your analysis. Scripts are often really short for something straightforward like a regression; most of the work is in data prep! But, if you're working collaboratively in industry, you're sharing in-process work and using collaboration tools, like GitHub (or Mode or any one of several others!), to get feedback on your work. You need to be sure that others can see, run, and understand what you're working on.

But you can tell me whether that's right, Laurel – I know you looked at my take-home assignment during my interview process.

Laurel I did. I think what you are saying is spot on.

Matt I love how both of you are emphasizing that folks should embrace the take-home assignment as another way to help interviewers understand their research approach and process. Commenting is a great way to "show your work." What else should candidates keep in mind when approaching those assignments?

Laurel I love it when people make histograms of everything – I know I do. It's a good idea to always look for outliers. That shows me the person is going beyond an "I'm going to run something and be done" approach. Looking for outliers signals that you're trying to learn something about the data. It shows that you're thinking about the data itself and not just about how you produce the final output that's going to go into the data set in your report.

Amelia That also gets to an important point about not assuming that all the data are good.

Laurel YES! Candidates should remember that employers are often sending "real" data sets. Or rather data sets that are transformations of the type of "raw" data people on the team are dealing with. We're not trying to mess with candidates or trick them by doing that. It's important for us to see what steps they take in approaching that (often messy) data. At CfA, our assignments are often transformed administrative data from different case management systems. So, as part of the assignment, candidates need to show sensitivity to the potential issues that data can create and that they have the skills needed to handle them. That's one area where I think academics can shine because we have a lot of experience thinking about data-generating processes, how data is collected, and what problems you can run into because of that. That contextual knowledge is really valuable and you want to show that you have it.

Amelia Like I mentioned earlier, in the peer review process or in trying to replicate something, I occasionally see an academic data set that kind of looks like it fell out of the sky. If you probe, the author can usually take you through how it was created and what the issues are (or might be). Those details are sometimes glossed over at first in academia, but they really matter a lot in industry – or at least they should. Candidates need to be able to connect those dots in their data-generating processes.

You also need to be able to understand and communicate what could go wrong, in the actual world, if there's a mistake in the data or your analysis. Not just like "Oh no, these standard errors are too narrow," but, at least in CfA's case, "lots of people could ultimately lose access to their benefits." It's a different level of impact and immediacy. That's one of the things that draws me to this work, but it does raise the stakes.

Matt Yes, that is definitely the reality of the work that we do in the social safety net space. I think it's always important to remember that the data that we work with are ultimately people. Admittedly in other industries, the data may not always have such dramatic implications, but they are still very important for the organization you're applying to.

Laurel So summing things up, there are two key things to keep in mind with take-home assignments. First, don't assume the data you're getting are clean and immediately ready to run analysis on. Second, never underestimate the importance of "showing your work" through the use of things like comments.

Other Tips for Interviewing

Matt We've covered a lot of ground. I'm wondering what other advice you all have for people preparing for interviews.

Kerry Behavioral questions are almost always part of the interview process. Questions like "Tell me about a time when you...." had a conflict with a coworker or had something go wrong on a project. You need to be able to describe what happened, how you resolved it, and what you learned from it. Those kinds of questions come up a lot, and it's good to have examples ready to go. This is especially true for those of us who are not great at thinking on our feet (and I put myself in that category). Research examples of these types of questions and think through how you could answer them. If you haven't worked in an industry setting, try to identify any and all collaborative projects that you have worked on in the past. Look for examples of interpersonal stuff that happened during those projects. What were some things that went well? What were some things that went badly? How did working on those projects change the way you'd approach things in the future? Being able to talk about collaboration, using past examples, is a very important part of the interview process.

Amelia This is a weak spot for me. There's often a lot of slack time in academic conversations (even academic interviews), and there's a tolerance for people sharing details or context that might not be immediately relevant. That isn't always the case during industry interviews. It's super important to have a repertoire of succinct examples of things that you've done and how they generalize. Also, it's important to practice sharing those examples. I got better at that as I interviewed for more positions.

Matt I'm so thankful this topic came up – especially for folks applying to roles in the tech industry or larger corporations. When we're interviewing candidates, we are often working from a script and have some specific questions we need to get through during our limited time together. The worst thing that you can hear as an interviewee (and I speak from personal experience here) is "I need you to speed up your answers so I can get through everything on my list." Having those answers prepared ahead of time is critical. And that's also something that a recruiter can help you with. Don't be afraid to ask about what specific questions you should prepare for or whether an organization has a specific framework that they want to hear the answers in. Helping you understand how to answer those questions is part of the recruiter's job.

Laurel Another thing that's important to keep in mind is that nonacademics may not understand the importance of some things you put on your resume. So, for example, if you list grants or awards, you need to be able to explain what those things mean because it's not necessarily intuitive from an outside perspective. It's fine to put them on there because they can help you show how you were successful on big tasks and that, if you are given some other tasks, you'll be successful with those as well. Just be proactive in explaining what they mean.

Amelia Honestly, one of the most important things I did was to ask a friend who transitioned to industry and works with data scientists to review my "first draft" resume. I had my academic positions listed separately and chronologically, but industry doesn't know or care what it means to transition from assistant to associate professor or the importance of particular journals.

Matt Yes. Being able to talk about things like grants gives you a chance to highlight other skills that are important to being successful at your work, not just all the writing and other skills that go into applying for and getting a grant (which are a lot), but also all the project and budget management experience that you get executing the grant.

Advice for People Making the Transition Right Now

Matt We've talked a lot about navigating the hiring process and sharing about your work. I'm wondering if there's any other advice you all have for people who are just at the start of making the transition.

Amelia Based on my experience, it's very difficult to get an industry job with just one coding language. If you're really applying for data science jobs, as opposed to quant research jobs, make sure that you actually know something about SQL and Python. That was my impression from the 50 or so jobs I applied to this summer.

Laurel I think it's really valuable to know that you have lots of job options. It might not immediately feel that way, but there are lots of jobs that you can potentially get and that are worth exploring. And you don't have to have a scarcity mindset. You don't need to settle for a job (even an academic one) that is making you miserable. I think there can be a sense when you're looking at academic jobs that you need to take whatever you are offered because there are usually so few positions open. But with industry, I feel like you can get a job offer, and, if it doesn't feel right, say "no thanks" without burning any bridges. I mean I don't recommend reapplying to that same organization 6 months later, but there are going to be other opportunities in other organizations.

Kerry In that same direction, in academia, it can be easy to get attached to the idea that your work is the core of your identity. It can take a long time to let go of that. And it's a good thing to let go of. It's so important to learn to not be too attached to the idea that you have a particular career trajectory and that's going to be your identity. Holding onto that mindset can lead to you thinking that every job you apply for has got to be the perfect one.

Matt I agree with that 100%! I tell people to treat their first job like a postdoc that pays better. In other words, you're not looking for a job or organization that you will stay with for the rest of your life. You're not trying to get tenure. In fact, in most cases, it's important to switch jobs every few years at the start of your career as you will often get your largest increases in pay when you change organizations.

Amelia I agree! On a slightly different note, one thing that really lightened my mental load in the last several months is knowing that outside of academia, quitting a job is not the same as quitting a career, and making that distinction has been really helpful.

Kerry Yes, it's important to embrace the fact that you're probably going to have a bunch of different jobs across your career. At each step of your career, you are going to make decisions based on what you need at that moment. And you can't possibly know upfront what all those needs are going to be. The factors that you're looking for are going to change over time as you get older. Take Laurel's story – she had a baby and realized she needed to shift careers. That's a change you didn't anticipate upfront?

Laurel Not in the least.

Kerry So, try to let go of being attached to any particular story about your career and where it's "supposed" to go. And I also recognize that that's not easy.

Laurel Yes, I totally agree it can be difficult for people. And it's also true that changing that mindset makes people feel less desperate. It's just a better place to be in your head.

Amelia One thing that can really help start that process is giving yourself permission to apply for every job you're even vaguely qualified for – even ones you don't necessarily want. That gives you space to iterate your approach. More importantly, it's a way for you to lower the stakes. I mean, I feel a little cringe about the first few applications I sent out before I understood what the hell I was doing. But that was a starting point, and it got me used to the process. And that approach is so different from academia! There the process always feels high stakes because there are so few positions, so everything has to be perfect. When you start to make the transition, embrace your power to make everything lower stakes. Seriously, I used to think I was bad at applying for jobs or handling rejection, but it turned out that what I am really bad at is *high-stakes* rejection. Once I realized I could control the stakes by applying for more positions, I realized I was actually pretty good at applying to jobs and handling rejection. This might not work for everyone, but it definitely helped me.

Matt Amelia that brings us to a topic I can't believe we didn't touch on until now: *impostor syndrome*. Let's be blunt here: graduate school is an environment that creates and reinforces imposter syndrome, especially in women, members of minority groups, and folks from other underrepresented communities. And that leads to people underestimating their capabilities and underrating their qualifications. It's so easy to fall into the trap of thinking everyone knows more than you do when the reality is that everyone knows a lot of different things. In any given area, you may have less experience than some people and more than others. The way you put that all together is unique to you and that's really valuable. And it's that unique approach you're going to be bringing to every job you apply for. For those of us who struggle with imposter syndrome – and I include myself, even at this point of my career – this may require a lot of practice, especially when you are having difficulty with the job search. But, if you focus on small steps, you'll hopefully find it easier to talk about all of your skills and talents.

Amelia Exactly! When I talk to young women who are starting their careers, they often have way more skills than they're actually listing on a resume. I know it can be scary, but give yourself permission to apply to all the positions and list all your skills. You'll be surprised at the positive responses you will get.

Wrapping Things Up

Matt We've covered a lot of ground during this conversation. Following Kerry's advice from before about always repeating the important points, here's the advice that really stood out to me:

When presenting past work,

- Make sure you are taking the time to relate the project and the approach you took to the job you are applying to.
- Repeat important points and make sure your audience is following your explanation of what you did. And be prepared to not always have your audience's full attention.
- Remember that your audience may include people who are not data scientists, so be sure you are able to explain your work on multiple levels.

With take-home assignments,

- Don't assume the data you are given is ready to go. You may be working with transformed "real" data and need to take time to check it for implausible values, outliers, or other issues.
- Use comments in your code to help reviewers understand the steps you took in processing your data.
- Demonstrate that you are able to write clean, portable, reproducible code. Think about file structure, abstraction, dependencies, and so on – and write accordingly.

During interviews,

- Think about the behavioral ("tell me about a time when you…") questions you could be asked ahead of time and have some answers ready.
- Interviewers often have a certain number of questions that they need to get through during an interview. The more you can help them by being prepared for that, the better off you are.
- Be prepared to explain more academic aspects of your resume to people who may not have much context or experience with them.
- When in doubt, you can always ask questions about an organization's interview process with people from their recruiting team.

Beyond all of that, embrace the idea that your career is going to be more than any one job and that there are a lot of opportunities out there for people with a data science background. As Kerry mentioned, you don't need to have your career path figured out right now. And to Amelia's point, you can also make this entire process lower stakes by applying for every job you can. That will help you get a lot of practice and revise your materials. Equally important, as Laurel mentioned, if you get a job offer that you don't feel is right for you, it's okay to say "no" and keep looking.

Finally, remember that your first job out of academia is exactly that: your first job out of academia. It doesn't define the rest of your career. The more you can take that pressure off yourself, the smoother your transition can be.

Does anyone have anything else to add?

Amelia *When in doubt, JUST ASK!* In academia, we often "play defense," in the sense of hoarding data, information, and even our questions and concerns, because we've been led to believe that only perfect candidates get jobs. That's somewhat counterproductive even in academia, but in other jobs, it's *really* counterproductive.

You want to show your future colleagues that you don't have to be the smartest in the room, that you're creative and collegial as well as smart and diligent. In that spirit, asking for help early in your process is key. Many organizations have referral bonuses, so people are usually happy to talk. More importantly, as you saw above, people who have made this transition are generally open to paying it forward. Ask for help and feedback early and often. Keep iterating. You've got this.

Matt Yes! Ask people, even those you haven't met, for help. It's normal for early-career people to reach out to folks further along to learn more about the work they do or just the field in general. A lot of us build time into our weekly schedules for those conversations.

Good luck to everyone who reads this in whatever the next step of your career is! Be kind to yourselves. The process of finding your first job can take a while and a lot of trial and error. Change is often difficult and scary. And as we've all shared, transitioning out of academia is very possible and can be very rewarding. We know you can do it.

Thriving in a Nonacademic Environment

Susan Navarro Smelcer and Meredith Whiteman Ross

You've done it. You figured out how to market yourself to private industry and you landed a great nonacademic job. Now what? Throughout your graduate career, you've worked hard to develop subject-matter expertise that you may or may not use, and your professional training has been focused on developing and contributing to that body of knowledge. In this chapter, we hope to provide some guidance on how to adapt those finely honed writing, research design, and analytical skills to your new corporate, government, or nonprofit environment.

Graduate school does not explicitly train you to work in the corporate environment, which is often collaborative and team based. You may find yourself feeling a bit at sea in the corporate world—both in terms of developing a new subject-matter expertise and needing to adapt your work habits to a new, collaborative environment.

Our goal in this chapter is to help you orient yourself in your new, nonacademic landscape. We have both been where you are now, and this chapter is, in part, a reflection on our experiences and what we wish we had known. Together, we have worked in a variety of roles outside academia—nonprofits, corporations, law firms, and government agencies. While corporate cultures differ, nonacademic environments tend to present similar challenges to the newly minted Ph.D.

First, you are likely to have gaps in your substantive knowledge of your company or industry—even if you bring expertise in writing, research design, or analysis. This is an uncomfortable spot, especially after spending so much time and energy becoming an expert in Supreme Court decision-making, international human rights

S. N. Smelcer (✉)
Wake Forest University, Winston-Salem, NC, USA
e-mail: smelcers@wfu.edu

M. W. Ross
Charter Schools USA, Fort Lauderdale, FL, USA
e-mail: mross@charterschoolsusa.com

© The Author(s), under exclusive license to Springer Nature
Switzerland AG 2023
N. Jackson (ed.), *Non-Academic Careers for Quantitative Social Scientists*,
Texts in Quantitative Political Analysis,
https://doi.org/10.1007/978-3-031-35036-8_19

organizations, or state and local policy making institutions. You will develop the necessary substantive expertise over time—and you can help increase your credibility at work by proactively seeking out that knowledge from your colleagues.

Second, your analytical and technical toolkit may be different than your colleagues. Perhaps you are one of many social scientists in your organization. But most likely you are not. As a result, knowing your audience is an important aspect to successfully communicating your work. Assumptions or conclusions that may be obvious to you may be totally opaque to your colleagues who are trained in different disciplines and vice versa.

Finally, working with data in private industry can bring with it unfamiliar ethical considerations. The diversity of technical skills on your team or within your company requires you to be doubly transparent about your assumptions and careful about how you use the data available to you. While these considerations shouldn't be totally foreign, your organization may be covered by federal statutes or regulations governing data use or otherwise constrained by professional rules or contractual obligations, such as nondisclosure agreements.

Throughout this chapter, we cover each of these challenges in turn. Our advice is general by necessity but drawn from our own experience about what we wish we would have known when starting our first nonacademic jobs.

Gap Between Substantive Knowledge and Quantitative Skills

Fortunately, many of the skills and strategies learned in the initial years of graduate work—reviewing the existing literature, developing questions, operationalizing measures, communicating results, and responding to reviewers' concerns—are transferrable to successful analytical work outside of academia. Think of these transferable skills as a toolbox. Whether you are using your tools to investigate citizens' attitudes about the legitimacy of international institutions or the relative performance of your company's product in the marketplace, a similar set of "tools" and processes will get the job done. In place of a traditional literature review, however, you may meet with relevant department contacts to get their perspective on the history of a problem, previous challenges, prior solutions, or how the state of the world may have changed since the problem was last addressed. Going into these meetings, you may already know the questions you were tasked to answer. But, more often than not, new questions or hypotheses arise. From these meetings, with the support of your team and the collaborating department(s), you define or refine the research questions at hand. Inventorying existing data and the inevitable tasks of collecting and operationalizing new metrics are still features of the nonacademic landscape.

Developing content knowledge and capturing the historical context of your industry and company are critical to your success. But when you enter a new industry, you might find yourself in the uncomfortable position of lacking domain-specific or qualitative knowledge of your market or field—knowledge that your new coworkers and teammates may have in spades. Your job will often be to translate your coworkers' qualitative knowledge and subject-matter expertise into well-formed quantitative hypotheses that can be rigorously tested. Your value-add comes from building off their foundational knowledge. Your own content knowledge will come with time and next we offer strategies that will aid you along the way.

One way to start building domain knowledge is by talking to the experts—your colleagues. In addition to project-specific discussions, consider setting up a regular communication schedule for non-project-related discussions. Pick their brains. Ask them about prior projects and outcomes. Sometimes these opportunities are formalized through substantive presentations or seminars highlighting a team's work, task forces, or committees to understand common issues that occur across units or other types of non-project-related meetings. Each industry calls them something different. But these groups and experiences are essentially learning communities that encourage growth and collaboration across departments and provide opportunities for staff to work toward solving common problems. For example, if you work somewhere with many divisions, say regional locations, and there are people holding similar positions (your position) in each of those divisions, it may be beneficial for regional team members to collaborate regularly. In a learning community, the group can solve problems together by bringing their range of experiences to the table. You, as the newest team member, will benefit from not only their knowledge of the requirements of the position but also their institutional knowledge.

You can also set up information-gathering meetings with team members who you work with regularly. These do not have to be project-related but should be on topics that provide insight into their work and responsibilities, especially in areas where you could provide support. Purposefully set aside time to listen to and learn from those coworkers with the content expertise to develop your own. Potential topics for these types of sessions could include:

1. "A year in the life"—if their work is cyclical, what are some of the reoccurring projects they tackle and high-level tasks involved?
2. Walk through an "after action" exercise with them, what was the last off-cycle project, was it executed effectively, and did they reach the intended outcome?
3. Review the project plan of an upcoming project—what assumptions will they make, what departments do they consult, and what is the timeline for completion, follow-up, and program evaluation? Of course, if appropriate and permissible in your role, offer your support where you can.

If applicable and whenever possible, go into the field to see your data or analyses in action. Putting faces, products, or processes to a name will elevate your work and bring you closer to the end user's perspective. The understanding garnered from practical experiences cannot be quantified. As district-level staff in K-12 education, I (Ross) love getting out of my office and walking the halls of a school building. This exercise not only puts names and faces to the dots on my screen, but it is a visual representation of how my work matters to the teachers and students I serve. Connecting your work product to first-hand end-user experiences provides immense value for your stakeholders. Never underestimate the knowledge that can be gained from simply being a fly on the wall for requirement gathering, hypothesis generating, or brainstorming sessions.

If you find yourself in an industry unrelated to your area of graduate study, do your due diligence. Does your industry have any professional organizations to join? Is there a research community affiliated with your work? Do any of the platforms and services your company or institution utilizes offer professional development or host conferences? These are all opportunities to hone your skills and do so in the "language" of your industry. And, just like in academia, these organizations and conferences provide the opportunity to network, share ideas, and give back.

These suggestions may be more or less relevant depending on your particular workload. Do you have or are you developing a specialty within your company, or are you part of a business intelligence team that supports a range of projects involving multiple business units across the company? If the former, investigations such as those described above would serve to put your work in context compared to other departments and teams. If the latter, getting a well-rounded understanding of various departments' priorities and project cycles will impact your ability to meet their needs and prioritize your work. You will be better equipped to have (sometimes difficult) conversations with units across your organization about what they *should* know—not just what they want to know. This foundational knowledge about your company and industry will be vital as you use your research design and analytical skills to support your colleagues.

Knowing the context of your work—and your role—within the larger ecosystem is an important element to knowing your audience. Acquainting yourself with the company's history of successes as well as their challenges and the end results in those trying times will be time well spent. The value of contextualizing your role relative to the current state and the desired state cannot be underestimated. Knowing where your audience has been and where they want to go will allow you to make connections in your own work, activating prior knowledge and adding a layer of credibility to your work.

Know Your Audience

Your job as analyst does not stop with your analysis; you are also the communicator. As a specialist, you and your team will likely have the responsibility of explaining and telling the story of your work beyond the boundaries of your team. Complicating matters for you, the storyteller, is the fact that your audience doesn't necessarily speak the social science or statistical jargon and shorthand you may be accustomed to. Your communication should be a balance of grounding new information in what they know and packaging it in a way they will understand and value. Using the tools described above, you should know something of your audience going into a presentation or delivering a memo or white paper. Depending on the formality of the situation and your relationship with your audience, the strategies below will make communicating quantitative results more palatable to a nonquantitative group.

Activate Prior Knowledge

Learning and knowledge acquisition increases when people can incorporate new information into their existing narrative or breadth of knowledge (Marzano 2004). Education research tells us that if you can make connections for your audience between what they know and what you are attempting to communicate, the odds that they will retain this information increases. In a classroom, when a teacher introduces a new topic, they will activate students' prior knowledge by asking probing questions, facilitating a brainstorming session, or using a "hook" such as an anecdote, demonstration, or video clip, which can provide some levity and an element of humor to the presentation.

In a boardroom, you may begin by providing the context for your work, the history of the problem, or essential questions your study was attempting to answer. To simplify statistical concepts, use examples from the real world or pop culture. For example, hurricane modeling and political polling can come in handy to explain confidence intervals and the uncertainty of estimations. Even those that live outside of the "danger zone" that is hurricane season are likely familiar with the dreaded "cone," or path of expected impact whose area widens as you move out from the storm's current position. The layman understands that the farther out we are trying to predict, the more uncertain we are of the area to be impacted. I have found this a great example to conceptualize confidence intervals and the likelihood of your results coming to fruition. I also use the margin of error in political polling as an example of quantifying how comfortable we should be with our results or how much our predictions could differ from the actual result in real time.

Sometimes less is more—and this will be a hard one. Time will usually be limited, either in a presentation format or the executive summary of a memo. You can liken your "pitch" in these situations to those you honed for your dissertation or thesis. You need a 45-min version for a job talk or conference presentation, a 15-minute version for a panel, maybe a 5-minute party or poster version, and a 1-minute elevator pitch. Count yourself lucky if you get an hour of time to review your findings. More often than not, you only have a 15-to-20-minute stretch, with time for Q & A, to explain potentially complex findings.

This seemingly short period of time represents the point at which the average adult's attention begins to wane (Cooper and Richards 2017; Jeffries 2014). It is not a coincidence that TED talks can be no longer than 18 min; they take advantage of the optimal chunk of time for retention (Rehn 2016). This means that your presentation needs to be clear, concise, and purposeful to efficiently communicate your results. Research in educational psychology has found that adults have capacity limits on the amount of information that can be retained in working memory—that is, the component of memory that is "extensively involved in goal-directed behaviors in which information must be retained and manipulated to ensure successful task execution" (Chai, et al. 2018). In general, adults will only be able to retain 4 ± 1 pieces of novel information at a time (Pass and Ayres 2014). Help your audience along and make sure they walk away with up to three to five "nuggets" or takeaways from your findings.

Simplify Versus Teach

There will come a time when you will be faced with the dilemma of providing sim-
plified content with less depth than you feel is warranted or spending the extra time
teaching your audience to get to more informed discussions. Incremental teaching
and learning builds capacity over time. Investing in this approach will not only
allow you to tackle more nuanced discussions, refined hypotheses, and research
questions, but it will also build your audience's trust in your findings. This trade-off
will become more obvious with time, but it's a challenging call to make—especially
as a new employee.

Consider this example from my (Ross') own work in quantifying student "success," traditionally measured in K-12 education by student proficiency on assessments. Just about every public-school student in America is required to sit for state
assessments annually beginning in third grade, continuing through high school
graduation. The proficiency rates of students, schools, and larger entities such as
school districts and states—calculated as the proportion of students achieving at a
predetermined level each year and from year to year—are informative. But proficiency alone does not complete the story. A significant number of students nation-
wide at any one time are performing below grade level or below what their state
would deem proficient. Many are multiple grade levels behind. As a result, many
states have also begun to incorporate measures of individual student growth. The
combination of achievement and growth measures holds schools accountable to not
only making sure students are performing at grade level but also to moving those
students who are behind toward grade level in a reasonable amount of time.

Explaining the importance and impact of individual student growth measures—
used in combination with proficiency scores—became a teachable moment. I spent
5–10 additional minutes walking through the proper interpretation of a plot with
four quadrants and a double axis. We have been able to build off the initial analysis
by adding layers such as student subgroups or special population status (special
education, English language learners) and swapping out axis variables to display
growth relative to a school's percent of students who are economically disadvantaged. This one extra step of explanation raised the level of analytical conversation
and is still paying dividends years later.

Feedback and Follow-Up

As an expert in social science methodology, your audience will inevitably have
questions for you—whether spoken aloud or not—that will require clarification.
Build in points of reflection and checks for understanding for your audience. If your
presentation takes the form of a white paper or executive memo, be sure to include
your contact information and a note explaining how the reader can provide feedback
or direct questions to the author. If you are presenting live (whether virtually or

in-person), be purposeful about where in the presentation you pause for questions. Be receptive to—and expect!—questions to come up in real time, be receptive to feedback, and make yourself available to field questions at a later point. If you are building dashboards and reports for your organization, provide a mechanism for the end user to provide feedback in real time while they are interacting with the deliverable. You could also include an open survey link on your email signature, which can act as a virtual suggestion box (of sorts).

At the end of the day, however, you must also *act* on your feedback. If you make a revision in response to a client's feedback or suggestion, be sure to highlight that update and its source in your next communication. This visible collaboration with your end user will only improve the quality of your product, and the efficacy gains on their end will perpetuate a continued open dialogue.

Existing Style Guides and Industry Norms

It sounds simple, but you will be better able to communicate your work if you carefully conform to company or industry norms and style guides. Familiar style elements, such as consistent color coding, citation scheme, or use of headings, offer a mental shortcut to the end user. In some cases, failing to follow style guides may actually lead your colleagues to misinterpret your work or tell a completely different story than you intended. A colleague tells the story of compiling a report as part of their work as a defense contractor. They constructed charts, drafted a narrative, and submitted their report to the appropriate military liaison. They did not realize, however, that the military had a norm governing which colors should be used for specific categories of troops, civilians, and combatants. Unknowingly, my colleague had used a red trend line to represent the popular opinion of US forces in Afghanistan, when traditionally red was reserved for the Taliban. If you find that your company or institution does not have a style guide, begin cultivating your own and be consistent with it. The familiarity fostered by regular interactions with the same colors, layouts, or icons will be one less thing you need to "teach" to your audience—saving you and them processing time.

Build Trust

Gaining and keeping your audience's trust is of the utmost importance. The strategies discussed in this chapter will help you not only build their confidence in your abilities but also their trust in your results. Some of the "greatest hits" around statistics and analysis do not help our cause: "You can make the data say anything," "98% of statistics are made up," and, my personal favorite, "Statistics are like bikinis. What they reveal is suggestive, but what they conceal is vital" (McGrath 2017, quoting Aaron Levenstein). There are even books that highlight all the ways manipulation is possible with titles that capitalize on these criticisms (e.g., Jones 2018; Huff 1993). The books themselves offer ways to avoid the pitfalls of common tropes and detail strategies to mitigate the chance of unintentionally misleading your audience. But being proactive and setting boundaries from the start will also dispel these perceptions. Be prepared for every meeting or deliverable, but do not answer questions to which you don't know the answers. Take down questions and answer them once you can confirm. You gain respect with your honesty and credibility in your follow-through.

Ethics of Data Analysis

You are unlikely to be the primary decision-maker in your organization—especially if this is your first job in private industry. But your work will likely be used to make decisions and drive changes in your organization. Unlike academia, which can be a solitary experience, you are unlikely to be a solitary researcher. Working on a team will require a good deal of humility, transparency, and communication. In this section, we provide some guideposts for ethical analysis of data in nonacademic settings—including specific applications that may require additional legal or institutional guidance.

The Importance of Humility, Transparency, and Communication

Humility might seem like an odd concept to discuss here—but it has everything to do with ethical data analysis in the corporate setting. Fundamentally, humility is about acknowledging that you may not be correct in your assumptions or that your analysis has serious limitations. You may be asked to prepare an analysis to brief a supervisor or colleague on an issue before an important discussion or meeting. You do your colleague a disservice—and misrepresent the data—if you do not explicitly disclose assumptions or unintentionally overgeneralize your findings by failing to note important shortcomings in the analysis. As a practicing attorney and trained social scientist at a law firm, I (Smelcer) was occasionally asked to perform statistical analyses using client data to help a partner prepare for discussions with expert witnesses. On one occasion, I remember writing a three-page memo detailing my analysis—with two of the three pages explaining its limitations.

In this way, humility is the progenitor of methodological transparency and good communication. While you may not be the domain expert on your team, you may be the research design or methodological expert. Research design choices that may be obvious to you based on your training may be foreign to other members of your team. It is your responsibility—both as a social scientist and colleague—to make sure that your team understands your choices and the limits of your analysis.

But how can you accomplish this? In most cases, thinking of yourself as an unbiased, outside observer will go a long way—but you can follow a few guiding principles to help make sure that your team is as prepared as possible. Lessons that you learned about data transparency in graduate school are doubly important here. You will likely not be the subject-matter expert, so you will need to be transparent about both your data sources and assumptions for your team—however comprised—to be confident in your results.

First, make sure that the goal of the project is clear—both to your team and yourself. What are you trying to achieve? This is not always obvious, and you may be serving multiple constituencies with conflicting goals. You can avoid this by being explicit with your supervisor(s) and team about the intended outcomes and use cases. Will your analysis be the basis of your firm's client outreach strategy? Or will your data be used internally to determine whether a certain marketing campaign was successful? Who will ultimately be receiving or relying on this analysis? These are all questions that should be asked at the beginning—not the end—of an assignment. Clearly defining the problem(s), goals, and audience ahead of time are the biggest timesavers when completing projects. When not done effectively, you may find yourself cycling through additional analyses due to a lack of a common understanding from the start.

Second, ensure that the scope of your data or analysis matches the project goal. This should be a familiar concept as a social scientist. In our graduate programs, warnings against overgeneralization were given early and often. The same is true in the nonacademic settings—though, now, you are the keeper of this discretion. When I (Smelcer) worked for a congressional agency, I was tasked with analyzing Congress' treatment of federal judicial nominations over time. Inevitably, my audience—usually congressional staff—wanted to use this information to generalize about how current congressional behavior did or did not conform to historical practice or norms. While I couldn't change *how* my audience used the data, I could be transparent about the scope and nature of the data I used.

Third, outline a timeline for your analysis and share it with your team or audience. Account for how long each step will take in the process, and include space to engage in a discussion of the hypothesis or research question prior to starting the analysis. Finally, always build in time to discuss preliminary findings with your team and adjust the analysis based on initial feedback. You improve your analysis (and protect your own credibility) by being transparent and communicative about the research process. There may be times when you will miss a deadline—but you must communicate with your teammates that you are going to miss it. If the deadline is not flexible, you may need to adjust your project plan or deliverable in response. Essentially, this boils down to communicating your time management plan and *involving your team in that planning!*

Finally, when providing or presenting your results, you have an ethical obligation to present your findings in an unbiased manner. You may think this is obvious—or possibly even borderline offensive that we are even mentioning this. But you can unwittingly create bias or misunderstandings in a multidisciplinary team when you fail to—wait for it—be transparent about your assumptions and methods. Moreover, in a multidisciplinary team, your colleagues may not fully understand what conclusions to draw from a particular result. It is your job to arm your team with sufficient information so that they can make well-informed decisions. And as a well-trained social scientist, you have an obligation to make clear the limitations on scope and generalizability inherent in your study.

A Note on Data Privacy Issues in Nonacademic Settings

Ethical data practices go beyond data and analytical transparency in nonacademic settings, however. Regardless of whether you are in a nonprofit or corporate environment, odds are good that you'll be working with proprietary data or data that are otherwise covered by a patchwork of state, national, and international data privacy regulations.

At the national level, data privacy is governed by a variety of general and domain-specific statutes and regulations. For example, the Federal Trade Commission (FTC) enforces Section 5 of its authorizing statute (the FTC Act), which outlaws "unfair or deceptive acts or practices in or affecting commerce." The FTC has interpreted this category to include a firm's failure to abide by its own published data privacy policies. Financial institutions, such as banks, must comply with regulations implementing the Gramm-Leach-Bliley Act's (GLBA) protection of nonpublic personally identifying information (PII). If your firm is associated with or performing services for a health plan, healthcare provider, or health data clearinghouse, the use of any data with PII may be subject to the Health Insurance Portability and Accountability Act (HIPAA). Data analysis for an educational institution involving student information and academic performance is subject to the Family Educational Rights and Privacy Act (FERPA). Note the absence of federal general data privacy legislation—an omission that makes the regulatory landscape all the more confusing.

States have enacted a variety of laws both mirroring and extending federal laws prohibiting unfair business practices and protecting PII. These laws include "baby FTC Acts" and consumer protection statutes that allow states to enforce unfair and deceptive consumer practices at the state level. In addition, some states have extended GLBA and HIPAA protections through "add-on" laws and regulations. In the absence of federal legislation, several states—most notably, Massachusetts and California—have enacted their own overarching general data privacy laws. These laws generally apply to a company's use of state residents' and employees' PII, even if that company is not located within that state.

Companies operating internationally may be covered by the European Union's (EU) General Data Protection Regulation (GDPR)—even if not explicitly operating in the EU! The GDPR is complex and covers a variety of firms that control, process, or otherwise act as an intermediary for protected data subjects' personal information. This regulation also controls how long PII can be stored, the methods by which it can be processed, and the legitimate purposes for which it may be used.

Data use may be governed by professional ethical standards or contractual agreements. Law firms or legal technology companies, for example, may be bound not only by attorney-client privilege but also any nondisclosure agreements, data sharing agreements, or terms of their engagement letter. This may prevent analysts and developers from not only using PII but also other, more aggregated forms of clients' data.

In each case—and others not mentioned here—it is important to connect with your organization's counsel about whether and how you can use client information in your analyses and application development. The regulatory landscape is confusing and complicated. Checking in with counsel both before starting a project with new data and extending existing analyses or applications can ensure that your work can be used to its fullest—and will help you avoid some headaches when you are trying to roll out products or services.

Conclusion

Moving from academia to private industry can be intimidating. In graduate school, we tend to learn how to do—and experience—research primarily as a solitary activity. Collaborative and team-based corporate environments turn that understanding on its head and will challenge your training. Open communication is crucial at every stage of a research project. But your success will rest largely on your ability to adapt your knowledge and expertise to a new ecosystem. This may mean starting from a place of relative ignorance about the industry or company in which you now find yourself, building your knowledge base over time, and gaining the trust of your peers. Communication, transparency, and a dose of humility will be important as you navigate your new environment. Our hope is that this chapter provides you with practical advice on figuring out what you *don't* know, how to build your capacity over time, and communicating what you *do* know. Remember, even if you feel discomfort from being (perhaps) a beginner all over again, you were hired for a reason. Armed with your methodological toolbox, you are more than capable of developing the additional skills and background knowledge you need to thrive in this new nonacademic environment.

References

Chai, Wen Jia, Aini Ismafarius Abd Hamid, and Jafri Malin Abdullah. 2018. "Working Memory from the Psychological and Neurosciences Perspectives: A Review." Frontiers in Psychology 9. https://www.frontiersin.org/article/10.3389/fpsyg.2018.00401

Cooper, Avraham Z., and Jeremy B. Richards. 2017. "Lectures for Adult Learners: Breaking Old Habits in Graduate Medical Education." AIMM Perspectives 130(3): 376–381.

Huff, Darrell. 1993. How to Lie with Statistics.

Jeffries, William B. 2014. Teaching Large Groups. In An Introduction to Medical Teaching. Eds. Kathryn N. Huggett & William B. Jeffries. Dordrecht: Springer Netherlands, pp. 11–26.

Jones, Gerald Everett. 2018. How to Lie with Charts. (4th ed.)

Marzano, Robert J. 2004. Building Background Knowledge for academic Achievement: Research on What Works in Schools. Alexandria, VA: Association for Supervision and Curriculum Development (ASCD).

McGrath, James. 2017. The Little Book of "Big" Management Wisdom: 90 Important Quotes and How to Use Them in Business. Pearson Business.

Pass, Fred, and Paul Ayres. 2014. "Cognitive Load Theory: A Broader View on the Role of Memory in Learning and Education." Educational Psychology Review 26(2): 191–195.

Rehn, Alf. 2016. "The 20-Minute Rule for Great Public Speaking—On Attention Spans and Keeping Focus." The Art of Keynoting (Medium blog), April 11. https://medium.com/the-art-of-keynoting/the-20-minute-rule-for-great-public-speaking-on-attention-spans-and-keeping-focus-7370cf06b636.

You Got Your First Job, What About Your Second? Conversations with Women Social Scientists on Landing Multiple Nonacademic Jobs

Mackenzie Price and Catasha Davis

By 2019, women out-paced men in the number of PhDs and master's degrees obtained across a number of academic fields. According to the American Enterprise Institute, women earned more master's and PhDs in 11 consecutive academic years between 2008 and 2019.[1] In the social and behavioral sciences, women earned 61% of the PhDs and approximately 64% of master's degrees in comparison to men at 39% and 36%, respectively.[2] Data also suggest that women show a disproportionate interest in careers outside of academia.[3] Women report wanting to leave academia for a host of reasons including considering academic careers to be undesirable (e.g., due to funding issues and high levels of competition) and finding the level of sacrifice to be too high (i.e., sacrificing family). With more women earning advanced degrees and moving into careers outside of academia, women must learn to expertly navigate the nonacademic job market.

---

[1] See American Enterprise Institute https://www.aei.org/carpe-diem/women-earned-majority-of-doctoral-degrees-in-2019-for-11th-straight-year-and-outnumber-men-in-grad-school-141-to-100/#:~:text=Women%20have%20now%20earned%20a,high%20first%20set%20in%202017. Last Accessed May 20, 2021.

[2] Ibid.

[3] The Guardian. (2012). Why women leave academia and why universities should be worried. Accessed from: https://www.theguardian.com/higher-education-network/blog/2012/may/24/why-women-leave-academia

---

M. Price (✉)
Ask MP, LLC, Washington, DC, USA

C. Davis
Parenthetic LLC, Arlington, VA, USA

© The Author(s), under exclusive license to Springer Nature Switzerland AG 2023
N. Jackson (ed.), *Non-Academic Careers for Quantitative Social Scientists*,
Texts in Quantitative Political Analysis,
https://doi.org/10.1007/978-3-031-35036-8_20

191

In academia, it is possible to spend an entire career – or at least many years – at one college or university. In contrast, careers outside of academia may require individuals to move around. The Bureau of Labor Statistics (2020) reports that the median tenure for an employee with a master's degree is 5 years – almost as long as the typical doctoral program and not enough time to save for retirement or pay off student loans. Thus, the nonacademic job market requires a mindset and knowledge base largely absent from academia. It is not simply about finding, interviewing, and securing the coveted tenure-track position. In other sectors, you are going to need to find more than one role. How can you find what you're looking for not once, but over and over?

Navigating between the public and private sectors and the various career opportunities requires knowledge and support. In this chapter, we ask women with master's and doctoral degrees across the social and behavioral sciences about their approach to career transitions. Their advice will help guide others attempting to transition between positions outside of academia.

Method

We wanted women who have made multiple transitions to guide the advice given to others. We sent a questionnaire to women who hold PhDs and master's degrees in the social and behavioral sciences. All of the women currently work outside of academia across nonprofit, public, and private sectors.

The women in the sample were recruited through a convenience sampling strategy. Both authors have social science PhDs and work in the private sector. Both have held multiple nonacademic positions and are connected with many other women working outside of academia. The authors used their connections to send out surveys to those willing to participate.

Questions in the instrument range from general background to questions about initially leaving academia and advice about transitioning between roles.

Sample Characteristics

We surveyed 13 social scientists who completed graduate programs and, at some point in their careers, took nonacademic jobs. Ten respondents hold doctorates, and three hold master's degrees. Most (~70%) identify as social scientists, and almost half have had over four post-PhD positions. Approximately 80% have had two or more positions outside of academia. At the time of the survey, the women in the sample had been out of academia between 1 and 10 years. About 69% were working in the private sector at for-profit organizations, with the remaining respondents divided between the public sector (one respondent), nonprofit sector (two respondents), and a think tank (one respondent). Thus, the women we spoke to have a multitude of private and public experiences, which make them valuable sources of career transition advice.

This chapter will discuss what drove these women to leave academia and what they have learned about moving from their first private sector position to their second, third, and beyond. Across the sections, we share the advice the women extend to others looking to transition in their private sector careers.

Walking Out of the Tower

The initial decision to look for employment outside of an academic institution is often to search for a different type of culture. Graduate school is a significant investment in time and other resources, and the experience is also a socializing one in which students develop an identity, knowledge, skills, professional associations, and exposure to the expectations of a profession.[4] The women in our sample made a critical decision to avoid adapting to and adopting the culture of academia. Looking for an entirely different culture was the unifying factor that drove their decision to initially look for jobs in other sectors and continue to find jobs and opportunities outside of academia.

Some of the women we spoke with made the initial decision to change sectors as an outright rejection of academia and its culture. Specific drivers of their first non-academic job search included looking for different compensation structures, wanting to focus on different kinds of projects and deliverables (i.e., less writing), and wanting to see their research used differently. One PhD in their first private sector position told us, "I wanted better pay and more fulfilling work." Another respondent who is building a career in the public sector shared, "The thought of seeking tenure was daunting; I wanted a dependable schedule with freedoms and not always worrying about publications." A PhD in their fourth role in the private sector reported, "I didn't like the culture of academia." Another respondent echoed the point of misalignment with the sectors' culture and pointed out that they were unwilling to live within the culture to have a career, "I didn't feel like I valued academia enough to put up with the competition and instability."

At least two respondents never intended to take a job in an academic setting. "I was always focused on application," reports a respondent with four nonacademic roles on their resume. Others realized that they would need to look outside of the academy to find the kind of jobs and the type of work-life they wanted. Another respondent told us, "I wanted my work to be connected to real-world impact, and that wasn't valued in my community." As one informant in the nonprofit sector reported, "Getting out of academia seemed like the only way I could have a career." Another social scientist who left the private sector to complete their doctorate and

---

[4] Liddell, Debora L.; Wilson, Maureen E.; Pasquesi, Kira; Hirschy, Amy S.; and Boyle, Kathleen M., "Development of Professional Identity Through Socialization in Graduate School" (2014). Higher Education and Student Affairs Faculty Publications. 12.

then returned to the private sector after graduate school shared, "[I had a] desire to have a more lucrative career to be able to create a better future for my children."

Change Jobs, Change Culture

But the story does not end with the first job. As fulfilling as it can be to set the goal to change sectors and walk out of academia, entering a new environment is challenging. Every industry has its own practices, values, expectations, and systemic issues. Those elements of a sector's culture can be the catalyst for more career change. "I realized very quickly that that place was not for me," shared a PhD reflecting on her first nonacademic role. She enjoyed using her skills to solve complex problems, but there were limits to how much she could learn and grow within the organization. She began actively planning to change jobs within the private sector as a result. Respondents in our sample all realized that even though they had left academia and wanted to stay outside of academia, having a career meant making multiple moves. As their careers progress, they continue to assess how the culture of the spaces they enter serves their interests, aligns with their goals, and speaks to their values. They build careers by interrogating their needs alongside the frustrations, shortcomings, and limitations of nonacademic roles.

Ultimately social scientists outside of academia must normalize moving between roles and reading the indicators of when it is time to transition. The women we queried acknowledge that you may not leave the culture even if you leave academia behind. Pieces of academia's culture can be recreated and referenced in different work environments, particularly in spaces that recruit large numbers of former academics.

Our respondents are clear that culture matters to them as they navigate the nonacademic job market. Not all positions and all organizations can measure up to what job seekers are looking for. A PhD doing research in the private sector told us, "I liked the idea of solving research problems pragmatically [but] non-academic jobs aren't perfect, and they have their own frustrations." For our respondents, transitions start with looking for a culture fit. As one social scientist described her decision to change jobs, "[I] was at a for-profit institution that was non-values consistent for me." In the words of a PhD employed by a think tank, "I don't want to join an organization whose values I don't share or an organization that seems to have no mechanism for discussing or mediating any lapses in their values."

Culture fit is reciprocal; organizations want to know if job seekers will do well within their organizational culture, and social scientists in transition also have to consider what makes a culture fit for them. Our respondents emphasize looking for clues about what you might take away or sacrifice in a given position in some of the same conversations they have with potential employers about their skills and ambitions. This process helped them leave academia and negotiate their subsequent transitions.

Transition Advice from Our Respondents

> Even though this is difficult to assess during one or two interviews, I try to be extra attentive to how people react to questions about org culture. – Private sector MA, four roles outside of academia

> Be mindful of what you want to learn. – Private sector PhD, four roles outside of academia

> Learn your non-negotiables. – Private sector PhD, two roles outside of academia

> Don't be afraid to take a leap of faith and try a position that is different from what you imagined. You don't have to work somewhere forever, there's plenty of time to move around and figure out what you like. – Private sector MA, three roles outside of academia

> Really make sure the place you are going to is stable. – Public sector PhD, four roles outside of academia

Clearly, culture is a catalyst for transitions. The transition from academia to other sectors is driven by the experience of culture. The transition from a first nonacademic job to the next role is inspired by culture and includes a revaluation process that repeats with each transition. But as you learn more about sectors and organizations, how do you actually get into the roles you want? In the next section, we share the critical steps to making repeated transitions that our respondents shared with us.

Network, Network, Network

Paying attention to and building a network is a familiar refrain for job seekers. The women in our sample talked about how networking can facilitate transitions in some cases and works as a barrier in others. Connections become a barrier when the people you are connected with have a very narrow network themselves. "I realized my advisor and my [dissertation] committee couldn't help me at a certain point. They didn't know anyone who wasn't on their same path." That realization, from a PhD in the private sector, inspired her to rethink who she needed to connect with and build a network more reflective of her long-term career goals.

Building a network is an active process. Making a connection can be reaching out for informational interviews, contacting people whose work interests you, or talking to alumni, graduates, or other peers about their work experiences. "You have to proactively gain connections" to expand your network, as a PhD with three roles outside of academia reminded us. Networking is not calling someone and saying, "I need a job." Our respondents described networking as asking questions, listening to people's stories, and sharing their own stories or information with people. Networking facilitates transitions by helping find people who have had the role you want in the past, who have insight into the culture of other organizations, or who even find out about new roles and opportunities before they are publicized.

Networking conversations, like informational interviews, are also a place to brainstorm work through ideas about transitions and career goals that are just taking shape.

However, having an established network to lean on is not automatic. Some may exit graduate school without an expansive network of people in the private sector. "Lack of networks [or] personal connections in organizations to which I applied" was a roadblock for one of our respondents, currently in their fourth nonacademic role. She credits connecting with former classmates, friends, and trusted colleagues across multiple sectors and types of work to hear their transition stories with facilitating her own transition. Network connections also allowed our respondents to workshop job application materials, connect with people with similar educational backgrounds, and get introduced to people with different backgrounds.

Our respondents offer essential advice on networking, including being unapologetic in reaching out to people you are not acquainted with. Just as you have expertise in your field, our respondents also suggest hiring experts (i.e., career coaches) to help facilitate career transitions.

Networking Advice from Our Respondents

> Talk to a career coach, or do a bunch of interviews and conversations with people in your network, to get feedback on your materials and your search. And network, because all kinds of positions are available that will never be listed. – Private sector PhD, two roles outside of academia
> Don't hesitate to send cold emails to people for informational interviews. If there are sectors that are hiring and seem interesting, but not completely in line with your imagined career, consider how you can apply your skillset in new ways. – Private sector MA, four roles outside of academiaThere's more out there than you know. People in your network might know about positions even before they are ever posted or circulated. Some roles are never posted. – Private sector PhD, two roles outside of academia

Learn the Language of Your Field and Other Fields

Networking, especially with people in a field you want to move into, can be "language immersion" for social scientists making transitions. As a student, you get to know your field's frameworks, methods, and points of view very intimately. Networking conversations are a method for learning more about other disciplines' frameworks, processes, jargon, and norms. Use what you learn to translate your interests into a new field's language and better envision what it would be like to bring your skills, interests, and experiences into that sector. As a PhD in their second consulting role shared, "learning how other fields saw my work changed how I explained my experience. I also started reading job ads differently."

When looking for your first job, you might have scanned job postings for activities and topics you had seen before. That approach can push you down a funnel that narrows quickly. Applying for jobs only because they replicate the activities you are used to doing limits what you come to believe you are qualified to do. When it's time for a career transition, think about how the skills you have (whether you developed them during graduate school or cultivated them more recently and in other parts of your life) could be put to use in a certain area. Also, acknowledge what you don't know; these are growth opportunities. When our respondents offered advice on the job market, they emphasized embracing the unknown and thinking about your skills instead of your knowledge.

Job-Search Advice from Our Respondents

Rarely will a job description say exactly, precisely, perfectly what you do. That doesn't mean you can't do it. – Private sector PhD, two roles outside academia

Don't sell yourself short. Academia makes you believe you only have super-specific skills that can't be applied elsewhere but that's totally wrong. Many of the skills you learn in a Ph.D. program are easily transferable. – Private sector PhD, two roles outside academia

Pitfalls and Tough Lessons

Throughout their time in nonacademic careers, our respondents learned a number of valuable lessons about career transitions. Stressing the importance of knowing when it's time to make a new transition and learning from the past, one respondent remarked, "I take red flags more seriously than I did early on in my career and don't give leadership the benefit of the doubt anymore."

Respondents also noted that transitioning is about having the right mindset. People can feel guilt, shame, and a high degree of uncertainty about leaving a position. One respondent mentioned, "I've actually seen people feel guilty for leaving a job." In a similar refrain, another informant mentioned how important it is to stop thinking that your current place of employment is the only place where you can thrive. Several respondents mentioned learning to be "okay" with leaving a job. Indeed, there are other positions and work environments that will embrace your skills and expertise, but you have to do the work to find them.

Other respondents stressed that it's essential not to make assumptions about the types of available positions or what others know about your experience and capacity to do work. One informant remarked, "[I assumed] that no one besides the place [I] worked now would hire PhDs." While another informant stated, "Having the knowledge doesn't mean the world will see you as a knowledgeable expert. You'll communicate this repeatedly. You'll give examples. You'll show your ability to apply skills and knowledge to problems in interview questions and on the job."

The women we spoke with also talked about how self-doubt and lack of information can lead to uncertainty during career transition periods. When asked about the pitfalls of transitioning between positions, one respondent remarked that "[Not] recognizing that you have agency over a transition" is one of the biggest. Another participant with an education PhD stated that a major pitfall was "Not having an adequate amount of information about how to make a transition." Having an advanced degree in the social and behavioral sciences gives you a lot of leverage in the private sector job market; you must learn to put that knowledge and those skills to work.

Additional Advice from Our Respondents

A PhD teaches you how to think. That's a skill that companies across industries need. And value. – Private sector PhD, two transitions outside of academia

Learn to become fluent in the language of the field/organization you wish to join, by reading, talking with people, etc. – Consulting sector PhD, four roles outside academia

There's a job market for researchers, there's job market for analysts, there's a job market for project managers. All of those are experiences you've had. You can get those roles. – Private sector PhD, three roles outside of academia

Conclusion

We set out to write this chapter because the narrative of finding a company that will host you for your entire career is not realistic. Data and the experiences of our respondents tell us that a nonacademic career is a series of transitions. To be realistic about those transitions is to be thoughtful and creative about finding and considering opportunities. A PhD in corporate role shared with us "you can do more than academia tells you can, but you also can't be everything for everybody. Learn about other industries and determine how you can be a part of them." Realistically, in the words of a PhD in their third private sector role, "be strategic about where you apply" since "sending hundreds of applications doesn't always equal more job offers."

Building a career in the private or public sectors is not easier than having a career in academia. It's simply different. The more you prepare yourself to deal with those differences at the outset of your career journey, the smoother your career transitions will likely be. It might take several positions or some time in multiple fields before finding a space that you want to be in. The women who talk about their experiences and offered advice in this chapter have and continue to successfully pursue careers outside of academia. Those who responded to our questions show that there is no one way to pursue a career outside of academia, but there are a couple of sound principles to remember. First, culture matters. Knowing your values and how they align with where you decide to work is important in any transition. Second, you must network. Across respondents, a consistent refrain is that networking with those you know and those you don't is critical to finding new positions. Some data suggest that up to 85% of positions are filled through referrals garnered through networking.[5] Networking can be intimidating and requires stepping out of one's comfort zone, but by all accounts, networking is worth the effort. Third, learning the language of the sector that interests you is just as important as learning your academic field. By learning the language of the sector, you will be able to meaningfully translate your skills and expertise to recruiters, hiring managers, and fellow networkers among others. Finally, remember that there will be pitfalls and lessons along the way. Learning from the experiences of others and acknowledging your own lessons will help move you forward. Finally, don't weigh yourself down with comparisons to others. To quote a respondent working in the nonprofit sector, "be patient with yourself and know that every individual['s] situation differs widely."

Bibliography

Alder, L. (2016, February). New survey reveals 85% of all jobs are filled via networking. LinkedIn. Retrieved from: https://www.linkedin.com/pulse/new-survey-reveals-85-all-jobs-filled-via-networking-lou-adler/?src=aff-lilpar;veh=aff_src.aff-lilpar_c.partners_pkw.10078_plc. Skimbit%20Ltd._pcrid.449670_learning;trk=aff_src.aff-lilpar_c.partners_pkw.10078_plc. Skimbit%20Ltd._pcrid.449670_learning;clickid=w9GSl5Tl%3AxyOTzLwUx0Mo38TUkiXy 1T3R1SRyY0;irgwc=1 Last Accessed: May 23, 2021

Freeland Fisher, J. (2019, December 27). How to get a job often comes down to one elite personal asset, and many people still don't realize it. CNBC. Retrieved from: https://www.cnbc.com/2019/12/27/how-to-get-a-job-often-comes-down-to-one-elite-personal-asset.html.   Last accessed: May 23, 2021.

Perry, M. (2020, October 15). Women earned majority of doctoral degrees in 2019 for 11th straight year and outnumber men in grad school 141 to 100. American Enterprise Institute. Retrieved from: https://www.aei.org/carpe-diem/women-earned-majority-of-doctoral-degrees-in-2019-for-11th-straight-year-and-outnumber-men-in-grad-school-141-to-100/#:~:text=Women%20 have%20now%20earned%20a,high%20first%20set%20in%202017.

Rice, C. (2012, May 24). Why women leave academia and why universities should be worried. The Guardian [online] Retrieved from: https://www.theguardian.com/higher-education-network/blog/2012/may/24/why-women-leave-academia. Last accessed May 23, 2021.

---

[5] See Alder, L. (2016, Feb.). New survey reveals 85% of all jobs are filled via networking. LinkedIn. Retrieved from: https://www.linkedin.com/pulse/new-survey-reveals-85-all-jobs-filled-via-networking-lou-adler/?src=aff-lilpar;veh=aff_src.aff-lilpar_c.partners_pkw.10078_plc.Skimbit%20 Ltd._pcrid.449670_learning;trk=aff_src.aff-lilpar_c.partners_pkw.10078_plc.Skimbit%20Ltd._ pcrid.449670_learning;clickid=w9GSl5Tl%3AxyOTzLwUx0Mo38TUkiXy1T3R1SRyY0;ir gwc=1 Last Accessed: May 23, 2021; Freeland Fisher, J. (2019, Dec 27). How to get a job often comes down to one elite personal asset, and many people still don't realize it. CNBC. Retrieved from: https://www.cnbc.com/2019/12/27/how-to-get-a-job-often-comes-down-to-one-elite-personal-asset.html. Last accessed: May 23, 2021.

Staying Academically Relevant in a Nonacademic Career

Angela Fontes

Introduction

So, you've landed in a nonacademic career! Whether you've landed here intentionally, on accident, or as a last resort, there are both great benefits and considerable challenges to a career outside of academia. For many of us, a nonacademic career may seem like a let-down to our Ph.D. advisors, our mentors, and maybe even ourselves. In my Ph.D. program, students were absolutely expected to enter academia, preferably at an R1, and anything else meant we had failed. Our career choices were binary – either you were in academia or you weren't.

But, often, life happens. For me, getting divorced during my Ph.D. program meant that I needed to stay within a few hours of where my ex-partner lived in order to co-parent, severely limiting my academic options. While I knew academia wasn't for me, at least right away, I didn't want to limit my options in the future or lose the momentum I had begun building in my personal research. I realized at that point that I needed to figure out how to stay relevant in academia in my nonacademic career. Now, 15 years after I finishing grad school, I feel I've had the best of both worlds; I've contributed to the scholarly conversation in my field (and taken the opportunity to dabble in others) while living where I want, earning a good salary, and not sacrificing a personal life to obtain tenure.

The purpose of this chapter is to share some thoughts on how straddling these two worlds can be done. Before I get into my tips, there are two important points I want to make:

A. Fontes (✉)
Fontes Research, Chicago, IL, USA

N. Jackson (ed.), *Non-Academic Careers for Quantitative Social Scientists*,
Texts in Quantitative Political Analysis,
https://doi.org/10.1007/978-3-031-35036-8_21

1. An "academic" career is not a 1/0 choice. While obtaining a tenure-track position is the traditional "academic" path, there are many in-between options, many of which I'll discuss in this chapter. Just because you aren't on a tenure track doesn't mean you can't be a relevant and accomplished "academic" researcher in your field.

2. Staying relevant in academia is not important to everyone, and that is 100% OK. While continuing to publish in academic journals and participate in academic conferences has been important to me personally, I recognize that it's not for others and feel no judgment. My brother, who is a Ph.D. in a different field, never intended to pursue an academic career and is happy to never publish again. We're all on different paths, and that's great.

Staying Relevant (If You Want to) 101

In this section I offer seven tips on how to stay relevant. But, before I dive in, what exactly do I mean by "staying relevant"? I don't think there's an exact definition, but for me it's been about growing my CV and continuing to contribute to the academic research conversation in my field through publication and presentations. My field is small, so "staying relevant" for me means having some level of name recognition, at least in the specific research domain I'm focused on. I think staying relevant means that you keep alive whatever passion you were following when you went to grad school, which will likely look different for different researchers.

Let's jump into my tips. I classify my tips into two sections; things you can do at your "day job" and things you can do outside of your primary employment. Many of these tips work together; for example, looking for academic partners is easier if you're willing to explore "neighbor" fields, and becoming involved in an academic association can make attending conferences easier and less expensive.

Staying Relevant, at Your "Day Job"

1. *Negotiate time for academic work with your employer.*

    As quantitative social scientists, we were hired outside of academia for our considerable research and/or analytic skills. While not always the case, employers often understand and value the desire to continue to publish and stay relevant in academia even when the job does not require these things. As such, don't be afraid to include "personal research time" in compensation negotiations. For example, you might take a slightly lower salary than you'd prefer, but negotiate in four hours a week to work on a paper or project of your own choosing. When you do, make sure you're communicating the benefits of this time for your employer. The ability to work on and publish your own research will not only make you a happier and more fulfilled employee, but may also elevate the status of your boss, team, or employer.

This was an important part of the compensation package I received in my first position out of grad school, as what we would now call a data scientist at a large advertising agency. I used that time to publish a part of my dissertation and would likely not have had the bandwidth to get that paper out had I not asked my employer for this time.

2. *Be flexible/willing to explore "neighbor" fields.*

I love this tip. After I left the ad agency, I took a position in the statistics department at a social science research center. At the time there was no work being done in my field within the organization, so I ended up as an internal analytics consultant to researchers in a number of other departments. While this did mean that I couldn't be laser-focused on work in my specific field, it did provide me with the opportunity to expand both how I thought about my field and my analytic toolkit. For example, as a researcher who generally used large national survey data, I had no experience with medical claims data until I worked on a public health project. Working in these "neighbor" fields allowed me to work with remarkable colleagues, publish in top-tier journals, and truly bring a new perspective to my own work. Although working on projects outside your main area of focus may at first feel like a waste of time, leaning into these opportunities can differentiate you from other researchers in your own field.

3. *Look for opportunities to turn what you're already doing into a paper or presentation.*

Unless you've left the research world completely, there may be ways to take something you are already doing for pay and expand or shift the work for presentation at an academic conference or a publication. Sometimes this could be as simple as taking a piece of research you are already working on as part of your "day job" and adding some additional analysis or rewriting for journal submission. Conference presentations (more on this below) are a great option for those of us not in tenure-track positions.

Think broadly about where your work might be relevant. Although I'm neither a marketer nor a business analytics researcher, I've done work in the past that fit more squarely in these fields than my "primary" area of research. As such, I've thought broadly about where my research might be relevant and had a surprising amount of success taking to conferences work that I was already doing for my job. Would the research you've conducted fit at a marketing conference? Are you working on some new and interesting analytics or survey methods? Does what you're working on have relevance to public policy? Find conferences and journals in those areas – even if that's not what you went to school for – and submit!

Staying Relevant, Outside of Your "Day Job"

4. *Get involved in one (or more) of the academic associations in your field.*

Academic associations – love them or hate them, most fields have at least one, and they can be extremely helpful in keeping up to date with what's happening in your field. Becoming involved in one or more of these associations will not only help you stay on top of recent developments in your area of study but these associations are great places to meet potential academic collaborators and showcase your work without going to the trouble of journal publication. In addition to getting on mailing lists, attending conferences and other events, and accessing any affiliated journal content your association might publish, consider volunteering in some capacity – this investment of time can reap great rewards in terms of feeling connected to the field and other researchers. For me, involvement in my association has been one of the most important – and rewarding – parts of staying relevant.

5. *Seek out academic partners to work with.*

    Many of us won't have the time to devote to solo academic publication, so looking to co-authors is important. Some of us may have colleagues at our "day job" who are interested in disseminating research in this way, but this is highly dependent upon your field and where you've landed. One strategy that has worked well for me is to seek out researchers in academia to partner with. I've often thought it a curious situation; it's not uncommon for there to be a plethora of data in private industry, often barely used by researchers within the organization with no time to publish, while those in academia have time, but are looking for data. Whether you have data to use, analytic skills to leverage, or just interest and time, you have something to contribute to an academic paper, and there is likely someone who would be happy to work with you.

    How do I find partners? I've found co-authors in a number of ways. First, academic associations and conferences are a great way to find out what people are working on and meet up for a conversation. I've asked people to work with me on my ideas, and I've also offered my methodology and analytic skills to work with a partner on an idea they were interested in researching – both have been fruitful opportunities. You can also simply email an academic researcher and start a conversation, particularly if you have data or expertise related to work that they are already conducting. In my experience, academic researchers are happy to have additional resources!

6. *Attend conferences and present when you can.*

    I've mentioned academic conferences a few times above, but I've found attending these events – even just one per year – to be a fantastic way to present my work, stay abreast of what's happening in my field, meet partners, and continue learning. Because much of my work over the years has not included developing a full paper based on the research I'm conducting, I've found conferences an ideal way to present my work as often the requirements for a conference presentation are an extended abstract, rather than a full paper. While not the same as a peer-reviewed article, conference presentations are a nice "add" to your CV, and many conferences produce some sort of proceedings that you can use to reference your work. Conferences are also a great way to meet partners and get ideas on how I might extend my "day job" research into the academic conversation.

Funding for conference participation or attendance is another thing you might try to negotiate into your "day job" agreement, whether through a direct agreement to attend a specific conference on an annual basis or a generic professional development fund. Crafting a request to send your employer outlining the benefits both to your work, maybe through learning new analytic techniques or methods, or meeting potential new hires for your organization, and to your job satisfaction, can often shake loose some funding or at least paid time to attend the event.

7. *Find a part-time adjunct position.*

Although I didn't take a tenure-track position when I finished grad school, I still felt strongly that I wanted to teach. I was fortunate to be in an area with many local universities and I relatively quickly found an opportunity to teach one course a year, at first, and soon every quarter, at a nearby school. With the explosion of online courses and programs, there are now more opportunities to pick up a course than ever.

Teaching provides me with a few important things. First is access to library resources that I didn't have in my nonacademic job. The ability to use the university library resources has been critically important as I've pursued my own research agenda and part of what has kept me teaching even as I've become increasingly busy in my "main" career. Second, teaching provides access to students and just the academic atmosphere. Even though I teach a methods course in a program only partially related to my own field, the ability to talk with students and other faculty, attend university events, and feel part of the university community has been invaluable.

Final Notes on Staying Relevant

I hope the above tips are helpful as you navigate staying academically relevant in a nonacademic career. Fifteen years ago, I would not have thought that I could continue to publish and be involved in an academic association if I wasn't on a tenure track, but I'm here to tell you that it's possible – if you want it. I'll end this chapter with three final thoughts to keep in mind as you consider how, or whether, you'd like to stay academically relevant:

- Keep both a CV and a resume. When job hunting, most of the time a resume will do, but use your CV as source material, drawing from it as appropriate for the resume or biographical sketch you are pulling together. Keep your public profile – whether on LinkedIn or another public-facing website – up to date with all the great work you are doing, whether it is for your job or not.
- Your ability to stay relevant will ebb and flow over the years. Some years I've been able to do several conference presentations and published a paper or two, and I've also gone several years without publishing a thing. One of the beautiful things about a nonacademic career is that that's ok. Make goals about how you'd

like to show up in an academic context, but don't ever beat yourself up if you don't meet your goals 100% of the time.

- Good research is good research, regardless of where it's published. While the primary topic of this chapter is about staying relevant in the academic community where journal publication is key, I think it's so important that we not discount work that is accessible and approachable to a broad audience – this work is rarely published in journals, but probably more impactful in terms of furthering social science. It's also incredibly freeing to be able to publish in the most appropriate journal instead of killing yourself to get in to only the journals with the highest impact factors!

In sum, you can absolutely stay part of the academic research world – if you want to – while taking a job outside of academia. For me, this has been the best of both worlds. I hope this chapter has helped you think about how you might have the benefits of a nonacademic career while still contributing to the academic conversation in your field.

Index

© The Editor(s) (if applicable) and The Author(s), under exclusive license to
Springer Nature Switzerland AG 2023
N. Jackson (ed.), *Non-Academic Careers for Quantitative Social Scientists*,
Texts in Quantitative Political Analysis,
https://doi.org/10.1007/978-3-031-35036-8

Printed in the USA
CPSIA information can be obtained
at www.ICGtesting.com
LVHW011924270823
756422LV00006B/434